THE
LAWLESS
STATE

THE CRIMES OF THE U.S. INTELLIGENCE AGENCIES

by
Morton H. Halperin
Jerry J. Berman
Robert L. Borosage
and
Christine M. Marwick

PENGUIN BOOKS

Penguin Books Ltd, Harmondsworth,
Middlesex, England
Penguin Books, 625 Madison Avenue,
New York, New York 10022, U.S.A.
Penguin Books Australia Ltd, Ringwood,
Victoria, Australia
Penguin Books Canada Ltd, 41 Steelcase Road West,
Markham, Ontario, Canada
Penguin Books (N.Z.) Ltd, 182-190 Wairau Road,
Auckland 10, New Zealand

A report by the Center for National Security Studies

First published 1976

Copyright © Center for National Security Studies, 1976
All rights reserved

ISBN 0 14 00.4386 1

Printed in the United States of America by
Offset Paperback Mfrs., Inc., Dallas, Pennsylvania
Set in Photon Times Roman

I speak of peace while covert enmity
Under the smile of safety wounds the world.

SHAKESPEARE, *Henry IV, Part II*

Acknowledgments

This book is the product of the collective effort of the staff of the Center for National Security Studies. Specific contributions should be noted. John Marks drafted the chapters on the CIA abroad. Susan Kaplan worked on the Martin Luther King, Jr., case study and provided general support throughout. Summary of the CIA's domestic programs is the work of Christy Macy. David Klaus prepared the IRS chapter and assisted David Cortright and Heidi Pasichow in the work on military intelligence. Judy Mead put together the grand-jury chapter with the assistance of Rhonda Copelon of the Center for Constitutional Rights.

As for the named authors, Jerry Berman wrote the FBI chapters; Morton Halperin helped edit the CIA portions and worked with Christine Marwick on the NSA chapters and on the last two chapters. Robert Borosage reviewed almost everything in the book and wrote the chapter on the Lawless State. These four are solely responsible for interpretation and mistakes.

The Center for National Security Studies owes much to many. Three gentlemen deserve particular mention. Leslie Dunbar got us started and has kept us on course through his insistence on principle and his example of decency. Randolph Compton, Chairman of the Fund for Peace, has furnished support in rocky moments and encouragement always. And W. H. Ferry—writer, friend, teller of unvarnished truths—has offered protection for our work and a sanctuary at his home, where the conversation sparkles and the roof doesn't leak. Like men and women, institutions cannot survive without bread, and for this, thanks be to the Field Foundation, the Veatch Committee of the Unitarian Church, and the many friends of David Hunter.

CONTENTS

Introduction   1

THE CIA ABROAD   13

1
The CIA's Campaign against Salvador Allende   15

2
The CIA: Covert Action around the World   30

THE FBI AT HOME   59

3
The FBI's Vendetta against Martin Luther King, Jr.   61

4
The Bureau in War and Peace   90

THE OTHER AGENCIES AT HOME   133

5
The CIA   135

CONTENTS

6

Military Intelligence   155

7

The National Security Agency   171

8

The Internal Revenue Service   187

9

The Grand Juries   209

10

The Lawless State   220

CONTROLLING THE INTELLIGENCE AGENCIES   237

11

Have the Crimes Stopped?   239

12

Designing Effective Reforms   255

Notes   280

Bibliography of Major Sources   315

Index   319

INTRODUCTION

For the past four years, the crimes and abuses of the secret realm of government have been unearthed, in fascinating and finally numbing detail. What began as an inquest of Richard Nixon's offenses slowly became a descent into the hellish activities of the secret intelligence agencies: the Central Intelligence Agency (CIA), the Federal Bureau of Investigation (FBI), the Military Intelligence apparatus, the National Security Agency (NSA), and the Internal Revenue Service (IRS).

These agencies represent the major part of the large, secret realm of government. They consume some $8 to $10 billion yearly, an estimated 10 percent of controllable federal spending, virtually all of it appropriated in false budget categories so that even most legislators do not know the true figures. Together they employ an estimated 175,000 persons, not counting the fathomless ranks of contract agents, informers, mercenaries, and provocateurs on retainer at any moment. They operate in secrecy at home and abroad, beyond the normal view of citizen, judge, or public official.

Only in the past years have some portion of their activities been held up to public light, and that all too brief exposure has now just about ended. The Watergate and impeachment hearings provided the first clues about serious abuses in the intelligence agencies. In late 1974, newspaper articles exposed the CIA's "destabilization" of the Allende regime in Chile and its massive domestic surveillance programs. These articles were based primarily on leaks from patriotic or disgruntled employees and they finally forced an official response. President Gerald Ford's Rockefeller Commission began by detailing many of the CIA's illegal domestic activities in a report issued in 1975. The House and the Senate set up separate investigating committees. The House committee, chaired by conservative Congressman Otis Pike, sought to reassert the legislature's powers. It subpoenaed documents, held public hearings, resisted compromises, and looked into activities that the agencies preferred to keep secret. Its subpoenas were resisted; its investigators frustrated; in the end, its final report was suppressed by the Congress itself. Portions of it were later printed in the *Village Vice;* the remainder remains unpublished. The Senate committee, chaired by Senator Frank Church, preferred compromise to conflict. It negotiated with the agencies for material, allowed CIA officials to screen all documents it was given, rarely issued a subpoena or held a public session. Its voluminous reports, published in the summer of 1976, unearthed many intelligence agency crimes but are still incomplete. The Church Committee even permitted the CIA to censor significant portions of the report, including four of its five case studies of secret CIA interventions abroad.

These official investigations have been supplemented by private ones. The finest investigative reporters have published the results of their own digging. Civil litigation by the victims of agency programs has pried out further documents. Some further information will still come out, but on the whole, the intelligence agencies are slipping back into their secret routines. While the eyes of the bureaucrats are still blinking from the unaccustomed exposure, we may begin to sort out the crimes and abuses of the past and the implications for the future.

The investigations have shown that every intelligence

agency had one or more surveillance programs that spied on law-abiding American citizens, in violation of the laws, the Constitution, and the traditions of the country. Their ominous scope is best portrayed by the code names used by the agencies: the CIA ran CHAOS, SETTER, HT-LINGUAL, MERRIMAC, and RESISTANCE; the FBI added COMINFIL, VIDEM, STUDEN; the military had CABLE SPLICER and GARDEN PLOT; the NSA managed MINARET and SHAMROCK; the IRS had LEPRECHAUN and the SSS (Special Service Staff). All the techniques associated with secret police bureaus throughout history were used to gather information: black-bag break-ins, wiretaps and bugs, mail openings, cable and telegram interceptions, garbage covers, and informers.

The number of citizens who have been the objects of the professional voyeurs is truly staggering. The FBI headquarters in Washington alone has over 500,000 domestic intelligence files, each typically containing information on more than one group or individual. Nearly a quarter of a million first-class letters were opened and photographed by the CIA in the United States between 1953 and 1973, producing a computerized index of nearly one and one-half million names. The CIA's six-year Operation CHAOS produced an index of 300,000 individuals. Uncounted millions of international telegrams and phone calls have been intercepted by the National Security Agency. Some 100,000 Americans are enshrined in Army intelligence dossiers. The Internal Revenue Service created files on more than 11,000 individuals and groups. During a three-year period, from 1971-74, political grand juries subpoened between 1,000 and 2,000 persons.

In addition, both at home and abroad, the intelligence agencies went beyond the mere collection of information. They developed programs to disrupt, "neutralize," and destroy those perceived as enemies—as threats to the political order at home and abroad. The CIA's covert action programs around the world were paralleled by the FBI's COINTELPRO at home, by the misuse of the IRS and the grand jury—all were part of a purposeful effort to live up to the mandate of a classified report of the 1954 Hoover Commission on Government Organization that "we must learn to subvert, sabotage, and destroy our enemies by more clever, more sophisticated and more effective methods than those used against us." Thus the illegalities exposed by the investigations were not isolated incidents of zealous agents exceeding their authority in the field, however frequently such may occur. Rather, the abuses were ongoing, bureaucratic programs, often continuing over decades, involving hundreds of officials, aimed at thousands of citizens, and ordered and approved at the highest level of the executive branch of government.

The secret realm of government is the deformed offspring of the modern presidency, an expression of the powers claimed by presidents in the area of national security. The origins of the intelligence agencies, like those of the modern president, can best be traced from World War II. The CIA is modeled after the wartime Office of Strategic Services (OSS), which ran secret intelligence, sabotage, and paramilitary activities behind enemy lines during the war. The FBI's authority to spy on citizens derives from a secret directive issued by President Franklin D. Roosevelt in 1936 in response to opposition to the war at home and rumors of possible Nazi sabotage of American preparedness efforts.

War greatly expands a president's powers and capabilities, for he acts not simply as the chief executive, but as the commander in chief. The legislative role naturally contracts as open deliberation is replaced by secret command. Political liberties are constricted; citizens are called to soldiery; obedience and sacrifice replace independence and questioning. Fear and hatred of the enemy provide the political base for the expanded authority of the president and the military.

War also requires intelligence, to discover plans of the enemy and to prevent the uncovering of one's own. Intelligence agencies operate at home and abroad, to spy and to frustrate the spies of others; to subvert and to deter the subversion of others; to sabotage and to guard against sabotage.

For the United States, the wartime emergency never ended. After World War II, America assumed the mantle of Britain as guarantor of world stability. Open warfare was followed by permanent cold war; Hitler's Germany was replaced by Stalin's Russia; Nazi fifth columns were replaced by Communist parties. The nuclear balance of terror made the president a literal arbiter of life and death. Thus the wartime powers of the president were never relinquished; the wartime institutions never dismantled. Intelligence activities born in total war were given permanent institutional homes. The CIA replaced the OSS in 1947; the FBI's authority to spy on Americans was reaffirmed by Harry Truman in 1946. The president claimed the right to act alone to defend the "national security," which would be defined within the White House.

"National security" is an inescapably political concept; one man's subversion is another's salvation. The power to define threats to the "national security" is the power to draw the limits of acceptable behavior for leaders abroad and citizens at home. The postwar presidents claimed the power not only to define national security, but also to act —often in secret—to enforce it. The ability to act secretly both bolstered the president's claim of authority and allowed administrations to engage in permanent intervention in politics at home and abroad in ways that were by design offensive to American values. As a result, a secret realm of government developed to watch and, if necessary, disrupt political opponents at home and abroad.

Using secret intelligence agencies to defend a constitutional republic is akin to the ancient medical practice of employing leeches to take blood from feverish patients. The intent is therapeutic, but in the long run the cure is more deadly than the disease. Secret intelligence agencies are designed to act routinely in ways that violate the laws or standards of society. As long as an overwhelming consensus exists on who the enemy is, few are troubled by the incompatibility. Over time, however, the secret activities of the intelligence agencies inevitably become removed from the popular conception of what is necessary. Eventually the society disagrees about the nature of the enemy. At that point, those who lead the dissent become a threat to the intelligence agencies, an enemy to the secret definition of national security.

In the 1950s, the anti-Communist consensus amply supported the secret activities of the government. "Soviet imperialism" had to be contained, and that in turn was equated with stopping Communist expansion abroad and Communist infiltration at home. The unified enemy made resolute presidential activities at home and abroad popular with the vast majority of Americans. Those who disagreed were few, and were generally dismissed as dupes or fellow travelers, if not actual Communists.

In this atmosphere, presidents enjoyed a free hand; constitutional checks and balances folded completely. Congressional oversight of the intelligence agencies was negligent and negligible. The few legislators entitled to information did not inquire; the agencies did not volunteer information. Judicial review was rarely available for secret activities. The press helped the agencies protect their secrets by suppressing stories, and journalists served as spies and informants. Within the executive branch, no attorney general seriously attempted to control the FBI or the CIA. Internal bureaucratic controls—the inspectors general and general counsels of each agency—were either ignored or asked to report only on matters of efficiency rather than legality or propriety.

In this atmosphere, the activities and targets of the intelligence agencies naturally expanded as time went by. The CIA started by opposing what were believed to be Soviet-controlled Communist parties in Western Europe, but was soon involved in opposing Third World leaders whom even the CIA considered independent and nationalist, but who were too Marxist, too friendly to the Soviet Union, or too charismatic for the agency's taste. Thus the most recent CIA operations to come to light have been the attempt to "destabilize" the democratically elected Allende government in Chile, to provide "electoral support" against the independent Communist party in Italian elections, and to supply arms and mercenaries to intervene against an independence movement in Angola.

Similarly the FBI started with a mandate to monitor wartime sabotage, but quickly expanded that to include more and more of the politically active in its files. After the war, each successive movement for political change became a target for FBI surveillance or disruption: the "old left," the civil rights movement, the student movement, the antiwar movement, the women's movement, the public interest community, the consumer and environmental movements. By 1972, the FBI found it had a significant portion of the delegates to the national convention of the Democratic party under surveillance, and many of the organizations to which they belonged singled out for disruption.

The cancerous growth of programs—in size, scope, and targets—often came in response to presidential urging. Dwight Eisenhower and John Kennedy pressed an anti-Communist crusade abroad which led to CIA assassination efforts in Africa and the Caribbean. Lyndon Johnson urged the agencies to respond to urban disorders and the antiwar movement, and Richard Nixon increased the pressure, demanding that a range of political opponents be watched or harassed. Often the secret agencies would expand upon the vague directives that established their programs. The army was directed to prepare for policing American cities in case of urban riots. This directive was translated into a massive intelligence program that spied on thousands of civilians, including environmental, civil rights, and antiwar groups. The CIA's Office of Security was charged with protecting agency installations; in the 1960s, this provided the excuse to infiltrate agents into political groups in Washington, including the Urban League, the Humanist Society, and Women Strike for Peace.

Sometimes programs were initiated without the direct

order or approval of the president or the attorney general. The FBI's COINTELPRO activities were started on J. Edgar Hoover's authority alone. The CIA's mail-opening program and NSA's "watch-list" operations were also begun without express orders from the White House. Although such programs may not have had the specific approval of a president, they seldom exceeded the official consensus on what needed to be done to political dissenters.

Many of the programs involved illegal techniques or activities, or developed without legal authority. Internally, national security provided the absolution for law-breaking; higher orders provided the authority. Agents in the field rarely questioned their orders, and seldom survived in an agency if they did. The widespread assumption was that the agencies were above the law, doing what had to be done for the nation's security.

Concern for illegality generally was expressed by increased secrecy. Illegal operations had a high "flap potential" if exposed, and the agencies developed special procedures to cover them up. The IRS and the NSA both issued special warnings to keep their political programs secret. The FBI developed a special Do Not File file for illegal techniques such as break-ins, or highly questionable operations like bugging columnist Joseph Kraft in Europe. Similarly the CIA constantly reiterated warnings that exposure would lead to "flap," and that an adequate cover story had to be developed.

By the mid-sixties, the dangers posed by a permanent secret realm in a constitutional republic became apparent. The executive branch had developed a conception of national security that had little to do with the defense of the country or the security of the people. The debacle in Vietnam ended the consensus that had survived for over a decade. A growing number of people began to doubt the wisdom and question the authority of the president and his national security bureaucracy. President Johnson and President Nixon both accurately viewed the protests as a threat to their ability to act abroad, a challenge to their

"UH— THESE ARE SORT-OF SECRET ORGANIZATIONS THAT OUR GOVERNMENT HIRES TO SEE THAT WE ENJOY THE RIGHT KIND OF —UH— LIBERTY"

COPYRIGHT 1976 BY HERBLOCK IN *THE WASHINGTON POST*

definition of national security. The secret intelligence agencies were marshaled to spy on and disrupt the antiwar dissenters. During the Nixon years, when a majority of the population opposed the war, the president and his secret police were at direct odds with most of the politically active citizenry. Thus Nixon kept calling on a "silent majority" to come to his aid.

Under these conditions, programs initially protected merely by secrecy had to be covered up by lies. As the covert activities of the secret agencies conflicted more and more with the views of the public, legislators and reporters began to inquire about different activities. Deception was the routine response to public inquiry. Thus CIA Director Richard Helms found it necessary to lie under oath about both the domestic and the international exploits of the CIA. Helms has not been indicted for perjury because of the general feeling within the Justice Department that his duty was to lie. Nixon made the same transition from secrecy to lies in the attempt to avoid the Watergate probes.

Exposure or the possibility of it moved the agencies to end some of their illegal programs. No internal control mechanism was so effective. J. Edgar Hoover curtailed the FBI's wiretap, break-in, mail-opening, and garbage cover operations in 1966 for fear their revelation might "embarrass the Bureau" (read "J. Edgar Hoover"). Hoover also scuttled the Huston Plan (see p. 120) by reciting fears of its exposure. The FBI's formal COINTELPRO program was terminated in 1971 in response to disclosures about it in the press. IRS payments to confidential informants were suspended in reaction to a journalistic investigation of Operation LEPRECHAUN. The NSA's Operation SHAMROCK, the program of obtaining international telegrams from telegraph companies, was discontinued in the face of the Senate Select Committee's investigation of the program in 1975.

Exposure came because of the failure in Vietnam and the excesses of Richard Nixon; the policy consensus broke apart before the independent institutions—the press, the Congress, and the courts—had been entirely desiccated. The struggle to bring Richard Nixon to justice demonstrated what a close call it was. The investigation of the intelligence agencies reveals that the conflict is far from resolved.

This book provides an account of the abuses of the secret realm of government. The activities described are all fully documented in official public sources. Our focus is on abuses and threats to the American constitutional system. We leave to others a full statement of the activities of these agencies and of the economic and political roots of presidential power on which their actions depend. The first part of the book describes the two major agencies and their principal activities—the CIA abroad and the FBI at home. Two case studies—one on the CIA campaign against Salvador Allende and the other on the FBI vendetta against Martin Luther King, Jr.—graphically illustrate how these agencies operate. The second part of the book reviews the activities initiated by each of the other intelligence agencies in response to the protest movement of the sixties. In each chapter, a brief background of the specific bureaucratic history of political spying is provided.

The book concludes with a review of the controls and restructuring necessary if these agencies are to be curtailed in the future. This last part is most important, because the intelligence agencies are still engaged in many of the activities detailed in the text. Although the book deals in large part with the past—the history of programs of the secret realm—the abuses continue. In this the investigation of the intelligence agencies differs from the inquest into the crimes of Richard Nixon. The impeachment proceedings ended with the president resigning in disgrace, his aides and co-conspirators removed from office, many indicted and convicted. The investigations of the intelligence agencies have, thus far, provided no significant reforms. The CIA's Clandestine Services still engages in covert operations abroad; the NSA still monitors the international communications of American citizens without a warrant; the FBI still spies on citizens engaged in political activities protected under the First Amendment. No legislation has yet been passed by the Congress to limit in law the activities of the intelligence agencies. The only "reforms" have been ordered by executive directive, and these have generally legitimated the past abuses. The political struggle to control these agencies still lies ahead. Its outcome depends—as did the impeachment proceedings—on the reactions of American citizens throughout the country.

The question is whether or not the secret realm can be dismantled and curtailed, so that the political liberties of American citizens will be respected and the secret intervention of America abroad ended. If not, we may leave a legacy predicted by Malcolm Muggeridge when he wrote:

In the eyes of posterity it will inevitably seem that, in safeguarding our freedom, we destroyed it; that the vast clandestine apparatus we built up to probe our enemies' resources and intentions only served in the end to confuse our own purposes; that the practice of deceiving others for the good of the state led infallibly to our deceiving ourselves; and that the vast army of intelligence personnel built up to execute these purposes were soon caught up in the web of their own sick fantasies, with disastrous consequences to them and us.[1]

THE CIA ABROAD

THE CIA'S
CAMPAIGN AGAINST
SALVADOR ALLENDE

1

Few Americans knew much about Chile before the military coup that toppled Marxist President Salvador Allende in 1973 and established a totalitarian regime. Only later was it understood that the coup ended a remarkable period of constitutional and democratic government. From independence in 1818 to 1973, Chile had enjoyed freedom under democratic rule with only three brief exceptions, the last in 1932. Chile had, and has, the preconditions for a stable democracy. It is an urban industrial country of 11 million people. Almost all of its industrial population is literate, and proportionately it has the largest middle class in Latin America. Moreover, Chileans have long held a strong commitment to democratic norms. Power changed hands as a result of free elections, and the military believed that it should be subordinate to civilian rule.

Had they known of these conditions, most Americans would have assumed that American policy was geared to supporting this democratic system. After all, Americans were the leaders of the "free world." Their self-professed goal was to defend and expand democracy in the world. However, while this was public policy, America's postwar presidents, working secretly through the CIA, were pursuing a quite different goal.

Since the early 1960s, American policy in Chile was directed at one objective—to keep Salvador Allende from coming to power. To accomplish this, Presidents Kennedy, Johnson, and Nixon, with the willing cooperation of the CIA, were prepared to destroy constitutional government in Chile.

Why did the White House and the CIA fear Allende so much? Why were they prepared to subvert what the United States claims to stand for? The answers are by no means clear. However, a detailed look at the CIA role in Chile provides unique insights into how American presidents used their secret armies to fight wars they feared Congress and the public would not support. The operations in Chile also demonstrate what the CIA was and is doing elsewhere. The staff of the Senate Intelligence Committee, which had access to information on a number of covert operations, concluded that "the pattern of United States covert action in Chile is striking but not unique. . . . The scale of CIA involvement in Chile was unusual but by no means unprecedented."[1]

WHY ALLENDE?

Who was this man who brought down upon himself the ire of American presidents and the CIA? Allende was not a Soviet puppet, plotting to bring Soviet troops to Chile to destroy democracy. He was a committed democrat, considered a moderate by Chilean socialists, leading a coalition of Marxist parties in the election place. His program was the same each time he ran for president from 1958 onward: he pledged to reshape the Chilean economy (beginning with nationalization of major industries), to redistribute income through tax and land reform; and to begin a policy of better relationships with Cuba, the USSR, and other socialist states. Despite the warnings of his personal friend Fidel Castro, and despite the vicious campaign orchestrated by the CIA, Allende continued to respect the democratic traditions in Chile after he was elected in 1970. The intelligence community's own assessments showed that local, student, and trade-union elections continued to be held regularly; the press remained free, and continued to attack the government; the military was not used to suppress other parties.

Allende's government also posed no strategic threats to the United States. In 1970, a high-level interdepartmental group concluded that the United States had no vital interests in Chile, and that Allende posed no likely threat to the peace of the region. Allende pursued a policy of nonalignment, entering into relations with Cuba and the Soviet Union, and demonstrating independence from the United States. United States intelligence estimates agreed that none of this was of strategic concern.

Yet to Henry Kissinger, it might as well have been 1948, with the Red Army looming just over the horizon. On September 16, 1970, he told a group of editors in a "background" briefing that an "Allende takeover" (i.e., victory in a democratic election) was not in United States interest. "There is a good chance that [Allende] will establish over a period of years some sort of Communist government," warned Kissinger, and that could pose "massive problems for us and for democratic forces and for pro-US forces in Latin America." In a stretch of his geopolitical imagination, Kissinger specified Argentina, Bolivia, and Peru as countries that would be adversely influenced by an Allende victory. Moreover, Kissinger feared that the "contagious example" of Chile would "infect" NATO allies in southern Europe.[2]

Kissinger was worried about the question of dominoes, "infection," and Western stability. Chile, like Vietnam before it and Angola after, had become a test case for America's imperial will. Not surprisingly, for the man who urged the carpet-bombing of Hanoi in order to "punctuate" his negotiating position against North Vietnam, Kissinger had little interest in either the condition of the Chilean people or their fate. "I don't see why we need to stand by and watch a country go Communist due to the irresponsibility of its own people," said Kissinger in 1970 at a supersecret meeting of the 40 Committee (the White House group chaired by Kissinger, which was supposed to approve major projects to manipulate other countries' internal affairs).[3]

Kissinger set the CIA against Allende, not to preserve democracy or to counter a Soviet puppet in Latin America, but to prevent a charismatic socialist from providing a democratic alternative to American policy. "Henry thought that Allende might lead an anti-United States movement in Latin America more effectively than Castro, just because it was the democratic path to power," commented an ex-staff aide.[4] In fact, it was precisely because Allende was widely regarded as a believer in democratic institutions that there was so much shock connected to his overthrow, especially in the Third World and southern Europe. What Kissinger was saying—and backing up with covert American power—was that adherence to democracy wasn't enough; that countries would not be allowed to switch over to a socialist way of running their economies, even democratically. The message of Chile was: no matter how unjust or corrupt the alternative, the United States would not allow meaningful economic or social change, at least with a Marxist label, and a willingness to have good relations with Cuba, China, and the Soviet Union.

Fidel Castro, on the other hand, received another message from American subversion of the Allende regime. He saw Allende's mistake as having allowed too much democracy. Castro told American interviewers in July 1974:

Allende respected all these rights. The opposition press conspired. There were newspapers conspiring for a coup d'etat every day, and they finally delivered the coup. Everyone had the right to conspire, and the results were that they overthrew the Allende government and set up a fascist regime.[5]

Castro believed—and Kissinger seemed to be comfirming—that there could be no socialism in Latin America with democratic freedoms and without armed power to back it up. In the end, the very specter that Kissinger raised for Chile if Allende stayed in power—abolition of basic freedoms—was the final result of the secret American foreign-policy goal of destablizing Chile.

The CIA's attempts to dislodge Allende from power in Chile were the culmination of a long agency campaign against Allende. Twice before—in 1958 and in 1964—Allende had run for the presidency, and on both occasions the CIA worked clandestinely to block him. To influence the outcome of the 1964 elections, the agency spent $3 million. As part of this effort, the CIA organized a media "scare campaign" (*campaña de terror*) and secretly paid over half the costs of the victorious Christian Democratic campaign.[6]

Philip Agee, who was a CIA operative in Uruguay in 1964, has described how some of this money was funneled into Chile through the Montevideo branch of the First National City Bank, with the help of the assistant manager, John M. Hennessy.[7] Five years later, Hennessy was the assistant secretary of the treasury for international affairs and in that post helped to coordinate the economic aspect of the Nixon administration's anti-Allende campaign.

Hennessy's dual role vividly illustrates the interlocking, overlapping nature of American corporate and government involvement in Chile—and, indeed, in all Latin America. United States corporations dominated the key sectors of Chile's economy—including the vital copper industry. By 1970, loans by financial institutions controlled or dominated by the United States—AID, the Export-Import Bank, the Inter-American Development Bank, the International Monetary Fund, and the World Bank—had given Chile the highest per-capita foreign debt in the world. With the knowledge and encouragement of the United States government, companies including Anaconda Copper and ITT contributed hundreds of thousands of dollars to anti-Allende candidates.

The Senate intelligence report indicates that in 1970 the CIA approached ITT for contributions to an Allende foe. Shortly thereafter, in the summer of 1970, a member of the ITT board of directors, John McCone, contacted the CIA in Washington to offer $1 million in ITT corporate funds for the anti-Allende effort. The CIA ostensibly rejected the offer but provided ITT with information on two "secure" funding channels that could be used to slip money to the National party and its candidate, Jorge Alessandri.[8]

John McCone wore several hats in this affair. In addition to being a director of ITT, he was the former head of the CIA itself, and was still secretly on the agency rolls as a "consultant." With his past CIA experience, McCone was fully aware that the CIA had "penetrated" virtually every sector of Chilean society. In intelligence parlance, the CIA for years had been steadily "building its assets" —placing and recruiting agents in key jobs all over Chile. In cooperation with—and often under cover supplied by— the AFL-CIO, the CIA had infiltrated the labor movement. It recruited Chileans in the media and among the country's most important politicians. CIA operators maintained regular "liaison" with the Chilean military and police services. In fact, according to a CIA source with direct personal knowledge, agency men in Chile were actively working as early as 1969 to "politicize" the armed forces and police in hopes of provoking a coup before the 1970 elections.[9]

The "asset-building" operations were part of the workaday routine for the dozen or so full-time CIA operatives assigned to the American embassy in Santiago and for the other CIA men in Chile disguised as students or businessmen. This permanent intervention in local politics had become a fact of life in Chile, as it had throughout Latin America. Presidential elections brought out spurts of CIA spending, but the "routine" level of covert action was not insignificant. Between 1964 and 1969, the agency spent close to $2 million on programs to train "anti-Communist organizers" working among Chilean peasants and slum dwellers. It subsidized or owned wire services, magazines, and newspapers. It directed projects to combat the left on Chile's campuses; supported a politically active women's organization; and tried to win influence in cultural and intellectual circles. The CIA even sponsored a group that specialized in putting up wall posters and heckling at public meetings.[10]

As the 1970 elections approached, the CIA and the United States ambassador to Chile, Edward Korry, again sought additional funds from the 40 Committee. In March of that year, the 40 Committee decided not to back any single candidate but to wage a "spoiling" campaign against Allende. (This policy was apparently circumvented by the CIA when it advised ITT on how to use agency funding conduits in feeding money to the National party candidate.) In all, the CIA spent close to $1 million to influence the 1970 elections. Some of the money went for "political action" and "black" (false) propaganda to break up the leftist coalition that had formed around Allende. The lion's share, however, went into another shrill media scare campaign. An Allende victory was equated with violence and Stalinist repression, and the message was sent out, the Senate Committee reports, by

an editorial support group that provided political features, editorials, and news articles for radio and press placement; and three different news services. . . . Sign-painting teams had instructions to paint the slogan "su paredon" (your wall) on 2000 walls, evoking an image of communist firing squads. . . . Other assets, all employees of *El Mercurio*, enabled the Station to generate more than one editorial per day based on CIA guidance. Access to *El Mercurio* had a multiplier effect, since its editorials were read throughout the country on various national radio networks.[11]

Despite the CIA's efforts, Allende won a narrow plurality in elections on September 4, 1970. But since he did not win a majority, formal selection of a president was left to the Chilean Congress, which was to meet on October 24. Chilean tradition dictated that, Allende, the candidate receiving the most votes, would be elected by the Congress.

The Nixon administration entertained other hopes, as the Senate Select Committee noted:

The reaction in Washington to Allende's plurality victory was immediate. The 40 Committee met on September 8 and 14 to discuss what action should be taken—prior to the October 24 congressional vote. On September 15, President Nixon informed CIA Director Richard Helms that an Allende regime in Chile would not be acceptable to the United States and instructed the CIA to play a direct role in organizing a military coup d'etat in Chile to prevent Allende's accession to the Presidency. . . .[12]

The Nixon administration policy to keep Allende out of power proceeded on two tracks. Under Track I, which had 40 Committee approval, the CIA used a variety of covert political, economic, and propaganda tactics to manipulate the Chilean political scene. One scheme to which the 40 Committee gave its assent was an allocation of $25,000 to bribe members of the Chilean Congress. This money was apparently never spent, but other CIA funds flowed into the ever more shrill propaganda campaign. According to the Senate report:

Themes developed during the campaign were exploited even more intensely during the weeks following September 4, in an effort to cause enough financial and political panic and political instability to goad President Frei or the Chilean military into action.[13]

The CIA moved quickly to create chaos on the Chilean scene. Agency Director Helms left the September 15 meeting with President Nixon with the following scribble among his notes: "Make the economy scream."[14] An interagency committee was set up (with representatives from the CIA, State, Treasury, and the White House) to coordinate the attack on Chile's economy. American multinationals, including ITT, were approached to take such actions as cutting off credit to Chile, stopping the shipment of spare parts, and causing runs on financial institutions. "A major financial panic ensued," noted the Senate Select Committee.[15]

Track II involved direct efforts to foment a military coup. Neither the State Department nor the 40 Committee was informed about these activities. The chain of command ran directly from Nixon to Kissinger to Helms at the CIA. Helms was told that $10 million or more would be available to do the job.[16] President Nixon was so adamant that Allende be stopped that Helms noted later about his orders: "If I ever carried a marshal's baton in my knapsack out of the Oval Office, it was that day."[17]

The CIA proceeded to make twenty-one contacts in two weeks with key Chilean military personnel to assure them that the United States would support a coup. At the time the primary obstacle within the military to such a move was Chief of Staff General René Schneider, a strong supporter of the Chilean military's tradition of non-involvement in politics. The CIA's reaction was to propose removing Schneider. American officials supported the coup plans, which included kidnaping General Schneider as a first step. After two unsuccessful attempts by the plotters, the CIA passed three submachine guns and ammunition to Chilean officers still planning to kidnap Schneider. The Senate committee found:

In the third kidnap attempt on October 22, apparently conducted by Chileans other than those to whom weapons had been supplied, General Schneider was shot and subsequently died. The guns used in the abortive kidnapping were, in all probability, not those supplied by the CIA to the conspirators. The Chilean military court . . . determined that Schneider had been murdered by handguns, although one machine gun was at the scene of the killing.[18]

Schneider was murdered, his fatal error being a firm belief in democracy and an apolitical military. His death was a shocking event in Chile, which had almost no past experience with political violence, but the armed forces still did not move, despite CIA urging. On October 24, 1970, Salvador Allende was confirmed as president of Chile.

DESTABILIZATION

While Henry Kissinger and his chief aide, Alexander Haig, have both testified that Track II ended even before General Schneider was killed, Thomas Karemessines, who headed the CIA's Clandestine Services at the time, claimed the contrary:

But what we were told to do was to continue our efforts. Stay alert, and to do what we could to contribute to the eventual achievement of the objectives and purposes of Track II. That being the case, I don't think it is proper to say that Track II was ended.[19]

Publicly, United States officials were pledging a low-key policy of non-interference in Chilean affairs, but secretly the Nixon administration was putting together a program designed to make it impossible for Allende to govern. Henry Kissinger provided the overall policy guidance, and special emphasis was placed on destroying the Chilean economy. This economic pressure included a virtual cut-off of economic aid; denial of credits to Chile in international financial institutions; and encouragement of United States corporations to cut off credits to Chile—which fell by 90 percent. The Treasury under John Connally and John Hennessy orchestrated this policy, which

intensified the effect of the economic measures taken by opposition groups within Chile, particularly the crippling strikes in the mining and transportation sectors. For instance, the combined effect of the foreign credit squeeze and domestic copper strikes on Chile's foreign exchange position was devastating.[20]

Kissinger meanwhile moved to create a new "country team" in Chile. Henry Hecksher, the CIA station chief who had predicted Allende would lose the election, was replaced in October 1970 by Raymond Warren, an experienced agency operative with past service in Columbia, Bolivia, and Chile itself. In 1971, Ambassador Edward Korry, an independent if hardline political appointee, was moved out in favor of Nathaniel Davis, a career Foreign Service Officer. Davis had served as ambassador to Guatemala at the time of the ongoing "pacification" program there in the late 1960s, and he was known as someone who could be counted on to follow Kissinger's orders.

After Allende's inauguration, the CIA funneled over $6 million into its attempts to subvert his government. Ambassador Davis had overall supervision of the effort, but Station Chief Warren held day-to-day control. Warren was able to call on the CIA's many clandestine assets scattered throughout Chilean society. His role can be likened to that of an orchestra leader, drawing maximum effect out of a wide assortment of instruments. Former Clandestine Services chief Richard Bissell explained how this worked:

Covert intervention is probably most effective in situations where a comprehensive effort is undertaken with a number of separate operations designed to support and complement one another and to have a cumulatively significant effect.[21]

This philosophy was put into action in Chile with staggering effect. The CIA concentrated its efforts in four key areas: Adding to its previous subsidies, the CIA spent another $1.5 million in support of *El Mercurio*.[22] Under the agency's guidance, the paper was transformed from a publication resembling the *Wall Street Journal* to one in the style of the *New York Daily News*, complete with screaming headlines and pictures of Soviet tanks on the front page.[23] The CIA justified this heavy expenditure on *El Mercurio* to the 40 Committee on the grounds that the Allende government was trying to close the paper and, in general, threatening the free press in Chile. On the contrary, according to the Senate report, "the press remained free," and even the CIA's own intelligence estimates stated that *El Mercurio* had been able to maintain its independence. The supposed threat to the press was the most important theme the CIA used in an international propaganda campaign aimed against Allende. With the fabricated charge, the CIA was able to convince newspapers around the world—including most of the American media—that Allende posed such a threat. Additionally the CIA circulated its propaganda throughout Chile by means of a complex assortment of captive newspapers, magazines, and radio and television outlets.[24]

CIA operations were supplemented by clandestine aid from sympathetic Brazilians and the secret services of other "allied" countries. Brazilians, themselves trained by the CIA for their own 1964 coup against a leftist president, seem to have played a major part in the disruption of Chile. The head of a Brazilian "think tank," Dr. Glycon de Paiva, boasted in a post-coup interview with the *Washington Post*: "The recipe exists and you can bake the cake any time. We saw how it worked in Brazil and now in Chile."[25] In Chile as in Brazil, the CIA heavily subsidized right-wing think tanks, which were used to coordinate intelligence, distribute propaganda, and organize paramilitary units.

Some of the CIA's money flowed into paramilitary and terrorist groups such as the notorious Patria y Libertad, an extremist private vigilante group. Other funds went, through conduits, into support of strikes that plagued the Allende regime. One hundred and eight leaders of the white-collar trade associations—some of which received direct CIA subsidies—received free training in the United States from the American Institute for Free Labor Development (AIFLD), an AFL-CIO affiliate which, according to ex-agency operative Philip Agee, was set up under the control of the CIA. While the 40 Committee turned down specific CIA proposals for direct support to two truckers' strikes that had a devastating effect in 1972 and 1973 on Chile's economy, the CIA passed money on to private-sector groups, which in turn, with the agency's knowledge, funded the truckers.[26]

Although the Nixon administration cut off economic aid to Allende's Chile, it continued to send in military assistance. The administration wanted to remain on good terms with the Chilean officer corps, with which there had always been considerable American contact. Starting in 1969 and continuing through 1973, the CIA established a special project to monitor coup plotting—which the CIA was encouraging at least in 1969 and 1970. The Senate Select Committee reported:

In November [1971], the Station suggested that the ultimate objective of the military penetration program was a military coup. Headquarters responded by rejecting that formulation of the objective, cautioning that the CIA did not have 40 Committee approval to become involved in a coup. However, Headquarters acknowledged the difficulty of drawing a firm link between monitoring coup plotting and becoming involved in it. It also realized that the U.S. government's desire to be in clandestine contact with military plotters, for whatever purpose, might well imply to them United States support for their future plans.[27]

On September 11, 1973, a group of military and policy officers—a group that the CIA had penetrated—overthrew the Allende government. The following month, CIA Director William Colby—using the surgical language of the bureaucracy—told a House committee that the CIA "had an overall appreciation" of the "deterioration" of the economic and political situation, and with the Chilean navy pushing for a coup, it had become "only a question of time before it came." Henry Kissinger testified in 1973, under oath:

The CIA had nothing to do with the coup, to the best of my knowledge, and I only put in that qualification in case some mad man appears down there, who, without instructions, talked to somebody.[28]

If Kissinger is telling the truth about the absence of direct CIA involvement, it is at best disingenuous for him to claim that the United States—and the CIA especially—had nothing to do with the overthrow of a government it had worked for three years to destabilize. The CIA's own internal documents, quoted by the Senate Select Committee, credit the anti-Allende propaganda campaign as having played a significant role in setting the stage for the coup.[29] The Chilean military had to have been influenced by the propaganda themes the CIA was spreading all over Chile—themes that promised firing squads for Allende's opponents and that falsely indicated that Cubans were taking over the Chilean intelligence services and gathering data on the Chilean high command.[30] The CIA had directly encouraged these same Chilean officers to pull off a coup in 1970 and then stayed in intimate touch with them through 1973 while they plotted. As Clandestine Services chief Thomas Karamessines testified: "I am sure that the seeds that were laid in that effort in 1970 had their impact in 1973."[31]

In 1974, President Ford defended the CIA's action in Chile by stating, "I think this is in the best interests of the people of Chile and certainly in our best interests."[32] One wonders what the president had in mind. A brutal military dictatorship has replaced a democratically elected government. All political parties have been effectively banned; the Congress has been shut down, the press censored; supporters of the last legal government have been jailed and tortured; thousands have been killed; and elections have been put off indefinitely.

And what American interests have been served? Our government has once again aligned itself with a repressive junta. Our leaders have once again been caught telling a series of lies to Congress and the American people about their actions in a foreign country. Once again the CIA has used the free press and free elections to subvert a country's regime. The lawlessness and ruthlessness of the CIA's operations have brought us opprobrium around the world. The terrorism sanctioned and encouraged by the CIA will surely only instruct others in its use.

Only American corporations seem to have profited by the CIA's intervention, and even their interests were poorly served. If corporate investment can be protected only by repressive regimes, then surely those investments are a poor risk. No country can long violate its own citizenry's sensibilities and principles simply to preserve corporate investments abroad.

The CIA's operations in Chile are not merely of historical interest. Congressman Michael Harrington, after reading secret CIA testimony on Chile, wrote: "The Agency activities in Chile were viewed as a prototype, or laboratory experiment, to test the techniques of heavy financial investment in efforts to discredit and bring down a government."

The "experiment" was a bureaucratic success in Chile (although the patient died). The next casualty was apparently Argentina. Jamaica or perhaps Italy might be a future victim.

President Ford was asked at a September 1974 press conference about the legality of the CIA's destabilization operation in Chile. He responded: "I'm not going to pass judgment on whether it's permitted under international law. It's a recognized fact that historically as well as presently, such actions are taken in the best interest of the countries involved."[33]

The president did not specify which country would next have its "best interest" served by covert action.

THE CIA:
COVERT ACTION
AROUND THE WORLD

2

"I don't see why we need to stand by and watch a country go communist due to the irresponsibility of its own people."[1] So spoke Henry Kissinger at a secret June 1970 White House meeting. The topic under discussion that day was, as noted in the previous chapter, what covert actions the CIA should take against Salvador Allende, but the sentiment reflected American behavior in many countries and could have come from the lips of any of the key American foreign-policy managers of the post-World-War-II era. These men—presidents and their chief advisers—felt that they knew best; that if other countries acted in a manner they considered irresponsible, they had the right, and even the duty, to intervene with American power.

For the last thirty years, the United States has stood almost alone as the activist leader of the West, and American officials have become the arbiters of what sort of economic and political systems other nations should have. When such countries as Greece and Vietnam were threatened from the left, the United States intervened. When leftists took power in countries like Guatemala, Iran, and Chile, the United States helped to overthrow them. Stated American policy may have been that foreign countries should be free to choose their own system of government, but the reality has been that this freedom of choice applied only within American-defined limits. Successive American administrations claimed that the American objective was to spread democracy, but in fact American objectives were different and more specific.

Essentially the United States has demanded three things of foreign regimes: (1) that they support the anti-Soviet and anti-Chinese foreign policy of the United States; (2) that they allow and safeguard the investment of outside—particularly American—capital; and (3) that they maintain internal stability—which has usually translated into their repressing their own internal lefts. The intensity of American intervention has also been influenced by such other factors as the brashness or charisma of a foreign leader and a country's physical proximity to the United States.

With some help from its allies, the United States generally imposed its standards on other countries, particularly those of the Third World, though American intervention was not always effective. In effect the United States has served as the world's policemen. And the secret policeman —the enforcer—of this system has been the CIA.

The CIA was established by Congress in 1947 at a time when the cold war with the Soviet Union was just beginning but when American leaders had taken up the role of Western leadership. Britain and France had long maintained colonial empires with comparatively small occupying forces and actively functioning secret services. Their technique was to use "dirty tricks" to divide and confound native opposition.[2] The United States had little experience with such clandestine agencies (although U.S. cavalry agents were known in the nineteenth century to have given blankets from tuberculosis wards to hostile Indians). In World War II, President Franklin D. Roosevelt created by executive order the Office of Strategic Services (OSS), a military agency designed to promote resistance movements and to use the techniques of secret war against the Axis powers. America's first covert operatives largely learned these arcane skills from their more experienced British allies.

The OSS was disbanded after the war ended in 1945, but many of its components were transferred intact to other government agencies. Its veterans had enjoyed their clandestine wartime experiences and much preferred spy work to the ordinary routine of civilian life. These OSS alumni were closely connected to some of the most powerful figures in American government, law, industry, and finance. Led by former OSS chief William "Wild Bill" Donovan and OSS operational chief in Switzerland, Allen Dulles, they formed a potent lobbying group for a peacetime intelligence service. By 1947, the Truman administration had accepted their belief that such an organization was needed to counter the Soviet threat covertly. In the National Security Act, passed that year, Truman and his top advisers proposed the command structure that would be used to fight a cold war: the National Security Council (NSC) was established as the chief decision-making body; the armed forces were unified into the Defense Department; and the Central Intelligence Agency was formed.

In considering this package, Congress was not informed that the CIA would take an activist covert role. Rather, the CIA was presented to the lawmakers and the public as an entity whose function would be the coordination and analysis of intelligence within the government. The failure of the various military intelligence agencies to provide a clear warning of the Japanese attack on Pearl Harbor was frequently cited as the reason the United States needed a central intelligence agency to pull together in one place all the information available from all the government agencies. The CIA then would be expected to give the president the best possible estimate of the situation.

The National Security Act did not mention that the CIA would collect intelligence, although the Truman administration apparently did privately inform some members of Congress.[3] However, no member of Congress was informed that the CIA would also be using the techniques of covert action to manipulate the internal affairs of other nations secretly. The Senate Select Committee on Intelligence noted that "authority for covert action cannot be found" in the 1947 act and that Congress was not aware of any such purpose.[4] The CIA's own general counsel conceded in a memorandum written shortly after the passage of the act that the legislative history showed no congressional intent to authorize covert action.[5] Nevertheless the CIA continues to claim that its authority to interfere in other countries' affairs came from a vaguely worded section of the National Security Act, which directed it "to perform such other functions and duties related to intelligence affecting national security as the National Security Council might from time to time direct."[6]

No one in a policymaking position in the executive branch was really concerned about whether Congress had authorized covert actions. Such activities were, they believed, necessary and hence the president could order them. Thus the first year of the CIA's existence, the NSC had assigned the agency responsibility for conduct of se-

" HELLO CHIEF ?..... I THINK WE'RE IN FOR SOME MORE BAD PRESS ....."

COPYRIGHT 1975 BY *DAYTON DAILY NEWS*

cret psychological, political, paramilitary, and economic operations.[7] There may not have been a legal mandate for such activities but there was something approaching a national consensus for "stopping Communism." To many Americans, including a commission headed by former President Herbert Hoover, that meant acting "more ruthless" than any foe. The Hoover Commission concluded in a secret annex on intelligence quoted in part in the Introduction:

It is now clear that we are facing an implacable enemy whose avowed objective is world domination by whatever means and at whatever cost. There are no rules in such a game. Hitherto acceptable norms of human conduct do not apply. If the U.S. is to survive, longstanding American concepts of "fair play" must be reconsidered. We must develop effective espionage and counterespionage services and must learn to subvert, sabotage, and destroy our enemies by more clever, more sophisticated, and more effective methods than those used against us. It may become necessary that the American people be made acquainted with, understand and support this fundamentally repugnant philosophy.[8]

Until recent years when CIA abuses were repeatedly exposed, the agency never found it necessary to tell Americans about its "fundamentally repugnant philosophy" that the end—"national security" as defined by the CIA and successive presidents—justifies the means, virtually every technique imaginable, including most of the criminal methods known to man. The American press was little more accurate in describing the CIA and its major place in American foreign policy. With only a few exceptions, not until the myth of "national security" was punctured by the Vietnam War and then Watergate, did parts of the media start to investigate United States intelligence. Newspapers like *The New York Times* actually conspired with the CIA to suppress stories, such as the 1961 invasion of Cuba at the Bay of Pigs[9] and the CIA's "secret war" in Laos.[10] As late as 1975, CIA Director William Colby was able to convince nearly a dozen media outlets not to publish the story of how the CIA had secretly contracted with a company owned by the late Howard Hughes to build the *Glomar Explorer*, a ship capable of retrieving a Soviet submarine off the ocean floor.

With the press abdicating its responsibility, and with the public quiescent on the subject, Congress was under no meaningful outside pressure to examine America's spy agencies. Within Congress itself, members were largely content to leave oversight to a handful of senior members who were distinguished by their age and their conservative political views. As a result the supposed congressional overseers served more as protectors of the CIA than as watchdogs of the public's trust. For example, a 1973 CIA memorandum released to the House intelligence committee showed that Senate oversight subcommittee member Henry Jackson worked behind the scenes to shield the CIA from investigation by a Senate Foreign Relations subcommittee. "Senator Jackson repeatedly made the comment that in his view the CIA Oversight Committee had the responsibility of protecting the Agency. . . ."[11]

For more than twenty-five years, the Congress and the press have given the executive branch virtually a free hand to carry on whatever clandestine operations it chose. The checks and balances that were written into the American system by the founding fathers were bypassed. The legislature, the courts, the media, and public opinion were not a real restraint on the CIA because none of the potential checkers or balancers knew what the secret agency was doing.

Despite earlier revelations of extensive CIA operations in Indochina and other foreign places, not until December 22, 1974 when *The New York Times*'s Seymour Her h exposed the CIA's illegal spying on Americans within the United States was there any real change in the media's or the Congress's attitudes.[12] The CIA had come home, with all its dirty tricks. The press, for its part, started to investigate CIA activities almost as it would those of other government agencies. In tacit admission of the failure of earlier oversight groups, both houses of Congress approved the formation of special committees to make in-depth studies of American intelligence. The Senate followed up with the creation of a permanent oversight committee.

Seymour Hersh's *New York Times* story on CIA domestic activity paved the way for an extensive investigation of the CIA and other intelligence agencies, but it was other revelations that focused attention on the CIA's covert actions abroad. First it was the secret war in Laos, then the overthrow of Allende and charges by Congressman Michael Harrington that the administration was lying about the CIA role in Chile. Later, in the midst of the congressional investigations, came word that the United States was secretly intervening in Angola. Congress for the first time cut off funds and halted the CIA intervention. The Congress and the public were finally ready to take a close look at covert operations.

This first attempt at meaningful investigation by Congress came after twenty-nine years, in which the CIA had grown dramatically in a manner far different from what Congress had originally authorized or envisioned. The CIA has retained the coordination and analytical role that the 1947 National Security Act gave it, but the CIA's first priority from its earliest days has been the operational work of its Clandestine Services (the common name for the agency's operational component, which has been officially known as the Directorate of Plans and currently as the Directorate of Operations).

By 1952, President Truman and his successors gave specific functions to the Clandestine Services and the rest of the CIA through a series of secret executive orders that became known as National Security Council Intelligence Directives (NSCIDS). By June 1948, President Truman had expanded the CIA's functions to include

propaganda; economic warfare; preventive direct action, including sabotage, demolition and evacuation measures; subversion against hostile states, including assistance to guerrilla and refugee liberation groups, and support of indigenous anti-communist elements of the free world.[13]

George Kennan, one of those instrumental in creating the CIA's covert capability, would later recall how the CIA's "dirty tricks department" quickly expanded well beyond what had originally been envisioned:

We had thought that this would be a facility which could be used when and if an occasion arose. . . . There might be years when we wouldn't have to do anything like this.[14]

Whatever the original intentions of officials like Kennan, the CIA—with one-third of its personnel drawn from OSS —quickly made concealed action, as the Senate Select Committee found, into a "routine American program of influencing governments and covertly exercising power, involving literally hundreds of projects" each year.[15]

The CIA's early efforts were centered on Western Europe where it labored mightily to shore up America's war-ravaged allies. United States leaders perceived a threat to these countries from the Red Army in the East and from local Communist parties, which had been in the forefront of the resistance against the Axis. On the overt level, the United States fought this threat—and helped its own economy in the process—by pouring billions of dollars in Marshall Plan aid into Western Europe and Turkey. On the clandestine level, the CIA conducted a "Marshall Plan" meshed with the overt. The agency brought money, manipulation, and violence to bear to aid its friends and counter the Communists. In the process, the CIA gave secret subsidies and guided the affairs of individual politicians, political parties, labor unions, newspapers, and cultural groups.

In Germany, both major political parties and most of their leaders received secret CIA subsidies.[16] In the spring of 1974, West German Chancellor Willy Brandt resigned in the wake of reports that one of his assistants was an East German spy. Ironically Brandt himself was one of many aspiring young German politicians put on the CIA payroll right after World War II. In Italy, according to a CIA document quoted in the House intelligence report,

The United States was concerned in 1948 that the Communists would emerge from the national elections sufficiently strong to enter the government as a major if not dominant force. As a counter, it was decided that CIA should give $1,000,000 to the center parties for this election with the bulk going to [deleted, but actually the Italian Christian Democratic Party].

Other CIA funds went to an anti-Communist labor federation, as well as church and civic groups. The House committee noted that between 1948 and 1968, the CIA spent over $65 million for secret-action projects in Italy.[17] CIA funding of Italian politics has continued into the present day. In December 1975 President Gerald Ford personally approved payment of $6 million in secret subsidies to anti-Communist forces in Italy in preparation for the elections that were held in June 1976.[18]

The CIA programs in Western Europe were considered quite successful by agency operatives. Coupled with acknowledged economic and military support—as well as strong anti-Soviet feelings in Western Europe—the CIA effort may have played a real part in the recovery of Western Europe and the maintenance of parliamentary systems in most countries. The CIA was seen as countering Soviet attempts at subversion, and it had more or less a blank check to be "more ruthless" than its Soviet counterpart, the KGB, or anyone else it opposed.

Spurred on by the Communist victory in China and the Korean War and its own successes in Western Europe, the CIA grew in personnel from less than 5,000 in 1950 to about 15,000 in 1955. By 1953, there were major covert operations in forty-eight countries.[19] By 1952, the Clandestine Services accounted for 74 percent of the CIA budget (*not* including the Directorate of Administration's costs in support of such secret activities as communications, logistical back-up, etc.). That figure had fallen to 54 percent by the end of the 1950s,[20] but with supporting administrative costs added in, clandestine work still accounted for more than two-thirds of the CIA's expenditures (of about $750 million per year) into the early 1970s.[21]

During the 1950s, it became clear that Western Europe

would stabilize around the NATO and Common Market countries, and that Soviet domination of most of Eastern Europe would not change markedly. Moreover, efforts to penetrate the Soviet bloc countries were almost universally unsuccessful. During those early years the CIA actively supported guerrilla movements in such places as Albania, Poland, and the Ukraine in futile efforts to "roll back the iron curtain."[22] In Poland, agency attempts to establish an underground apparatus involved millions of dollars of gold and many agents. For years CIA agents in Poland maintained regular contact with their case officers in West Germany. Again and again the CIA sent in more gold and more agents in response to requests from the underground. Only after several years did the agency realize that the Polish Secret Service had captured the entire network from the beginning, and kept it going to bilk the agency of millions of dollars in gold and to trap some of its best agents.

While the CIA had enjoyed comparatively little success in Eastern Europe, the Soviet Union, and China, it found more fertile territory in less developed nations where corruption and poverty tended to be endemic.[23] Noted the CIA's former chief of Clandestine Services, Richard Bissel:

Simply because [their] governments are much less highly organized there is less security consciousness; and there is apt to be more actual or potential diffusion of power among parties, localities, organizations, and individuals outside the central government.[24]

Two spectacular "successes" in the early 1950s overthrowing constitutional but "leftist" governments in Iran and Guatemala set the tone for agency Third World operations. Mohammed Mossadegh in Iran and Jacobo Arbenz in Guatemala were charismatic leaders who, like Castro, Patrice Lumumba, and Allende, sought to lead a leftist revolution.[25] They were all labeled "Communists" and the CIA, directed by successive presidents, sought to drive them from power. In each of these cases (except

Cuba) and in others, the agency was "successful" in that the feared charismatic leader was removed from the scene. Whether American ideals or even strategic interests were served by these actions is another matter.

Overthrowing governments is but one type of CIA activity. The Church Committee reported that since 1961 the CIA had conducted "several thousand covert action projects."[26] The techniques used in these operations have run the gamut from military actions to planting stories in newspapers. The Senate intelligence report describes how such action projects increased dramatically in the Third World during the 1950s:

Financial support was provided to parties, candidates, and incumbent leaders of almost every political persuasion, except the extreme left and right. The immediate purpose of these projects was to encourage political stability, and thus prevent Communist incursions, but another important objective was the acquisition of "agents of influence" who could be used at a future date to provide intelligence or to carry out political action. Through such projects, the CIA developed a world-wide infrastructure of individual agents, or networks of agents, in a variety of covert activity.[27]

One former CIA station chief told the Senate committee how it was in his country:

Any aspiring politician almost automatically would come to CIA to see if we could help get him elected. . . . They were the wards of the United States, and . . . whatever happened for good or bad was the fault of the CIA.[28]

Philip Agee, who spent twelve years in CIA operational work, describes in minute detail in his book *Inside the Company: CIA Diary* how the agency in Ecuador recruited as secret agents the country's vice president, members of the cabinet, the head of police intelligence, key chiefs of labor and student unions, important journalists and military officers, heads of political parties, and both the nephew of the country's president and his personal doctor. In short the CIA, during Agee's assignment in Ecuador in the early 1960s, was manipulating if not controlling all the key sectors of that country's society. The cost for holding this near total sway over a whole country: under a million dollars a year for the CIA station's budget.[29]

The meddling in these societies had little to do with our national interest or security. For example, the Shah of Iran had a border dispute with the Iraqi government and wanted to feed the Kurdish revolt against the Iraqis. The Shah prevailed on Nixon and Kissinger to provide money to the Kurds and to assure them of American support. After three years, the Shah settled his dispute with Iraq. The CIA suddenly cut the Kurds off without a penny as the Iraqis launched an all-out search-and-destroy mission the day after the secret agreement was signed with Iran. The result was thousands of casualties and more than 200,000 refugees. Kissinger even refused to provide humanitarian assistance to the refugees, stating: "Covert action should not be confused with missionary work."[30]

In Ecuador the CIA helped to overthrow two governments, with only about ten American operators working there full time. In more complex societies like Brazil, Iran, and Vietnam, the CIA assigned considerably more personnel.

In some places the CIA—always at the order of the White House—went well beyond behind-the-scenes manipulation and fought "secret wars." Although the Constitution says only the Congress shall declare war, a succession of presidents has committed the CIA's paramilitary forces to combat. In virtually all these cases most members of Congress were not even informed that United States forces were involved in fighting. Yet, as the Senate committee found, "Paramilitary operations have great potential for escalating into major military commitments.[31]

Against mainland China during the 1950s, the CIA sponsored guerrilla raids—the only results of which were the deaths of many Chinese and the capture and imprisonment for twenty years of two young CIA operatives, John Downey and Richard Fecteau. In Guatemala, in 1954, the CIA organized a small army to overthrow a leftist government.[32] In Indonesia in 1958, the CIA supplied rebels fighting against President Sukarno, and agency planes—belonging to an agency "proprietary," or front, called Civil Air Transport—bombed government forces.[33] In Burma during the 1950s, the CIA supported about 12,000 Nationalist Chinese who had fled China in 1949. These forces became heavily involved in the opium trade—as were the CIA's Meo allies in Laos. The United States ambassador to Burma, who was not aware of the CIA involvement, wound up lying about their presence to the Burmese government.[34]

The largest CIA military operations took place in Indochina. The CIA's involvement in Vietnam had started in support of the French colonial regime before 1954. Thereafter the CIA and General Edward Lansdale, one of its legendary operators, played a key role in installing President Ngo Dinh Diem in power. Lansdale's subordinates ran guerrilla raids against North Vietnam; spread false propaganda that caused large increases in the flow of refugees from North Vietnam; and financed and trained Diem's secret police and palace guards.[35] United States Special Forces, or "Green Berets," which were under CIA operational control until 1963, recruited an army of ethnic minorities to fight secretly along Vietnam's borders and in Cambodia, North Vietnam, and Laos.

Inside Laos itself the CIA organized another, even larger, "secret" army, which contained at its peak 35,000 Meo and other minority tribesmen. When that force had been nearly decimated in the early 1970s, 17,000 Thai troops were hired by the agency.[36] Congress had by law forbidden the hiring of such mercenaries from neighboring countries, but the Nixon administration gave the CIA the go-ahead to recruit the Thais anyway, under the thin subterfuge that they had signed on not in Thailand but locally in Laos.[37]

Despite the tens of thousands of foreign soldiers on its payroll, the CIA was able to keep its war in Laos concealed from most members of Congress until 1969.[38] While it was no secret from the enemy soldiers who were being bombed and shot, the agency's involvement was largely invisible to the outside world because of a wide variety of covers. Its operatives hid as political and economic officers in the American embassy in Vientiane, as CIA persons do around the world; 25 percent of so-called State Department officials worldwide are actually with the CIA.[39] The U.S. Army and Air Force also provided cover, as military units have long done for the CIA both at home and abroad. The Agency for International Development (AID) was another front for the CIA and allowed it to set up under AID cover a "requirements Office" and a "Research Management Branch." By 1971, almost 50,000 American military men and women based outside Laos were supporting the "secret war: logistically and with massive bombing strikes."[40]

Within Laos the CIA's L'Armée Clandestine was being flown around and supplied by two "private" airlines, Continental Air Services and Air America. Continental was owned by the domestic United States airline of the same name, and its Laotian service had been set up in cooperation with the CIA. Ostensibly it was flying for AID, under lucrative contracts, but in actuality it was with the CIA, and its top officers had been given special security clearances by the agency.[41]

Air America, on the other hand, was a fully owned and operated subsidiary of the CIA—called a "proprietary." It, in turn, was a spin-off of Civil Air Transport (CAT), the CIA airline that had used B-26s to bomb Indonesia in 1958. A CIA operative had written about CAT in 1961:

CAT had demonstrated its capabilities on numerous occasions to meet all types of contingency or long-term covert air requirements in support of U.S. objectives. During the past 10 years, it has had some notable achievements, including support of the Chinese Nationalist withdrawal from the mainland, air drop support to the French at Dien Bien Phu, complete logistical and tactical air support for the Indonesian operation, air lifts of refugees from North Vietnam, more than 200 overflights of Mainland China and Tibet, and extensive air support in Laos during the present crisis. . . .[42]

By 1970, CIA proprietary airlines, including CAT, Air

America, and Southern Air Transport, owned considerably more aircraft than Pan American Airlines.[43] With the end of direct American participation in the Indochinese wars in 1973, the CIA sold its largest air proprietaries. The purchasers have been individuals or companies with long relationships with the agency, who will presumably be willing to let the CIA lease back its old "assets."

The CIA also made extensive use of proprietaries in its second largest operation, mounted against Cuban leader Fidel Castro. Starting in the late 1950s, the CIA organized a Cuban exile army to overthrow Castro. The result was the CIA's greatest fiasco ever: the total routing of its forces at the Bay of Pigs. The agency did not give up, however, as the Kennedy brothers remained more determined than ever to get rid of the Castro government. CIA paramilitary forces continued to make regular raids against Cuba, destroying crops, blowing up installations, and generally attacking the Cuban economy, in operations code-named MONGOOSE.[44]

The most extreme of the CIA's anti-Castro programs were its repeated attempts to assassinate the Cuban leader. Time after time, during the Eisenhower, Kennedy, and Johnson administrations, the CIA failed in its murder attempts. From 1960 to 1962, the agency worked in tandem with Mafia leaders to dispose of Castro. The CIA's mob accomplices included Sam Giancana of the Chicago family, the Trafficantes of Havana and Tampa, Florida, and convicted card cheat John Rosselli of the West Coast. The agency tried poisoners and riflemen. Explosive seashells and a deadly fountain pen were some of the murderous devices the agency's Technical Service Division came up with. In 1963, the technicians specially prepared a skin-diving suit to be presented as a gift to Castro. It was dusted inside with a fungus that would produce a chronic skin disease called Madura foot. Just to make sure, the breathing apparatus was contaminated with tubercle bacillus.[45]

The CIA's ill-fated attempts to kill Castro were only one episode in agency assassination plots. Murder was viewed within the CIA as an important enough weapon that an assassination capability was institutionalized in 1961. The agency, which has a particular knack for euphemism, called the program "executive action." Preferring to keep the actual blood off their own hands, agency officials hired people like mafiosos and an agent code-named WI/ROGUE to do the dirty work. WI/ROGUE is described in CIA documents as a "forger and former bank robber":

He is indeed aware of the precepts of right and wrong, but if he is given an assignment which may be morally wrong in the eyes of the world, but necessary because his case officer ordered him to carry it out, then it is right, and he will dutifully undertake appropriate action for its execution without pangs of conscience. In a word, he can rationalize all actions.[46]

WI/ROGUE was involved in the CIA's attempts to kill Patrice Lumumba in the Congo (now Zaire). The Senate Select Committee found that the CIA sent highly toxic poisons to the Congo and took other "exploratory steps" as part of its plots to kill the popular leftist leader.[47] In 1961, in the Dominican Republic, Rafael Trujillo was shot by Dominican dissidents who were in close touch with the CIA and the State Department. Reported the Senate Select Committee:

Some Government personnel were aware that the dissidents intended to kill Trujillo. Three pistols and three carbines were furnished by American officials, although a request for machine guns was later refused.[48]

The CIA was also involved in plots that led to the assassinations of Ngo Dinh Diem and his brother Nhu in South Vietnam, and that, already detailed, of General René Schneider in Chile.[48] Whether the CIA directly planned for these men to die or whether their shootings were outside the agency's control is not clear from the record available. In any case the CIA was certainly a witting accomplice in both the Vietnamese case, where it gave its approval to the coup plotters, and the Schneider incident, where it provided machine guns and other equipment to those plotting against him.

In Vietnam the CIA became involved in a different kind of assassination program. This was a series of operations —generally referred to as PHOENIX—which were designed to "neutralize" the political infrastructure of the National Liberation Front (NLF). In the first two and one-half years of PHOENIX, 20,587 suspected NLF cadre were killed, according to figures supplied Congress by William Colby, the man who supervised the program and then was promoted by President Nixon to head the CIA. Linked to PHOENIX were CIA-run and -financed Provincial Interrogation Centers and Counter Terror (CT) teams in every Vietnamese province. Wayne Cooper, a former State Department official with direct knowledge of the CT program (whose name was changed by the CIA in 1966 for public relations reasons), observed:

CIA representatives recruited, organized, supplied, and directly paid CT teams, whose function was to use Viet Cong techniques of terror—assassination, abuses, kidnappings and intimidation— against the Viet Cong leadership.[49]

To mount large-scale operations abroad and to maintain its worldwide espionage and concealed-operations apparatus, the CIA developed a massive secret infrastructure within the United States. Many segments of American society have become involved, wittingly or unwittingly, in CIA operations. Proprietaries, whose role in air operations was described above, performed a wide variety of other services for the CIA. One proprietary called Southern Capital and Management Corporation invested agency funds in stocks and bonds and stood at the center of a tangled web of proprietary insurance and other financial companies.[50] Another, called International Police Services, Inc., was a training school for thousands of foreign policemen and part of an even larger police program that the CIA ran in cooperation with AID.[51] Yet another, Psychological Assessment Associates, did psychological research on ways to assess potential CIA agents and employees in an effort to identify their vulnerabilities and their truthfulness.[52]

The CIA realized from its very beginning that its operations stood a better chance of remaining hidden and being effective if they could be concealed behind private proprietaries and could use the facilities of other institutions. The covert operatives understood that they could reach out deeper into foreign societies they wished to penetrate and manipulate if they could work through legitimate United States corporations and organizations. In the process, virtually no sector of American society was immune from CIA use, and the agency was able to build up a secret constituency and operational network across the United States.

CORPORATIONS

The CIA makes wide use of legitimate multinational corporations. Financial institutions such as the First National City Bank help the CIA move large sums of money into target countries.[53] During the mid-1950s, Pan American Airlines had an arrangement with the CIA to provide agency personnel access to baggage in planes transiting the airport in Panama City, Panama, and even to provide the operatives with mechanics overalls—better to disguise them. In Chile from 1970 to 1973, ITT worked closely with the CIA in a whole variety of secret operations.[54]

Multinational corporations also provide cover to CIA operatives abroad. Companies known to have concealed CIA personnel on their payrolls are ITT, Pan Am, and Grace Shipping Lines.[55] In February 1974, a "high government official," who was in fact CIA Director William Colby, told reporters that the CIA had over 200 operatives working under corporate cover. A rare public glimpse of the inner workings of such an agency-corporate arrangement came in 1975 when Ashland Oil Company admitted to the Securities and Exchange Commission that it had received $98,968 from the CIA from 1968 to 1973. The money was reportedly to pay Ashland the costs of providing cover to an agency operator for those five years in Western Europe. Of the money, $50,000 wound up in a fund that Ashland used to make illegal campaign contributions in the United States.[56] Ashland obviously had its own use for the untraceable "laundered" funds the CIA uses to pay its debts.

LABOR

Starting in the late 1940s, the CIA has worked extremely closely with George Meany and much of the American labor movement to build strong anti-Comunist unions and to destroy the effectiveness of leftist unions. The agency funneled money for European unions in the early years through such labor leaders as Walter Reuther of the United Auto Workers and the AFL's Irving Brown.[57] CIA funds went to the international programs of individual unions, including the American Newspaper Guild and the American Federation of Federal, State, and Municipal Employees[58] (which served as the CIA's principal instrument for fomenting a general strike and helping to overthrow the government of British Guiana in 1962-63).[59]

THE PRESS AND PUBLISHING

The CIA's activities in the media area are as varied as the most diverse conglomerates. Since 1947, the agency has published over 1,250 books that were not identified as being connected with the United States government. These works were distributed around the world—and in the United States—to support propaganda themes the CIA was pushing. Wrote the CIA's covert propaganda chief in 1961: "Books differ from all other propaganda media, primarily because one single book can significantly change the reader's attitude and action to an extent unmatched by the impact of any other single medium."[60]

In addition to book publishing, the CIA has also owned or subsidized for propaganda purposes magazines, newspapers, news services, and radio and television stations.

Although the CIA's propaganda activities are supposed to be limited to foreign audiences, events and ideas described in agency publications are often widely distributed in the United States. *The Penkovskiy Papers*, which the CIA wrote, was a best seller at home, and information put out by the CIA in its Chilean media operations in 1970 was picked up by both the *Washington Post* and *The New York Times*.[61] Clandestine Services head Desmond Fitzgerald commented in 1967: "Fallout in the United States from a foreign publication which we support is inevitable and consequently permissible."[62]

While the CIA apparently is not bothered by the prospect of putting out misleading propaganda inside the United States, it has established safeguards to make sure that top officials outside the agency do not accept falsehoods it is spreading as truth and use these misleading data as a basis to make policy. Regular coordination exists between the CIA and the State Department to prevent the deception of these officials through CIA "black" propaganda.[63]

The CIA uses the press in another way by disguising some of its operatives as news personnel. In 1973, CIA Director Colby revealed that some "three dozen" American newsmen worked for the agency.[64] In February 1976, the CIA announced it would no longer make use of "accredited" reporters, but the announcement was worded in a way not to give away the fact that the Senate Select Committee would reveal two months later: namely, the CIA was still using more than twenty-five *unaccredited* journalists—freelancers, stringers, and news executives.

CHURCHES AND MISSIONARIES

As the Senate Intelligence Committee confirmed, the CIA has been using small numbers of missionaries and church personnel in operational activities and as intelligence sources.[65] Some of these included American missionaries in Bolivia who passed to the CIA information on dissident groups, a South Vietnamese bishop on the CIA payroll, CIA-financed radio broadcasts to promote literacy and spread anti-Communist propaganda in Colombia, and use of a Jesuit (Roger Vekemans) in Chile as a conduit for millions of dollars in political-action funds.[66]

UNIVERSITIES

The CIA has used United States universities as recruiting grounds. One target is foreign students whom the agency wants to turn into spies in their home countries. Another is American students who may be recruited to be secret CIA operatives. A third group is professors, including visitors from abroad and those on the faculty, who may be recruited as permanent agents or persuaded to take on a single assignment. For this purpose the CIA maintains secret contractual relationships with several hundred academics on over a hundred campuses.[67] The principal job of these CIA professors is to identify and help evaluate potential agents. After a potential recruit is spotted, his name is passed on to the CIA, which secretly investigates the individual. If a person is an American, a cover story—such as a credit-agency check—is used to gather the information. If the individual passes the security review the CIA secret recruiters will often be used to introduce the potential recruit to his would-be case officer. Some professors also are used to write CIA propaganda and to carry out specialized undercover missions. A professor or student (or someone posing as one of these) has a perfect excuse to travel around the world, asking all sorts of questions of interest to the CIA. Sometimes a professor thinks he is gathering information for a private business firm or research group when in fact the organization is a CIA front. Additionally the CIA sponsors considerable research on campus, and in most cases the agency's involvement is hidden—even from students and graduate assistants helping in the research. At the Massachusetts Institute of Technology, the CIA funded from 1951 to 1965 the

Center for International Studies, and from 1952 to 1967 it paid much of the budget of the National Student Association, whose officers attended international conferences as American representatives and sometimes carried out operational tasks for the CIA.[68] During the early 1960s, the CIA used Michigan State University programs as a cover for agency police training programs in South Vietnam,[69] and it continues to assign covert missions to academics—or people pretending to be academics.

DRUG TESTING AND BEHAVIOR MODIFICATION

Perhaps the most alarming research sponsored by the CIA in support of its clandestine programs was its extensive program on drug testing and behavior modification.

Early Saturday morning, on November 27, 1953, New York City policemen found the body of Frank Olson on the pavement by the Statler Hilton Hotel; he had hurled himself through the window of his room on the tenth floor. When the police asked the man who had been sharing Olson's room for an explanation of the apparent suicide, his companion mentioned that Olson suffered from ulcers. Twenty-two years later, it was revealed that Olson had commited suicide as a result of a CIA drug-testing program, in which he had unwittingly been administered a dose of LSD in a glass of Cointreau.

In response to growing fears that "hostile" foreign countries were using chemical and biological substances against United States agents, the CIA began to develop a defensive program of drug testing in the late 1940s and early 1950s, which turned into behavior modification experiments on unsuspecting individuals. Various programs expanded to include the stockpiling of lethal and incapacitating drugs, and the study of biological agents to be used against crops and animals. In 1953, the agency discussed a $240,000 purchase of 10 kilograms of LSD—enough for 100 million doses. Whether the purchase actually took place is not yet known. Over a ten-year period additional avenues of research were initiated, including experimentation on the effects of radiation and electric shocks. At one time the CIA flooded the New York subway system with a "harmless simulant" of a disease-carrying gas, as a trial study on the vulnerability of subway riders to sneak attack.

The major drug-testing program, known as MKULTRA, began to test volunteers at the Lexington Rehabilitation Center in Kentucky, a hospital for drug addicts. Willing volunteers were also tested in cooperation with the Bureau of Narcotics. But agency officials, concerned that testing under controlled conditions did not constitute a true test of the drug's effect, began to experiment on unwitting individuals. Agents working on the project would randomly choose a victim at a bar or off the street and, with no prior consent or medical prescreening, would take the individual back to a safe house and administer the drug. For many of the unsuspecting victims, the result was days or even weeks of hospitalization and mental stress. For Frank Olson, a civilian employee of the army who was assigned to work on the drug-testing program with the CIA at Fort Deitrick, Maryland, it meant the death by suicide described above.

Although the agency made sure that Olson's widow and three young children received financial benefits, no explanation was ever given, and the family endured unknown anguish in its search for a reason for Olson's suicide. In a statement written by the family accompanying the release of CIA documents detailing the history of the twenty-two-year cover-up, the pain of those years was expressed. "We are one family whose history has been fundamentally altered by illegal CIA activity, the family of the only American so far identified as having died as a result of CIA treachery." The family spoke of the shadow of doubt and guilt that hung over the children, and the "inevitable trauma and day-to-day consequences" for Alice Olson, his wife.

The CIA's reaction to Olson's suicide was quite different. After agonizing consideration involving CIA chief Allen Dulles and future agency chief Richard Helms, a punishment appropriate to a clandestine organization was concocted. A letter was prepared and signed by Dulles telling those involved in causing Olson's death that they should not have done what they did. This letter was hand carried to each of those involved and they were permitted to read it but not to keep a copy. To preserve security, copies of the letter were not placed in the personnel files of those involved.

The drug-testing programs continued to expose unknown numbers of people to the risk of death or mental or physical injury for the next ten years, the only changes being a tightening of security precautions. An inspector general's study in 1957 warned that knowledge of the program "would have serious repercussions in political and diplomatic circles." Fear that the program would be leaked led CIA Director Helms to destroy all records of its activities, in 1973, including 152 separate files. Helms himself continued to push for an expanded drug-testing program, even after it had been terminated. Referring to its usefulness, Helms stated, "While I share your uneasiness and distaste for any program which tends to intrude upon an individual's private and legal prerogatives, I believe it is necessary that the Agency maintain a central role in this activity."

FOUNDATIONS AND VOLUNTARY ORGANIZATIONS

In 1967, *Ramparts* magazine exposed the CIA's use of a network of front and cooperating foundations, which acted as conduits for tens of millions of dollars in covert funds.[70] The Senate committee found that from 1963 to 1966 the CIA funded nearly half of all grants made by all foundations, other than Rockefeller, Ford, and Carnegie, in the area of international activities. In addition to the

National Student Association, recipients of the CIA largesse included the International Commission of Jurists, the National Education Association, the African-American Institute, the American Friends of the Middle East, the Congress for Cultural Freedom, and *Encounter* magazine. The money was generally used to pay for the international activities of supposedly independent groups, which could then counter leftist groups.[71] Reacting to the *Ramparts* revelations, the Johnson administration adopted a policy that no CIA funds should go to any United States educational or private organizations. Not to be deterred, however, the CIA kept undercover relationships with individuals connected to such groups, and it continued funding Radio Free Europe and Radio Liberty until Congress in 1971 provided alternate funding.[72]

ÉMIGRÉ GROUPS

The CIA regards ethnic groups in the United States—from Eastern Europeans to Cuban to Chinese—as fair game for its clandestine operations. While the stated targets of the agency are supposed to be overseas, the CIA is authorized to work clandestinely at home if the information it seeks has to do with foreign places and is gathered from foreigners. The millions of Americans belonging to some ethnic group are potential targets under this standard. In Miami during the mid-1960s, the CIA organized an intelligence service among Cuban exiles, which operated extensively among that city's Cuban community.[73]

While supporters of the CIA have complained that the agency's capabilities have been greatly damaged by the ongoing CIA scandals, the fact remains that even at the scandals' height, the agency continued to have the operational structure in place to pour millions of dollars in arms and support into Angola and to fund election support in Italy.

All over the world the CIA maintains the capability to carry out covert operations. As the Senate Select Committee found:

There is no question that the CIA attaches great importance to the maintenance of a worldwide clandestine infrastructure—the so-called "plumbing" in place. During the 1960s the Agency developed a worldwide system of standby covert action "assets," ranging from media personnel to individuals said to influence the behavior of governments.[74]

This clandestine infrastructure has been cut back to some extent in recent years, but the power of the CIA to

intervene should not be underestimated. The agency is always reluctant to give up a useful asset, and under procedures in force as late as the summer of 1976 the CIA needed to consult no outsiders, whether in the executive branch or Congress, before recruiting and making payments to key foreigners able to manipulate events in other countries.

To be sure, before those assets could be used in a large-scale operation to overthrow a government or mount a major propaganda campaign, the CIA would have to seek permission of a National Security Council panel, the Operations Advisory Group (a body made up of the assistant to the president for national security affairs, the secretaries of state and defense, the chairman of the Joint Chiefs of Staff, and the director of central intelligence; earlier versions of this panel have been called the Special Group, the 54/12 Committee, the 303 Committee, and the 40 Committee). Nevertheless, of the several thousand covert-action projects carried out by the CIA since 1961, the Senate Select Committee found that only fourteen percent were individually considered by this executive branch review group.[75]

Moreover, the Operations Advisory Group has no oversight at all over CIA operations directed toward intelligence gathering or counter-intelligence work. While CIA recruitment of the interior minister in Bolivia or penetration and training of the police in Uruguay can have an explosive effect on United States foreign relations, the agency submits to no high-level review before taking such actions. Reportedly, in recent years as covert action has come under increasing attack, the CIA has designated more and more of its assets—in its internal bookkeeping system—as "FI/CI" (foreign intelligence/counter-intelligence) agents. While these agents may be in key positions where they can have a profound effect on their country's affairs, the CIA is able to claim they are used only for informational purposes. That may be true in the short run, but these intelligence agents remain a crucial part of the CIA's covert-action "plumbing in place."

The president's secret enforcer still operates across the globe. The day-to-day routine meddling continues unabated. Larger programs—with the exception of Angola and Italy—may have been postponed while the agency was under investigation. But if no reforms are made, the CIA will remain at the president's hip, ready to be triggered wherever he aims.

THE FBI AT HOME

THE FBI'S
VENDETTA AGAINST
MARTIN LUTHER KING, JR.

3

In the early evening on December 1, 1955, Mrs. Rosa Parks boarded a Montgomery, Alabama, bus to return home from work. Mrs. Parks sat down in the first seat behind the section reserved for whites. When several white passengers boarded the crowded bus, the driver turned and issued his customary order to Mrs. Parks and three other blacks to stand and give up their seats to the white passengers. Mrs. Parks quietly refused and was arrested and jailed.

Although other blacks had been arrested that year—and one man shot and killed by police—for disobeying bus drivers in Montgomery, the arrest of Mrs. Parks sparked a response. Within five days, local civil rights leaders and clergymen, among them a young minister, Martin Luther King, Jr., led Montgomery blacks in launching an effective 382-day bus boycott to end segregated seating.

The bus boycott in Montgomery ended one form of segregation in one southern city and began a new phase in the civil rights movement, a decade of protest and non-violent confrontation designed to break down patterns of segregation and discrimination that had existed since the end of Reconstruction.

To do so, the civil rights movement marched: from

Montgomery to Greensboro, North Carolina, and then back to Birmingham and Selma; and from the South to the North and the cities of Washington, D.C., and Chicago, and to the suburb of Cicero. It was a decade of sit-ins, freedom rides, economic boycotts, and marches: a peoples' movement for dignity and equality.

The nonviolent civil rights movement was made up of many leaders and organizations: Roy Wilkins and the National Association for the Advancement of Colored People (NAACP); James Farmer and the Congress of Racial Equality; James Forman and the Student Nonviolent Coordinating Committee; John Lewis and the Voter Education Project. But it was Martin Luther King, Jr., and the Southern Christian Leadership Conference that came to symbolize the nonviolent movement.

Through his speaking, marching, and passive resistance, King became the personification of the movement and its aspirations. Others, like the Reverend Ralph Abernathy and John Lewis were organizers and tacticians; King was the spokesman, the one who could express the hopes of the blacks, provide inspiration, state the philosophy of nonviolence, and communicate to the nation.

When Rosa Parks refused to give up her seat on that bus in Montgomery, King, president of the boycott organization, explained why the blacks resisted: "We are tired," he said,

tired of being segregated and humiliated. We are impatient for justice. But we will protest with love. There will be no violence on our part. There will be no cross burnings. No white person will be taken from his home by a hooded Negro mob and murdered. If we do this, if we protest with love, future historians will have to say, "There lived a great people, a black people who injected new meaning and dignity into the veins of civilization."[1]

When the organizers of the boycott decided on nonviolent protest, it was King who could articulate its essence: "We are simply saying to the white community, 'We can no longer cooperate with an evil system. We will use non-cooperation to give birth to justice.'"[2]

After success in the Montgomery boycott, King and

others active in the protest held a conference in Atlanta to consider the next steps. On January 11, the conferees, mostly southern black clergymen, founded the Southern Christian Leadership Conference (SCLC) and elected King president. SCLC was established so that black clergymen could assume leadership in nonviolent protest against segregation and to encourage blacks "to assert their human dignity by refusing further cooperation with evil."[3] Symbolic of its spiritual basis, one of SCLC's first actions was to join with the NAACP and A. Philip Randolph in a "Prayer Pilgrimage" to Washington, D.C. in May 1957. At that rally, Martin Luther King, Jr. spoke to 35,000 demonstrators about segregation and injustice and, in that famous ringing cadence, repeated the demand "Give us the ballot" over and over again.[4]

The call was sufficient for the FBI to open an investigation of King and SCLC. According to FBI reports, SCLC was designed "to organize a register-and-vote campaign among Negroes in the South."[5] The bureau marked it for overt surveillance under the FBI category of "racial matters." As J. Edgar Hoover put it:

In the absence of any indication that the Communist Party has attempted, or is attempting, to infiltrate this organization you should conduct no investigation in this matter. *However, in view of the stated purpose of the organization, you should remain alert for public source information concerning it in connection with the racial situation.*[6]

For the FBI, an organization seeking to register blacks in the South was clearly suspicious. Until 1962, the bureau would monitor King and SCLC under the "racial matters" category, which required agents to collect "all pertinent information" about the "proposed or actual activities of individuals and organizations in the racial field."[7] According to the Senate Select Committee, the FBI information on King was "extensive."[8]

The unfolding story of the civil rights protest movement and the leadership role of Martin Luther King, Jr., is a most ignoble chapter in the history of FBI spying and manipulation. As the civil rights movement grew and expanded, the FBI pinpointed every group and emergent leader for intensive investigation and most for harassment and disruption, the FBI's domestic version of CIA covert action abroad. The NAACP was the subject of a COMIN-FIL investigation. The Congress of Racial Equality (CORE) and the Student Nonviolent Coordinating Committee (SNCC) were listed by the FBI as "Black-Hate"-type organizations and selected for covert disruption of their political activities.[9] But the most vicious FBI attack was reserved for King and the Southern Christian Leadership Conference. All of the arbitrary power and lawless tactics that had accumulated in the bureau over the years were marshaled to destroy King's reputation and the movement he led. The FBI relied on its vague authority to investigate "subversives" to spy on King and SCLC; its vague authority to conduct warrantless wiretapping and microphonic surveillance to tap and bug him; its secrecy to conduct covert operations against him. The campaign began with his rise to leadership and grew more vicious as he reached the height of his power; it continued even after his assassination in 1968.

Parts of the FBI's vendetta were carried out with the knowledge, if not approval, of men in high political office who claimed to be King's allies and supporters. Presidents Kennedy and Johnson, Attorneys General Robert Kennedy and Nicholas Katzenbach, Assistant Attorney General Burke Marshall, and Special Assistant to the President Bill Moyers all knew of some of the bureau's activities. None of these men approved of the vendetta, but their failure to act gave Hoover free rein long after there was even a minimum pretext for continuing any kind of inquiry into King's activities. They must share the responsibility and blame for Hoover's actions.

Martin Luther King, Jr., and SCLC did not lead the sit-ins and freedom rides. The 1960 lunch-counter sit-ins that began in Greensboro, North Carolina, were sparked by young black college students and resulted in the formation of a new organization, the Student Nonviolent Coordinating Committee (SNCC). The 1961 "freedom rides" through the South that forced desegregation of the inter-state transportation system were organized by James Farmer and the Congress of Racial Equality.

However, King was present in Greensboro and provided inspiration to the student demonstrators. He rode the buses with James Farmer. SCLC attracted the funding used to underwrite the demonstrations, and the organization of SNCC. Most important, King was the key spokesman for the movement in negotiations with the White House and the Justice Department, a role that grew out of his national prominence and his impact on the 1960 presidential campaign.

In 1960, King was arrested in Atlanta, Georgia, for "parading without a permit" and sentenced to four months of hard labor. This took place during the heat of the 1960 presidential campaign, and advisers to John Kennedy persuaded him to intercede on behalf of King. He personally telephoned Coretta King to express his sympathy and his support for civil rights. King was freed on bail and Kennedy's act is credited with helping him win his narrow election victory. It also put the new president at least symbolically on record in support of the civil rights movement. And it opened a dialogue of critical import between King and the administration.

During the demonstrations in 1960 and 1961, King negotiated with the White House and the Justice Department. Repeatedly the Justice Department urged King to postpone demonstrations because of bad timing.[10] Convinced that the only way to pressure the administration to move more decisively in the civil rights area was through demonstrations, King refused. King was instrumental in persuading the Justice Department to send U.S. marshals to protect freedom riders in Birmingham.

Significantly the Justice Department did not send the FBI to Birmingham. The bureau was busy with its "racial matters" investigation, issuing reports on Communist influence in the racial area. On July 25, 1961, the FBI reported to Presidential Assistant McGeorge Bundy that the Communist party had "attempted" to take advantage of "racial disturbances" in the South and had "endeavored" to bring "pressure to bear" on government officials "through the press, labor unions, and student groups."[11] Already Justice Department officials were aware of Hoover's hostility to the civil rights movement and his repeated attempts to tie the movement to communism and "subversion." Instead of confronting the FBI, officials in the department preferred to ignore the reports and go around the FBI in their efforts to protect demonstrators.[12]

In 1962, Albany, Georgia, was the site of the first major campaign planned and led by King. In a massive effort to end *all* segregation in Albany's public facilities, King directed protests against every city facility. For one year, King and his followers marched on city hall, staged sit-ins in libraries, and held prayer vigils on downtown streets.

In February, King and over 700 fellow demonstrators were arrested for parading without a permit. Arrest followed arrest, and by the end of the year 1,000 demonstrators had gone to jail, charged with illegal assembly, unlawful parading, and disturbing the peace. However, local police handled the demonstrators with "sophistication." (Demonstrators were beaten, but never in front of television camera crews.) Public attention and sympathy were not marshaled. In the end the protests fell short of their goals: a personal and political setback for King.

Albany marked the beginning of the FBI's campaign against King. Several factors played a role in the FBI decision to single him out. In Albany, whether defeated or not, King emerged as a leader of a massive protest demonstration in his own right. More important, on January 8, 1962, the FBI was criticized in a report issued by the Southern Regional Council (SRC), an Atlanta-based civil rights support group with close ties to SCLC. The report found that FBI officials usually stood by when local citizens and police beat up demonstrators. The substance of that report was immediately communicated to Hoover.[13] Coincidentally—or perhaps not so coincidentally—January 8 was the day that Hoover sent a memo to Attorney General Robert Kennedy, which alleged that Stanley Levison, a close friend and confidant of King, was "a member of the Communist Party, U.S.A. [CPUSA]."[14] Alert to subversive activity, hostile to the civil rights movement and enraged at any criticism directed at the bureau, Hoover set his campaign in motion.

In February, on the day King was arrested on a charge of parading without a permit in Albany, Hoover, on receiving the full Southern Regional Council report, penned on it that King was "no good."[15] He then ordered a field review of FBI files for "subversive" information on King "suitable for dissemination." By May, the nonviolent civil rights leader was listed on "Section A of the Reserve Index." King was now a person to be rounded up and detained in the event of a "national emergency." King was indexed as "Communist."[16]

In June, Hoover sent another memorandum to Attorney General Kennedy; the FBI claimed that Jack O'Dell, on the staff of SCLC, was a "member of the National Committee of the Communist Party."[17] In October, Cartha DeLoach, head of the Crime Records Division, the FBI's public relations arm, was given a copy of the charges against King and O'Dell for "possible use by his contacts in the news media field in such Southern states as Alabama where Dr. King has announced that the next targets for integration of universities are located."[18] By October 28, the instructions had been carried out and the FBI's investigative files had been leaked to the press. The *Augusta Chronicle* wrote an article stating that O'Dell, a member of "CPUSA's National Committee," was serving as Dr. King's "Acting Executive Director."[19]

Communist party affiliation is hardly evidence that someone is a subversive foreign agent. Many members of the Communist party are and were patriotic citizens. But both King and officials in the Kennedy administration realized the political danger in the charge that Communist party members were associated with the civil rights movement.

Martin Luther King responded to the allegations on

October 30 by stating that "no person of known Communist affiliation" could serve on the SCLC staff. He denied knowledge of O'Dell's Communist party connections and announced that O'Dell had temporarily resigned from SCLC pending SCLC investigation of the allegation.[20]

The FBI launched its own investigation. Having discovered Levison and O'Dell, the bureau opened an intensive COMINFIL investigation of King and the Southern Christian Leadership Conference. Field offices were instructed to gather information on the members, associates, and activities of SCLC, and on any Communist party activities directed at influencing or infiltrating SCLC.[21]

Although the public record is incomplete, it seems that the FBI's move to investigate King stemmed primarily from the fact that this leader of a movement Hoover could not abide had criticized the Federal Bureau of Investigation.

In November 1962, an update of the SRC report was issued that specifically charged the FBI with failure to act responsibly to protect King and his followers in Albany, Georgia. In a section entitled "Where Was the Federal Government?" the report made the following observations about the FBI:

There is a considerable amount of distrust among Albany Negroes for local members of the Federal Bureau of Investigation.

With all the clear violations by local police of constitutional rights, with undisputed evidence of beatings by sheriffs and deputy sheriffs, the FBI has not made a single arrest on behalf of Negro citizens. . . .

The FBI is most effective in solving ordinary crimes, and perhaps it should stick to that.[22]

Upon release of this report, King himself backed up the charges with an explanation that was published in the press.

One of the great problems we face with the FBI in the South is that the agents are white Southerners who have been influenced by the mores of the community. To maintain their status, they have to be friendly with the local police and people who are promoting segregation.[23]

The bureau did dispatch eighty-six agents to Albany to conduct an investigation that led to the arrest of nine demonstrators on the charge of "obstructing justice."[24] Needless to say, "criticism" of the FBI is not a proper basis for opening an intensive investigation under COMINFIL or any other FBI category, even under the bureau's own standards. But according to William Sullivan, former head of the Intelligence Division, King's criticism and Hoover's dislike for the civil rights movement were the basis for beginning the campaign against King:

[Hoover] was very upset about the criticism that King made publicly about our failure to protect the Negro in the South against violations of the Negro civil liberties, and King on a number of occasions soundly criticized the Director. . . . I think behind it all was the racial bias, the dislike of Negroes, the dislike of the civil rights movement. . . . I do not think he could rise above that.[25]

If this was the "real reason" for the investigation, it was up to officials in the Department of Justice to discover it and end it. However, between January 8, 1962, when the FBI charged that King's associate, Stanley Levison, was a member of the Communist party, and October 1962, when the FBI opened its COMINFIL investigation, no Justice official took the logical step of demanding to see Hoover's evidence or "raw unevaluated files" to substantiate the allegation that King was under the control of the Communist party. Of course, it was not a common practice for the FBI to disclose its investigative files to the department, and the Kennedy administration accepted this policy that insulated the FBI from any accountability.[26]

If Justice Department officials had conducted an inquiry, they would have discovered that the FBI's evidence was at best thin and at worst sheer fabrication. The files showed that Levison had been associated with King from the early days of SCLC, but that as recently as November 1961 an FBI memorandum stated that there was no reason for a "security interest" in King.[27] The worst that Hoover was able to disclose to Attorney General Kennedy on his own initiative—and one would expect him to disclose the worst—was that an informer had alleged that Levison had been active in the Labor Youth League in 1954, a group which the FBI listed as "subversive" but not Communist.[28]

If the department had conducted its own inquiry, it would have learned that Levinson was indeed close to King. From the early days of SCLC, Levison had helped King with legal problems, fund raising, and strategy, and had encouraged his efforts in time of adversity. Levison himself has denied that he was ever a member of the Communist party or under its domination or control. And Bayard Rustin, the civil rights leader who introduced Levison to King, was convinced that Stanley Levinson's public and private positions over the years would make any Communists in the wings recognize him as an enemy.[29] Even if he were a Communist, there is absolutely no evidence that he ever engaged in espionage or spying. As one scholar who has considered the charges points out: "I *do* know he has never been indicted under the espionage laws; he has never been indicted for failing to register . . . as an enemy agent. . . ."[30]

But the attorney general did not confront the director or conduct his own inquiry. Instead, Robert Kennedy dispatched Assistant Attorney General Burke Marshall to warn King of the charges and persuade him to dissociate himself from Levison.[31]

In March, the attorney general also approved a "national security" wiretap and microphonic surveillance of Levison's New York office. From that date until October, the surveillance disclosed nothing indicating that Levison or King was under Communist influence; the attorney general learned only about King's civil rights activities.[32] Less is known about O'Dell. However, SCLC attorneys conducted an investigation of him, following his temporary resignation, and could find no evidence of membership in the Communist party.[33] The bureau was not concerned with criminal activity, nor did it seek evidence of espionage or Soviet control. It was enough that O'Dell and Levison might be Communists.

Robert Kennedy and other Justice Department officials voiced no objection when Hoover opened a COMINFIL investigation aimed at King and SCLC in October, even though it violated the FBI's own loose standard. According to the FBI *Manual*, a COMINFIL investigation required specific evidence that the "Communist Party has *specifically instructed* its members to infiltrate the organization" or that "Communist Party members have infiltrated the organization in *sufficient strength* to influence or control the organization."[34] In spite of the fact that there was no such evidence, the bureau was allowed to continue both the COMINFIL investigation and the tap on Levison's office phone. And significantly, there is no Justice Department or FBI record that indicates that the bureau was in any way reprimanded for obviously leaking investigative file information in October to the press.

As the FBI intensified its investigation of Martin Luther King, Jr., King and SCLC stepped up their protest efforts. Undaunted by the setback in Albany, King launched a major effort in Birmingham, Alabama, in 1963, a city King considered the "most thoroughly segregated big city in the U.S."[35] Everywhere "Whites Only" signs were prominently displayed. When the courts had ordered Birmingham parks desegregated, the response of city officials was to close the parks.

When King went to Birmingham, he took with him the lesson of Albany. To end segregation in Birmingham public facilities and obtain a commitment for equal job opportunities, King decided to focus his effort on an economic boycott of Birmingham businesses. Unlike his action in Albany, King would not carry out a general protest effort.

At first King had few supporters. Whites and blacks accused him of being an "outsider," and black clergymen thought his effort "ill-timed." In April, the city obtained a court order against further demonstrations. Bull Connor, commissioner of public safety, knowing that King never defied a court order, believed the campaign was over. But this time King decided to disobey the injunction. On Good Friday he staged a march, and was arrested and jailed.

King wrote his famous "Letter from a Birmingham Jail." Addressed to "My Dear Fellow Clergymen," the letter explained his position and asked for their support. "I am in Birmingham because injustice is here," he wrote. He could not be called an outsider, he reasoned, because "we are caught in an inescapable network of mutuality, tied in a single garment of destiny." Waiting for change, he said, was not the answer:

We know through painful experience that freedom is never voluntarily given by the oppressor; it must be demanded by the oppressed. Frankly, I have yet to engage in a direct-action campaign that was "well-timed" in the view of those who have not suffered unduly from the disease of segregation. For years now I have heard the word "Wait!" It rings in the ear of every Negro with piercing familiarity. This "Wait" has almost always meant "Never." We must come to see, with one of our distinguished jurists, that "justice too long delayed is justice denied."[36]

Released from jail on bond, King marched again. Now others flocked to join him. On May 2, 1963, Bull Connor and the local police waded into a march of hundreds of men, women, and children. On television, millions of Americans witnessed crushing streams of water flattening children; women beaten with clubs; and dogs ripping at men's flesh. They also heard the words of Connor: "Look at 'em run," he yelled, "look at those niggers run!" The public outrage was enormous, and the result followed quickly.[37]

On May 10, city businessmen met the demands of King and the demonstrators. This touched off a rash of violence by local Ku Klux Klan (KKK) groups, including bombings and beatings. Some blacks fought back and President Kennedy went on television to warn the violent and to state that federal troops were on standby alert. King also pleaded for "nonviolence" and by the end of the month, calm had returned to Birmingham.

The civil rights protests had worked. On June 11, President Kennedy announced that his administration was proposing legislation to end all segregation in public facilities, to guarantee voting rights and minority job opportunities. In a dramatic address, Kennedy said:

One hundred years of delay have passed since President Lincoln freed the slaves, yet their heirs, their grandsons, are not fully free. They are not yet freed from the bonds of injustice; they are not yet freed from social and economic oppression. And this nation, for all its hopes and its boasts, will not be fully free until all its citizens are free.[38]

That summer the attention of the civil rights movement was focused on the nation's capital. The president submitted his legislation to Congress, which began hearings on the measure. In July, civil rights leaders planned a march on Washington to urge Congress to act on the legislation. In August, over 250,000 persons converged on the city in a peaceful demonstration of support for civil rights.

That summer also involved private negotiations between King and the White House and Justice Department over these matters—but with one critical addition: what to do about Hoover's charges of Communist influence directed at King and SCLC, charges that threatened to destroy King, the prospects for civil rights legislation, and perhaps undermine the Kennedy administration itself. The parties negotiated about civil rights and FBI "blackmail" at the same time.

From January to June 1963, the FBI bombarded the Justice Department with a battery of memoranda on King and SCLC gleaned from its COMINFIL investigation and its electronic surveillance of Stanley Levison. The only "Communist activity" in the reports was information showing that King was continuing to associate with Stanley Levison and Jack O'Dell. The bulk of the information was a detailed account of the civil rights activities, plans, and strategies of King and SCLC, all gathered in violation of the FBI's own rule that COMINFIL investigations were to be limited to information on Communist infiltration and were not to include "legitimate activities" of organizations under investigation.[39] The violation drew no complaint from the Justice Department.

What troubled the Justice officials was King's association with Levison and O'Dell. During these months the attorney general, through his aides, continued to urge King to sever his ties with the two associates. Time and again during the Birmingham effort, King's aides were forced to deal with the Justice Department about this "grave and serious matter."[40]

During these discussions King's aides pressed the Justice Department to substantiate the Communist charges or obtain proof from the FBI. According to King's former aide (and now congressman), Andrew Young, Deputy Attorney General Burke Marshall said he had no proof and that he "couldn't get anything out of the Bureau." Young recalled that Marshall had said, "We ask [the bureau] for things and we get these big memos, but they don't ever really say anything."[41] Still Justice officials pressed King to cut his ties with the two associates.

On June 22, King met with Burke Marshall, Attorney General Robert Kennedy, and President John Kennedy in Washington. In those meetings, all three urged King to end his association with Levison and O'Dell. Now, however, the request was linked to the new civil rights legislative initiative. Unless King broke with these men, they argued, the civil rights legislation was doomed. As King reported to Andy Young, "There was an attempt [by the FBI] to smear the movement on the basis of Communist influence. The president also said, 'I assume you know you're under very close surveillance.' "[42]

The threat of FBI blackmail was real. Only a few days before the meeting, Hoover had told Robert Kennedy what was in store for the movement if King did not end his "Communist Party" ties. He described the conversation in a memorandum:

I pointed out that if Dr. King continues this association, he is going to hurt his own cause as there are more and more Communists trying to take advantage of [the] movement and bigots down South who are against integration are beginning to charge Dr. King is tied in with Communists. I stated I thought Marshall could very definitely say this association is rather widely known and, with things crystalizing for them now, nothing could be worse than for Dr. King to be associated with it.[43]

Hoover did not mention that the "charge" was being made with information from FBI investigative files.

With the civil rights legislation at stake, King agreed at the June 22 meetings to dissociate himself from Levison and O'Dell. King was forced to act or face a smear campaign. In fact, only a few days after the meeting, a story appeared in the *Birmingham News* stating that a "highly authorized source" had said that Jack O'Dell was on the SCLC payroll despite his temporary resignation in December 1962.[44] Soon after, Levison resigned his membership in SCLC and O'Dell received a letter from King terminating his employment with SCLC.

With King's commitment, the president and the Justice Department were prepared to defend King and the civil rights movement against charges of Communist influence, but not to end the FBI program directed against King. Moreover, by exacting that commitment from King, they had met Hoover's unjustifiable demands and had bowed to his threat of blackmail. As all the parties should have realized, the habit of blackmailers is to come back for more.

On July 29, Director Hoover sent the Justice Department a report from the New York office entitled "Martin Luther King, Jr.: Affiliation with the Communist Movement." According to a memorandum from Courtney Evans of the FBI, the reaction of the attorney general to the report was that "if this report got up to the Hill at this time, he [Kennedy] would be impeached."[45] The report has not been made public, but it is likely that it contained documentary evidence—perhaps from the Levison electronic surveillance—that King had not broken off his relationship with Levison. Both President Kennedy and the attorney general had publicly denied charges made by southern governors that King was associated with named Communists, which explains Kennedy's reaction. King had not kept his "commitment" and the FBI was asking for more—to tap the phones at King's offices and home, a request that the attorney general had previously denied.

In fact, King did not break off his ties with Levison; he was too close an adviser and friend. Levison, like O'Dell, had stepped aside, but as Victor Navasky writes:

Levison had booked speaking engagements for King, he had worked on drafts of manuscripts and speeches, he had handled legal problems. And so, despite King's promise to break with Levison, he would call—from time to time—to find out a date or a location or to get some files. . . . [A]s King checked unfinished business, facts, dates and memories with Levison, they gradually resumed communication.[46]

Learning that Levison and King were in communication, and knowing that Hoover knew about it, the attorney general reconsidered his decision on wiretapping King. After the wiretaps were found to be "feasible" by the FBI, Robert Kennedy authorized the taps in October. He directed the FBI to place a "national security wiretap on King at his current address or at any future address to which he may move" and "on the SCLC office at the current New York address or to any other address to which it may be moved."[47] The taps would continue for the next two years.

Former Kennedy associates have offered several justifications for the wiretaps aimed at King. According to those aides, Kennedy was angry that King had broken his commitment; worried that the civil rights legislation might be derailed if the activities of King *and* Hoover were not monitored; hopeful that the tap would convince Hoover that King was not a Communist; and anxious to get to the bottom of the FBI's Communist charges against King. There was also a desire to protect the administration from being smeared; if Hoover was going to discredit King, the Kennedy administration would be, as the attorney general put it, "impeached" along with him unless it established a record of cooperation in the investigation of King.

Under the law, however, these were not legitimate reasons to tap King's phones. Even by the Justice Department's own expansive legal interpretation at the time, a "national security" wiretap was to be authorized only in cases vitally affecting the internal security. The only way for the Kennedy administration to protect King, or civil rights, or the administration itself, was to obey the law and refuse Hoover's request. When a former aide to Robert Kennedy said that to interfere with the FBI investigation would have been interpreted as "political interference," what he was really admitting was that the FBI was beyond the control of the Justice Department and even of the president.

When the attorney general approved the King wiretaps, he did not know that the FBI planned to use them in a counterintelligence operation directed at King and SCLC. During the summer of 1963, FBI leaders engaged in their own series of internal private negotiations, and decided to conduct a covert operation to discredit and destroy Martin Luther King.[48]

In July, while civil rights leaders planned for a march on Washington, the FBI Intelligence Division opened a file on "Communist Influence in Racial Matters." On August 23, the division sent a report to J. Edgar Hoover that provoked an internal battle. The 67-page report concluded that there was "an obvious failure of the Communist Party of the United States to appreciably infiltrate, influence, or control large numbers of American Negroes in this country."[49]

Hoover's reaction to the report was angry and sarcastic. "I for one," he wrote, "can't ignore the memos . . . re King et al. [Levison and O'Dell], as having only an infinitesimal effect on the efforts to exploit the American Negro by the Communists."[50] When another memorandum followed on August 26 reporting that only 100 Communists planned to march with the demonstrators on August 28. Hoover penned on the report the sarcastic rejoinder: "just infinitesimal!"[51]

On August 28, 250,000 persons marched on Washington. The march, sponsored by a cross-section of civil rights, labor, and church organizations, was designed to support the enactment of civil rights legislation. That day, when Martin Luther King addressed the assemblage, he made his most memorable speech:

I have a dream
> that one day this nation will rise up and live out the true meaning of its creed: "We hold these truths to be self-evident, that all men are created equal."

I have a dream
> that one day in the red hills of Georgia sons of former slaves and the sons of former slave owners will be able to sit down together at the table of brotherhood.

I have a dream
> that one day even the state of Mississippi, a state sweltering in the heat of injustice . . . will be transformed into an oasis of freedom and justice.

I have a dream
> that my four little children will one day live in a nation where they will be judged not by the color of their skin but by the content of their character.

The speech brought the crowd to its feet, applauding, echoing the "Amens" that greet evangelical preaching, and shouting "Freedom Now!" The FBI reacted differently. In memoranda to the director, King's speech was characterized as "demagogic," and the presence of "200" Communists among the 250,000 marchers caused the Intelligence Division to state that it had underestimated Communist efforts and influence on American Negroes and the civil rights movement.[52] King was singled out:

He stands head and shoulders over all other Negro leaders put together when it comes to influencing great masses of Negroes. *We must mark him now . . . as the most dangerous Negro* of the future in this Nation from the standpoint of Communism, the Negro and national security.[53]

More ominously, the FBI suggested that "legal" efforts to

deal with King might not be enough. "It may be unrealistic," the memorandum went on,

to limit ourselves as we have been doing to legalistic proofs or definitely conclusive evidence that would stand up in testimony in court or before Congressional Committees. . . .[54]

It was up to the FBI to "mark" King and bring him down on its own—to take the law into its own hands.

On October 1, 1963, Hoover received and then approved a combined COMINFIL-COINTELPRO plan against the civil rights movement. The approved plan called for intensifying "coverage of Communist influence on the Negro." It recommended the "use of all possible investigative techniques" and stated an "urgent need for imaginative and aggressive tactics . . . to neutralize or disrupt the Party's activities in the Negro field."[55]

On October 10 and 21, Attorney General Kennedy gave the FBI one of those "investigative techniques" by approving the wiretaps on King.[56]

On October 18, 1963, the FBI distributed a different kind of memorandum on King, not only to the Justice Department, but to officials at the White House, the Central Intelligence Agency, the State Department, the Defense Department, and Defense Department intelligence agencies. It summarized the bureau's Communist party charges against King and went much further. According to Assistant Attorney General Burke Marshall, it was

a personal diatribe . . . a personal attack without evidentiary support on the character, the moral character and person of Dr. Martin Luther King, and it was only peripherally related to anything substantive, like whether or not there was Communist infiltration or influence on the civil rights movement. . . . It was a personal attack on the man and went far afield from the charges [of possible Communist influence].[57]

The attorney general was outraged and demanded that Hoover seek the return of the report. By October 28, all copies were returned. This was the first—and last—official action to deter Hoover's vendetta against King.

In November, John Kennedy was assassinated in Dallas, Texas. Lyndon Johnson became president and the Justice Department was in a state of confusion with the attorney general preoccupied with his personal grief. King viewed the assassination as a tragedy, and hoped it would spawn a new public concern for peace and reconciliation.

While the nation mourned, the FBI held a conference at the beginning of December to plan its campaign to destroy King and the civil rights movement. At that all-day meeting FBI officials put forward proposals that make G. Gordon Liddy's Watergate plan seem pale by comparison. Officials of the nation's number-one law enforcement agency agreed to use "all available investigative techniques" to develop information for use "to discredit" King. Proposals discussed included using ministers, "disgruntled" acquaintances, "aggressive" newsmen, "colored" agents, Dr. King's housekeeper, and even Dr. King's wife or "placing a good looking female plant in King's office" to develop discrediting information and to take action that would lead to his disgrace.[58]

From the nature of Burke Marshall's description of the October 18 report, it is obvious that the FBI was on to something it viewed as unsavory about King's private life. The report made the charges, but as Marshall said, there was no "evidentiary" support. Now the FBI was out to get the proof. By January, the FBI had initiated physical and photographic surveillance of King, deploying its most experienced personnel to gather information, and had placed the first of many illegal bugs in Dr. King's room at the Willard Hotel in Washington, D.C.[59]

According to Justice Department regulations at the time, microphonic surveillance, although it necessitated a physical trespass and was more intrusive than a phone tap, did not require the approval of the attorney general. Even under its own regulations, however, the FBI could only use this technique to gather "important intelligence or evidence relating to matters connected with national security." In this case the FBI planned to use "bugs" to learn about "the [private] activities of Dr. King and his associates" so that King could be "completely discredited." It was clearly illegal.

The Willard Hotel "bug" yielded "19 reels" of tape.[60] The FBI, at least in its own opinion, had struck pay dirt. The bug apparently picked up information about King's private extramarital and perhaps "inter-racial" sexual activities. This opened up the possibility of discrediting King as a Communist who engaged in "moral improprieties."

For J. Edgar Hoover, "immoral" behavior was a crime comparable to "subversive" activity—and of equal utility. Hoover gathered such information on prominent persons to use for political and blackmail purposes. Often he would share such "official and confidential" information with presidents when his surveillance uncovered "obscene matters" on the president's opponents or aides. Sometimes he would let people know he had such information on them, and that list includes Presidents John Kennedy and Richard Nixon. In this case, however, Hoover did not plan to let King know he had the information to gain a "political" power advantage over him; he planned to use it to destroy him politically. With the Willard Hotel tapes, the FBI campaign moved into high gear.

With Kennedy and Lyndon Johnson pressing action on civil rights legislation and calling for a "War on Poverty," Martin Luther King was a man the country and the world thought worthy of honor. In December 1963, *Time* magazine named him "Man of the Year." In 1964, while continuing his "nonviolent" activities on behalf of civil rights in St. Augustine, Florida, and other cities, King was awarded honorary degrees by universities; he was invited by Willy Brandt, the mayor of West Berlin, to speak at a ceremony honoring the memory of President Kennedy; he had an audience with Pope Paul VI in Rome; and, in October, he was named by the Nobel Prize Committee to receive the Peace Prize in December.

If for King 1964 was a year of honors and increasing

public recognition, for the FBI it was a year of concerted effort to dishonor him. Learning that King had been named Man of the Year by *Time*, Hoover wrote across a memorandum, "They had to dig deep in the garbage to come up with this one."[61] When Marquette University prepared to offer him an honorary degree (a university that had awarded Hoover the same honor in 1950), the FBI's reaction was that this was "shocking indeed."[62] When Pope Paul met with King, Hoover wrote on a memorandum about the audience: "astounding."[63] And the Nobel Peace Prize was viewed as an unmitigated disaster.

Hoover and FBI officials did more than express dismay. In 1964, through briefings, prepared "monographs," and even distribution of the "tapes," the FBI spewed out information on King's "Communist" activities and "private" behavior. In January 1964, the FBI briefed Presidential Assistant Walter Jenkins. On January 23, Hoover, in off-the-record testimony, told the House Appropriations Committee, and the chairman of the committee, Congressman John Rooney, was shown transcripts of the tapes. In March, the FBI briefed officials at Marquette University to head off the honorary degree. In that same month, a "Top Secret" memorandum was sent to Attorney General Robert Kennedy. In June, the FBI briefed officials of the National Council of Churches and other influential church bodies to encourage them to end their support of King. In September, Francis Cardinal Spellman was told to warn Pope Paul that it would be embarrassing for him to meet with King.[64]

When the Nobel Peace Prize was announced in October, the FBI prepared a monograph on King—an updated version of the one Robert Kennedy had recalled in October 1963—and distributed it to Presidential Assistant Bill Moyers, United Nations Ambassador Adlai Stevenson, United Nations official Ralph Bunche, Senator Hubert H. Humphrey, Governor Nelson Rockefeller, the United States ambassadors in London and Oslo, and to leading citizens in Atlanta who planned to honor King after his receipt of the prize in December.

Throughout the year, the FBI offered the tapes to newsmen and columnists, including Mike Royko of the *Chicago Daily News*. The monograph was also sent to Ralph McGill of the *Atlanta Constitution* and shown to columnist Carl Rowan.[65]

The reaction of official Washington was unconscionable. Not one official—especially those in supervisory positions over the FBI—took adequate steps to stop this vicious campaign. After the briefing of Walter Jenkins in January, President Johnson certainly learned about it but did nothing. In March, Attorney General Robert Kennedy was informed, but failed to intercede and expressed worry over its impact on his political future. In November, new Attorney General Nicholas Katzenbach and outgoing Assistant Attorney General Burke Marshall flew to the LBJ ranch to tell Lyndon Johnson about the FBI smear campaign and about the FBI's offer of tapes to the press. Although Johnson registered concern, Katzenbach and Marshall never made follow-up inquiries to determine whether the president had intervened. Attorney General Katzenbach himself certainly did not intervene.[66]

The trip to the LBJ ranch in November was a futile gesture. Johnson already knew about the campaign in January through Walter Jenkins, who thought the information should be distributed. In December, Bill Moyers, another Johnson aide, ordered the FBI monograph distributed. When Moyers reported that members of the press were warning about the FBI campaign, Johnson complained about the press criticizing the bureau.[67] Johnson came to the defense of Hoover!

The fact was, that Johnson was in no position to attack Hoover. It was always his contention that it was better to have the director, as he put it, "on the inside of the tent pissing out rather than on the outside of the tent pissing in."[68] Johnson was also worried about being enmeshed in a Communist smear campaign directed at the civil rights movement, since he was now supporting civil rights legislation. Most important, Johnson himself was compromised, since the warnings of Marshall and Katzenbach came after Johnson had made "political" use of the FBI surveillance against King.

In August, Johnson had dispatched thirty FBI agents under the direction of Cartha DeLoach, head of the Crimes Record Division, to Atlantic City, New Jersey, to "cover" the Democratic convention. Ostensibly sent to protect the president (the job of the Secret Service) and prevent civil disturbances (the job of the local police), the squad gathered political information for Johnson. According to its report, the squad was able to

keep the White House fully apprised of all major developments during the Convention's course by means of informant coverage, by use of various confidential techniques, by infiltration of key groups through use of undercover agents, and through utilization of agents using appropriate cover as reporters. . . . Among the "confidential techniques" were two electronic surveillances: a wiretap on the hotel room occupied by Martin Luther King, Jr., and a microphone surveillance of SNCC and CORE.[69]

Through the King tap, Johnson was able to gather intelligence on the potentially explosive challenge by the Mississippi Freedom Democratic Party (MFDP) to the all-white Mississippi delegation. As an example, the tap yielded information that

King and [an associate] were drafting a telegram to President Johnson . . . to register a mild protest. According to King, the President pledged complete neutrality regarding the selecting of the proper Mississippi delegation to be seated at the convention. King feels that the Credentials Committee will turn down the Mississippi Freedom Party and that they are doing this because the President exerted pressure on the committee along this line. The MFDP wanted to get the issue before the full convention, but because of the President's actions, this will be impossible.[70]

It was accurate reporting, albeit from an illegal tap, and took pressure off the president, who now knew exactly what the demands of the MFDP were, and how far it was willing to compromise. But it also made it impossible for Johnson to clamp down on Hoover.

With official Washington unresponsive, cowed, or compromised, only civil rights leaders, including King himself, took steps to blunt the FBI attack. Knowing about the smear campaign, they were particularly worried that Hoover would go public with the information after King and Hoover began to battle each other in public over the Communist party charges.

In April, Hoover was quoted in the press as having testified that "Communist influence does exist in the civil rights movement."[71] King reacted sharply:

It is very unfortunate that Mr. J. Edgar Hoover, in his claims of alleged Communist infiltration in the civil rights movement, has allowed himself to aid and abet the salacious claims of Southern racists and the extreme right-wing elements.

We challenge all who raise the "red" issue, whether they be newspaper columnists or the head of the FBI himself—to come forward and provide real evidence which contradicts this stand of the SCLC. We are confident that this cannot be done.[72]

Going further, King repeated the charge of FBI inaction in the South that had provoked the anti-King campaign:

It is difficult to accept the word of the FBI on Communist infiltration in the civil rights movement, when they have been so completely ineffectual in resolving the continued mayhem and brutality inflicted upon the Negro in the deep south.[73]

Hoover's first response was to say that it was incumbent on the civil rights movement to prove that there was no Communist influence. Then, in November, Hoover held a press briefing. Asked to respond to King's charges, Hoover, off the record, called King "one of the lowest characters in the country." On the record, he called King the most "notorious liar" in the country. Hoover's comments were widely publicized.[74]

King's response this time was designed to dampen the controversy. "I cannot conceive of Mr. Hoover making a statement like this," King said, "without being under extreme pressure. He has apparently faltered under the awesome burden, complexities, and responsibilities of his office." King also sent Hoover a telegram stating that while he had criticized the bureau, the director's response was "a mystery to me" and expressed a desire "to discuss this question with you at length."[75]

On November 27, Roy Wilkins was told by Cartha De-Loach that if King wanted "war" the FBI was prepared to engage in one, and the two of them discussed the FBI's "derogatory" material. Wilkins told DeLoach that if the FBI made it public, it could ruin the civil rights movement.[76] Obviously Wilkins reported this back to King, and a number of leaders, including King, agreed to take steps to set up a meeting with the director. Hoover agreed to meet with King on December 1.

According to all accounts, the meeting was exceedingly cordial. Hoover expressed support for the civil rights movement and then turned to what was on his mind—criticism of the bureau. The meeting consisted of a long monologue by Hoover on the FBI's efforts to protect civil rights demonstrators, enforce the laws in the South, and prevent terrorism. At the end of the meeting, King and Hoover agreed to a public truce.[77]

Only now do we know how close the FBI came to an all-out confrontation. Unknown to King or SCLC until later, the FBI, at the height of the public controversy, took its most distressing step. It mailed the "tapes" to the SCLC office in Atlanta with a covering letter urging King to commit suicide or face public revelation of the information on the tapes on the eve of the award ceremonies in Sweden. The letter said in part:

King, there is only one thing left for you to do. You know what it is. You have just 34 days in which to do (this exact number has been selected for a specific reason, it has definite practical significance). You are done. There is but one way out for you. You better take it before your filthy fraudulent self is bared to the nation.[78]

It was thirty-four days before the Nobel Peace Prize ceremonies.

Although public scandal was averted at the last moment, the FBI's campaign continued. From 1965 until

King's death, the covert effort of the FBI to destroy King and to topple him from "his pedestal" continued. Aside from the suicide note, there is no more graphic illustration of the mind-set and nature of this political police operation than the realization that while the campaign went on, the FBI had a parallel plan to find a "suitable replacement" for King.

The plan was simple. William Sullivan, the head of the Intelligence Division, had given it some thought and, in a January 1964 memorandum to Hoover, proposed that the FBI conduct a search to find a "suitable" successor to King. Hoover agreed. Sullivan, when asked about the memorandum by the Senate Intelligence Committee, responded in a way that speaks for itself: "I'm very proud of this memorandum, one of the best memoranda I ever

COPYRIGHT 1975 BY HERBLOCK IN *THE WASHINGTON POST*

wrote. I think here I was showing some concern for the country."[79]

While King was alive, the concern was shown again and again. From 1965 on, every major activity of King was an occasion for distributing an "updated" monograph on his "Communist ties" and sexual improprieties. For example, in 1967 when King spoke out against the Vietnam War, an updated monograph was sent to the White House, the secretary of state, the secretary of defense, and the Secret Service.[80] Then in 1968 when King announced his Washington Spring Project, which became the Poor Peoples' Campaign after his death, another monograph was distributed.[81] Even after his death, when Congress contemplated making his birthday a national holiday, the FBI officials briefed congressmen on King's private life.[82]

The FBI also engaged in other political operations directed at King and SCLC. It launched a rumor that King had a secret Swiss bank account and dispatched agents to see if it were true.[83] It triggered an Internal Revenue Service audit of SCLC's taxes to harass the organization.[84] It intervened at the Ford Foundation and at the National Science Foundation to attempt to cut off funding to SCLC.[85] The FBI even took steps to encourage magazines and publishers not to publish articles or books by King.[86]

In 1967, King and SCLC became key targets of an official FBI COINTELPRO directed at all "black hate-type" groups. One of its aims was to prevent the rise of a "black messiah," specifically Martin Luther King. Under the program, the FBI tried to leak stories to the press accusing King and SCLC of provoking violence during the Sanitary Workers' strike in Memphis in 1968 and sent out misinformation that the Poor Peoples' Campaign had enough donations to support its project.[87]

When occasions arose for official intervention by the Justice Department, little was done. In 1965, Lyndon Johnson enforced a strict limitation on electronic surveillance, which required a reauthorization of all national security wiretaps, the attorney general's approval for microphonic surveillance, and periodic review of all authorizations. When King's tap came up, Attorney General Nicholas Katzenbach reauthorized the wiretap and at least three microphonic surveillances. He cannot explain why he did it or how his name came to be on the authorizations. Finally, Attorney General Ramsey Clark refused to reauthorize surveillance of King in 1968 and 1969.[88]

As for governmental response to the smear campaign, there was none. The monographs were sent out and they stayed out. No one ever called them back.

While the FBI never went "public" with its charges, the total campaign had an enormous effect. The intensive surveillance put the movement in an electronic "fishbowl," according to SCLC legal counsel Harry Wachtel.[89] From 1962 on, the government knew every plan and strategy of King and SCLC, which could not but have adversely affected their negotiations with the government over civil rights matters. Heading off the Communist party charge drained energy and time that could have been devoted to the movement. Finally, the smear campaign caused donors to turn away from SCLC and created factionalism in the civil rights movement over whether King should continue to lead. The FBI did "expose" and "disrupt" the movement. And the anguish this caused for King is incalculable.

The FBI had turned its arsenal of surveillance and disruption techniques on Martin Luther King and the civil rights movement. It was concerned not with Soviet agents nor with criminal activity, but with the political and personal activities of a man and a movement committed to nonviolence and democracy. King was not the first such target, nor the last. In the end we are all victims, as our political life is distorted and constricted by the FBI, a law enforcement agency now policing politics.

As the Allende episode provides a rare insight into the standard procedures of CIA operations abroad, so the King story reveals much about how the FBI behaves at home. As the next chapter shows, King was not the only target of FBI operations.

THE
BUREAU IN
WAR AND PEACE

4

The Federal Bureau of Investigation is the nation's chief law enforcement agency. It is also an intelligence agency, the domestic counterpart to the Central Intelligence Agency. It does at home what the CIA does abroad: gathers information on those whose politics it distrusts, and uses covert techniques to disrupt their activities. Over the past forty years, the modern bureau, established in 1935, has grown in both power and size; from a small unit inside the Justice Department into a massive police bureaucracy having jurisdiction over 100 federal criminal matters. Deploying over 8,000 trained agents from the "Seat of Government" in Washington, D.C., to some fifty field offices and resident agencies across the country, the bureau investigates both politics and crime.[1] It has also grown into a nationwide spy apparatus that devotes 20 percent of its resources—more than twice the amount allocated to its fight against organized crime—to conduct intelligence operations directed primarily at American citizens engaged in political activity.

The growth of the bureau and its "dual" investigatory jurisdiction is in part a consequence of the historical transfer of political power from state and local to national government. It is also the result of wars and social struggles, which have led the national government to call on the bureau to conduct intelligence operations and to uncover subversion and civil unrest in addition to investigating crimes; and it is, finally, the work of J. Edgar Hoover, who presided over the bureau until his death in 1972.

Hoover was the "master builder" of the Federal Bureau of Investigation. He was a consummate bureaucrat who took over a scandal-ridden bureau in 1924 and cleaned up its operations and polished its image. His use of scientific methods in criminal investigative work gained him world-wide attention. Hoover was also a shameless publicist, who inflated bureau accomplishments to establish an image of the bureau—and himself—as incorruptible and invincible. Through highly publicized "gangbuster" operations, FBI "crime clocks," and the famous Hiss and Rosenberg "spy cases," Hoover built a political base of public support that allowed him to expand the bureau's investigative jurisdiction almost at will.[2]

When President Franklin D. Roosevelt called on the bureau to conduct intelligence and counterintelligence operations at the outset of World War II, Hoover was more than willing to cooperate. A rabid anti-Communist and supporter of the traditional American way of life, Hoover suspected every "ism" and had a prior record to prove it. Under the predecessor Bureau of Investigation, Hoover had headed up the General Intelligence Division, which launched extensive investigations and vigilante operations against aliens and radicals prior to and just after World War I. The new demands for intelligence at the outset of World War II permitted Hoover to reestablish his intelligence operations.

The scope and nature of FBI intelligence activities have only recently become public. Prior to 1971, bureau operations were conducted in secret and beyond public scrutiny. When charges were made that the FBI was a political police, they were brushed off as exaggerated rhetoric or paranoia, or as the fabrications of disgruntled ex-agents who told about The FBI Nobody Knows.[3] High government officials and even members of the press who *did* know what the bureau was doing—and that the charges were in fact understatements of the case against the bureau—kept silent. Some remained silent because they approved of the FBI's intelligence activities; others because they were compromised by their own participation or personal use of FBI intelligence information; and still others out of fear. For Hoover, in addition to his other attributes, was not above political blackmail. His "Official and Confidential" files, in which he deposited derogatory information on political men, were legendary—famed and feared. With such files, the official who challenged the bureau risked retaliation and public embarrassment. Through intelligence Hoover found the means to protect the bureau and himself from public scrutiny and accountability.

But finally the secret bureau that Hoover built has begun to surface. In 1971, a group of radicals raided the bureau field office in Pennsylvania, stole FBI documents, and published them. The "Media Papers" revealed the bureau's extensive use of informers on campuses, inside civil rights groups, and in organizations opposed to the Vietnam War. The Papers also provided the first evidence that the FBI was conducting secret operations to disrupt and discredit political organizations.[4] In the midst of the Watergate revelations, the FBI was discovered to have conducted at least seventeen national security wiretaps of former government officials and newsmen in order to plug "security leaks."[5] Civil litigation, notably a suit brought by the Socialist Workers party,[6] revealed more about FBI undercover operations; and the Rockefeller Commission, in conducting its inquiry into the CIA's domestic intelligence operations, uncovered a joint CIA-FBI mail-opening program aimed at American citizens.[7] With these revelations, the stage was set for full congressional investigations into the bureau's intelligence operations, the first such inquiry since the FBI was established. From these investigations has come knowledge of a range of abuses, from FBI burglary programs to the systematic gathering of political intelligence at the request of various presidents.[8] Now a public understanding of the FBI's intelligence activity is possible.

For forty years the FBI's domestic intelligence mission has been to contain "the spread of communism" and to protect the dominant political order. It is a mission that parallels the CIA's efforts abroad. Like the CIA, the FBI has carried out extensive surveillance programs, intervened in political events to shape their outcome, and engaged in covert operations to disrupt the activities of political groups and movements. However, the FBI's primary targets for surveillance and disruption have been American citizens and political movements.

ORIGINS IN WAR

"We are an intelligence agency," the FBI proclaimed in one internal bureau memorandum.[9] Yet nowhere in the statutes of the United States is there mention of the FBI's intelligence authority. By statute the Congress established the FBI strictly as a law enforcement agency, with no other duty except assisting the Justice Department in the detection of crimes committed against the United States. No law gives the bureau the authority to investigate political activity not closely related to criminal activity.[10] In fact, between 1924 and 1936, the FBI exercised no other investigative function except to gather evidence of criminal conduct.[11]

The period is significant because America was not at war or threatened by war. Move backward in time, and the FBI is deeply involved in intelligence activity as a consequence of World War I. Move forward in time, and the FBI is again engaged in extensive surveillance operations on the eve of World War II. When confronted by the specter of war, the executive branch has called on the bureau to conduct intelligence and counterintelligence operations in the United States. FBI intelligence has its roots in war and its authority to engage in intelligence activity derives not from statutes but from executive orders and instructions issued during wartime emergency.

Just prior to World War I, administration officials made repeated requests of the Bureau of Investigation (the predecessor to the FBI) to conduct intelligence operations to counter possible sabotage and espionage operations in the United States. Once pressed into operation, the bureau showed broader concerns, particularly the alleged threat posed by America's resident immigrant population. The General Intelligence Division, headed by J. Edgar Hoover, conducted investigations of "potential enemy aliens" and developed an index of persons it believed should be arrested and detained in time of war. After the outbreak of World War I, the government, on information supplied by the bureau, arrested over 6,300 resident aliens and detained more than 2,000 of them without due process of law.[12]

During the war, the bureau expanded its operations. Assisted by private vigilante groups, the bureau conducted "slacker raids" in 1918 and, "without warrants or sufficient probable cause for arrest," arrested 50,000 men suspected of possible draft evasion.[13] The bureau spied on citizens who criticized the war, opposed the draft, or participated in militant labor organizing efforts. When Congress enacted an Espionage Act that punished "disloyal utterances," United States attorneys across the country prosecuted nearly 2,000 persons under the act, largely based on information gathered by the bureau.[14]

When the war ended in 1918, the bureau turned its attention to monitoring the activities of American radicals. When a rash of bombing incidents blamed on radicals touched off a "red scare," the bureau took action. In January 1920, after the home of Attorney General A. Mitchell Palmer had been bombed, the bureau conducted a series of coordinated raids across the country. Agents arrested 10,000 persons believed to be members of the Communist and Communist Labor parties and denied them the right to post bail. The arrests, carried out without warrants or probable cause, constituted a massive infringement of individual liberties. The "Palmer Raids" provoked a tide of public criticism, congressional investigations, and finally an administration response.[15]

In 1924, Harlan Fiske Stone became attorney general and set out to reform the Justice Department and end the bureau's political police operations. Stone named J. Edgar Hoover, widely respected for his administrative skills and honesty, to head the then disorganized and discredited bureau. The attorney general abolished the bureau's General Intelligence Division and declared that the business of the bureau was to investigate crimes, not political activities:

The Bureau of Investigation is not concerned with political or other opinions of individuals. It is concerned only with their conduct and then only with such conduct as is forbidden by the laws of the United States. When a police system passes beyond these limits, it is dangerous to the proper administration of justice and to human liberty. . . .[16]

Stone's resolute actions curtailed bureau intelligence activity. For the next decade Hoover and the bureau observed the prohibition. When asked to intervene in labor or other domestic political struggles, the director refused. He would explain that these were either local matters or activities that did not violate federal criminal statutes. Stone's response had one negative effect: it preempted congressional efforts to enact a statute to prohibit bureau intelligence investigations.[17]

As World War II approached, the executive branch once again called on the FBI to conduct domestic intelligence and counterintelligence operations in the United States. Overturning Stone's prohibition on domestic spying, President Franklin D. Roosevelt issued a series of *secret* instructions to J. Edgar Hoover that authorized the bureau to conduct broad surveillance programs directed at American citizens. At a meeting with Hoover in 1936, Roosevelt ordered the bureau to monitor "subversive activities in the United States, particularly Fascism and

Communism." The president wanted a "broad picture of the general movements and its activities as may affect the economic and political life of the country as a whole."[18] In a 1940 memorandum, the president gave the FBI the power to employ warrantless wiretaps and bugs against "persons suspected of subversive activities against the government of the United States, including suspected spies."[19]

These sweeping instructions expressed both the president's and the director's prewar concerns. When Roosevelt met with Hoover in 1936, he was primarily worried about German spy operations and the possibility that Nazi elements in the United States might impede the war effort. In fact, the president had ordered the FBI to conduct a limited investigation of the Nazi movement in 1934.[20] Reporting to the president at this meeting, Hoover first mentioned the effort of the pro-Fascist Father Coughlin to have "General Butler lead an expedition to Mexico." But then Hoover devoted the rest of the time to warning the president that the Communists could "paralyze the country" through their control of the West Coast Longshoremen's Union headed by Harry Bridges, if they were successful in their attempts to take over the United Mine Workers, and by virtue of their influence over the Newspaper Guild which, according to Hoover, had "strong Communist leanings."[21] Apparently convinced, Roosevelt issued his broad instruction to the bureau to gather information on both the Communist and Fascist movements in the United States.

On September 6, 1939, Roosevelt issued a press release that instructed local law enforcement agencies to turn over all information regarding "espionage, counterespionage, sabotage . . . and violations of the neutrality laws" to the FBI, including information relating to "subversive activities."[22] Historically, this press release is the most important order issued by a president to the bureau. It was the only *public* acknowledgment made during the war years that the FBI had been authorized to conduct intelligence operations. It was based solely on a presidential claim of inherent power; and it was the order on which the FBI

THE BUREAU IN WAR AND PEACE

relied until 1973 to justify its extensive surveillance activities.[23]

Although the president's press release "announced" the FBI's intelligence mission, its growth was entirely a product of a secret executive action. A conscious decision was made *not* to seek legislative authority for intelligence operations, despite their questionable legal basis. As Hoover explained in a memorandum to President Roosevelt:

[I]t is believed imperative that [the intelligence structure] be proceeded with, with the utmost degree of secrecy in order to avoid criticism or objections which might be raised to such an expansion by either ill-informed persons or individuals having some ulterior motive. . . . Consequently, it would seem undesirable to seek any special legislation which would draw attention to the fact that it was proposed to develop a special counterespionage drive of any great magnitude.[24]

When Congress finally did learn about FBI intelligence work, it was after World War II had begun in Europe and years after bureau operations were in place. When Hoover reported to the House Appropriations Committee in 1939, he informed the committee that the bureau had *already* compiled "extensive indices of individuals, groups and organizations engaged in . . . subversive activities, in espionage activities, or any activities that are possibly detrimental to the internal security of the United States."[25]

With war in progress, Congress deferred to the executive. Now the "criticism and objections" Hoover had feared evaporated as the country closed ranks in the face of conflict abroad. At war's edge, the Congress was in no mood to question the bureau. Even though the bureau was once again "concerned with the political . . . opinions of individuals," Congress appropriated monies to allow the FBI to conduct its intelligence investigations and enacted repressive measures of its own. In 1940, Congress passed the Smith Act, which made it a federal crime to advocate the violent overthrow of the government, and in 1941, the

97

Voorhis Act, which required the registration of all subversive organizations having foreign links and advocating the violent overthrow of the government.[26]

The threat of war had once again transformed the FBI into a political police. On the eve of World War II, the FBI had the authority to conduct domestic intelligence and counterintelligence operations, including the investigation of possible "subversive activities." It had a mandate to employ covert surveillance techniques, such as wiretaps, against selected domestic groups and individuals. And the Congress had appropriated the monies for the conduct of this intelligence activity.

MODUS OPERANDI—THE WAR YEARS

Once authorized to investigate the political beliefs and associations of Americans, J. Edgar Hoover moved swiftly to establish an updated version of the General Intelligence Division he had headed during World War I. The operations were almost identical, from the categories of groups under surveillance to the secret collection techniques employed.

Hoover immediately launched a massive surveillance program to provide the president with the "broad picture" he requested. However, Hoover never restricted his agents to collecting information on organizations that owed "allegiance" to foreign countries with whom America might be in conflict. In 1936, he directed his field offices "to obtain from all possible sources information concerning subversive activities being conducted in the United States by Communists, Fascists, representatives or advocates of other organizations or groups advocating the overthrow or replacement of the Government of the United States by illegal methods."[27]

The FBI search for subversion was conducted in every area of American social and political life. All information "of a subversive or general intelligence character" was reviewed and filed at FBI headquarters, with index cards on individuals which made it possible to identify the persons "engaged in any particular activity, either in any section of the country or in a particular industry or movement."[28]

During the war years, the FBI investigated possible Fascist or Communist influence in such groups as the Christian Front and Christian Mobilizers (who followed Father Coughlin), the American Destiny party, the American Nationalist party, and America First on the right; and organizations from the Communist party to the NAACP on the left. The FBI also probed the League of Fair Play, which furnished "speakers to Rotary and Kiwanis Clubs and to schools and colleges" to determine whether it was infiltrated, and the Independent Voters of Illinois because of reports that it was Communist-infiltrated. The bureau went so far as to monitor a New York child-care center because it was "apparently dominated and run" by Communists, to determine whether it was a "front" for implementing the Communist program.[29]

The sweep of Hoover's surveillance operations was matched by the public drumbeat of his alarmist statements. In 1940, he publicly announced that foreign "isms" had "succeeded in boring into every phase of American life, masquerading behind front organizations."[30] By 1944, the FBI estimated that "almost 1,000,000 people knowingly or unknowingly had been drawn into Communist-front activity."[31]

After President Roosevelt authorized FBI use of warrantless domestic security wiretaps in 1940, the bureau increasingly resorted to covert techniques to gather information. Although the president had requested that wiretaps be restricted "insofar as possible to aliens,"[32] the primary targets for electronic surveillance were leaders and members of the Communist party and the Socialist Workers party.[33] Without legal authorization, the FBI also operated its first mail-opening program (called "Z-Coverage"), and monitored the international mail of Americans suspected of being sympathetic to hostile foreign countries.[34] The bureau developed a network of informers to penetrate and report on the activities of suspect organizations.[35] Field offices were authorized to obtain information from "public and private records, confidential sources of information, newspaper morgues, public libraries, employment records, school records, et cetera."[36]

Throughout the war—even after the United States and the Soviet Union became allies in 1941—the FBI prepared to use its information against Americans and alien residents. In a throwback to World War I the bureau, with the initial approval and participation of the Justice Department, developed a "Custodial Detention List" of persons the bureau believed should be arrested and held in case of national emergency because their "presence at liberty . . . would constitute a menace to the public peace and safety. . . ." Under the bureau's criteria, persons were dangerous if they showed "strong Nazi tendencies" or "strong Communist tendencies."[37]

As the FBI mounted this campaign, it increasingly became an agency beyond accountability. The president, who initiated the FBI intelligence mission, left it to the Justice Department to oversee the bureau. The Justice Department did not monitor the FBI; it agreed with Hoover that the bureau should not have to disclose the details of its program, because confidential sources of information and the identities of informers might be compromised. The bureau became so insulated that when the Justice Department terminated the Custodial Detention List program in 1943 because it did not believe the program was legal, Hoover simply changed the name of the list to "Security Index" and continued to update it without telling Justice officials.[38]

Congress had no standard to which it could hold the bureau accountable because it had not enacted a statute to define FBI intelligence. Congress deferred to the FBI's desire for secrecy by permitting the House Appropriations Committee to oversee all bureau operations and to hear testimony on FBI surveillance in secret sessions. Over time this committee became a "captive" of the bureau and refused to question its appropriations requests. The full

Congress also authorized bureau funds without debate.

Public scrutiny was impossible because the FBI program was secret. Moreover, the public was of no mind to criticize the bureau. Through his skillful use of public relations techniques, Hoover had established an image of himself and the bureau in the public consciousness as incorruptible, efficient, and above reproach. The president, the Justice Department, and the Congress hesitated to challenge a man whose pronouncements on communism were received as gospel. Fear also played a role, since both the executive and the Congress knew that Hoover maintained "Official and Confidential Files" on public officials.[39] (President Roosevelt and his top advisers knew this because Roosevelt had used the FBI to run "name checks" on his opponents for political purposes, and Hoover had supplied the president with a steady flow of "confidential" and derogatory information on those opponents.[40])

With FBI operations conducted in secret and with no laws governing its intelligence activities, the bureau was also beyond the scrutiny of the courts. Citizens did not know or could not prove that the FBI was infringing on their civil liberties. The insulation of the FBI from effective accountability was complete.

Much of this was justified as wartime necessity. When Congress approved the bureau's intelligence and counterintelligence operations to meet the wartime crisis, worried congressmen were assured by Hoover that when the hostilities ended the bureau would cease its intrusive investigations. When Hoover approached Congress for appropriations in 1941, he engaged in this significant exchange with members of the Appropriations Committee:

MR. LUDLOW. At the close of the present emergency, when peace comes, it would mean that much of this emergency work necessarily will be discontinued.

MR. HOOVER. That is correct. . . . If the national emergency should terminate, the structure dealing with national defense can immediately be discontinued or very materially curtailed according to the wishes of Congress.[41]

COLD-WAR INSTITUTIONALIZATION

When World War II ended, America did *not* return to peacetime conditions, but moved into a new phase: a cold war against communism. The institutions of war were not dismantled; the presidency remained ascendant, and a permanent national security structure was created.

One part of this structure was a permanent intelligence establishment. In 1947, Congress enacted legislation establishing a Central Intelligence Agency. The Federal Bureau of Investigation became its domestic counterpart. The executive branch, first by way of a secret National Security Council Directive and then by order of President Truman, reauthorized the bureau to conduct internal security investigations relating to espionage, sabotage, and subversive activities.[42] The bureau was not only put firmly in place but was allowed to expand its internal security operations. Policymakers campaigned for a peacetime military establishment by convincing the public of the imminent threat of Soviet expansion, generating widespread public fear and anxiety. In this charged atmosphere, the critical distinction between the "international" threat of communism and the "domestic" dangers of subversion was erased. As a result, the bureau received even wider latitude to conduct surveillance of American citizens. J. Edgar Hoover not only accepted this new authority but did all in his power to obtain it—even to the point of personally misleading the nation as to the extent of the dangers posed by "subversive activity."

At the outset of the cold war, officials did fear the possibility that agents of the Soviet Union might attempt to use domestic Communists for espionage purposes. The Canadian government published a report documenting such efforts in Canada in 1945. The discovery that "classified" State Department documents had been published in a small Communist journal coming on the heels of the Canadian report led to public apprehension. The House Un-American Activities Committee (HUAC) launched an investigation into government security and heard charges by Elizabeth Bentley and Whittaker Chambers that Alger Hiss and other government officials had provided classified information to the Soviet Union during World War II. After these charges and the Rosenberg spy case, apprehension turned into alarm.[43]

Public demagogues and anti-Communists rose to the occasion to exploit the new fears; the climate was ripe for overreaction. Shaken by the Soviet Union's testing of the atom bomb, the "fall" of China, and the outbreak of the Korean conflict, the public was on the verge of hysteria. When HUAC and Senator Joseph McCarthy's Senate Internal Security Committee leveled charges that the nation was overrun with Communists and "fellow travelers" sympathetic to the aims of the world Communist movement, many were prepared to listen, to believe, and increasingly to join in a demand for government action to do something about "subversion."[44]

The agency that could have calmed public fears was the Federal Bureau of Investigation. The bureau had monitored the Communist party and political left throughout the war years and was in a position to state the "real" danger posed by domestic communism. At the time, Hoover knew that the threat was almost nonexistent or at least unprovable. Significantly, his files showed that the number of *potential* "Government Communist Underground" employees did not exceed 100 persons and FBI records on these individuals did "not have *evidence, whether admissible or otherwise, reflecting actual membership in the Communist Party.*"[45] Hoover also knew that membership in the Communist party had dwindled substantially since the signing of the Nazi-Soviet Pact in 1939 and that the overwhelming majority of American Communists and radicals were anti-Soviet.[46]

Hoover chose not to reveal this critical intelligence information. On the contrary, he used every opportunity to play on public fears, to erase the distinction between foreign and domestic threats, and to press for more repressive measures to deal with subversion. When Hoover appeared before the House Un-American Activities Committee in 1947 to discuss the "spy" problem, he did not mention his intelligence estimates or confine his remarks to the danger of Soviet espionage. He warned that the Communists constituted "a menace to freedom, to democratic ideals, to the worship of God and to America's way of life." He went on to praise all, including the committee, who joined in the "fight against Communism" by seeking to identify and expose Communists.[47]

J. Edgar Hoover released statements that warned of subversion in all areas of American political life. When the Justice Department cautioned against "political" investigations by the Congress, Hoover undercut the department and fueled the fires of public alarm:

The forces which are most anxious to weaken our internal security are not always easy to identify. Communists have been trained in deceit and secretly work toward the day when they hope to replace our American way of life with a Communist dictatorship. They utilize cleverly camouflaged movements, such as some peace groups and civil rights organizations, to achieve their sinister purposes. While they as individuals are difficult to identify, the Communist Party line is clear. Its first concern is the advancement of Soviet Russia and the godless Communist cause. It is important to learn to know the enemies of the American way of life.[48]

The public hysteria generated by Hoover's dire warnings, the charges of the congressional investigating committees and the cold-war atmosphere led to repressive measures. By executive order, President Truman initiated a Loyalty and Security Program in 1947. Government boards investigated the loyalty of federal employees, and the attorney general compiled a list of subversive organizations to guide the boards in determining whether an individual's political associations indicated disloyal behavior.[49] In 1950, the president also reauthorized the bureau to investigate "subversive activities."[50] In this same year, Congress approved the Loyalty Program by prescribing security board procedures for the State, Justice, Commerce, and Defense departments, and empowered the president to extend the process to other agencies as he thought "necessary in the best interests of national security." Congress also authorized agency heads to summarily suspend employees suspected of disloyalty.[51]

Overriding President Truman's veto, Congress enacted the Internal Security Act of 1950, which required Communists and Communist fronts to register with the government and set up procedures for the arrest and detention of persons who might engage in espionage and sabotage during a national emergency.[52] Finally, Congress passed the Communist Control Act of 1954, which stripped the Communist party of all "rights, privileges, and immunities attendant upon legal bodies under the jurisdiction of the laws of the United States."[53]

All of these measures were supported by J. Edgar Hoover, and all of them increased the FBI's authority to spy on American citizens. Already investigating "subversive activities," the Loyalty Program gave the FBI exclusive jurisdiction to conduct "name checks" and full field investigations of government employees suspected of disloyalty, as well as the authority to conduct investigations to determine which organizations should be placed on the "Attorney General's List."[54] The Internal Security Act gave a congressional stamp of approval for the bureau's ongoing secret program of compiling a "security index" of persons marked for arrest and detention in case of national emergency. The Registration Act legitimized the bureau's efforts to uncover Communist "fronts" that could be prosecuted for failure to register with the government.

The FBI's new political police powers were a measure of its continuing insulation from accountability. Moderates and liberals offered little opposition and often gave their support to these repressive measures while expressing *private* apprehension about the danger to civil liberties. After exploiting public fears to generate consensus in favor of the national security state, moderates and liberals were caught in the whiplash of their own political rhetoric. President Truman established the Loyalty Program, even though he feared it would turn the FBI into a "Gestapo."[55] His top aides expressed alarm when the president issued a statement supporting the bureau's investigation of "subversive activities." "How in H— did this get out?" one presidential assistant asked. Another noted, "This is the most inscrutable Presidential statement I've seen in a long time."[56] But nothing was done to retract or narrow this grant of power. Congressional liberals, anxious to engage themselves from the label "Communism," joined conservatives in voting to override President Truman's veto of the Internal Security Act.

COLD-WAR INTELLIGENCE

The FBI instituted its most sweeping intelligence probes into American life during the cold-war period. It initiated COMINFIL, a program aimed at determining Communist "infiltration" in America. It developed hundreds of thousands of files on Americans and maintained a number of "detention lists." It employed a vast array of investigative techniques to gather information on citizens. It often acted beyond the law.

While the bureau investigated *all* members of the Communist party USA, and other radical organizations like the Socialist Workers party, it was also engaged in a wide-ranging search for Communist "infiltration" in America. Communists were said to use other groups as "fronts" for their purposes. The only way to discover if any group was a front was to spy on it. The only way to decide which groups to watch was to pick those whose positions—on peace, racism, economics, civil liberties—paralleled the Communist "line." From the beginning, the theory of COMINFIL enabled the bureau to monitor the entire range of liberal and left groups. Over the years, it became the excuse for Hoover to go after any group he didn't like.

Under COMINFIL, bureau agents and informers penetrated liberal organizations such as the American Friends Service Committee to find out if Communists were influencing or controlling its activities. The bureau operated inside the NAACP and other civil rights groups to monitor Communist activity in the civil rights area. Organizations that advocated "peace," such as SANE, were suspect because peace activities "paralleled" the "Communist line" and might indicate Communist influence, control, or sympathy. Bureau agents and informers gathered information on the political opinions and activities of university professors, student groups, and labor unions as part of the same intensive effort to determine whether America was in the grip of an "epidemic." Any group or organization that advocated social change or reform was fair game for the bureau. Even a coalition of lawyers and civil liberties organizations, including the National Lawyers Guild and the American Civil Liberties Union, was spied on because it advocated the abolition of the House Un-American Activities Committee. According to the bureau, this could only be Communist-inspired.[57]

By the bureau's own estimates, membership in the Communist party never exceeded 80,000 persons at any time during the cold-war period.[58] Yet the bureau opened approximately 432,000 headquarters files on individuals and groups in the "subversive" category during this decade.[59] By 1955, the attorney general could report that the FBI was conducting surveillance of "the entire spectrum of the social and labor movement."[60]

The collection techniques used by the FBI over the next two decades were perfected in the 1950s. The FBI deployed nearly 1,600 agents to conduct "security" work. This amounted to one-third of the bureau's total investigative force.[61] These agents recruited and controlled as many as 5,000 "subversive informants" who penetrated organizations to collect information for the bureau.[62] Although in many ways more intrusive than wiretaps or bugs, "informer plants" are legal, and the FBI placed few restrictions on them. Bureau informers, paid on an "incentive basis," acted as "vacuum cleaners," gathering any and all information without regard for the privacy of political association and activity. Informers noted everything about an organization and often stole confidential documents. Bureau reports, based on information supplied by informers, provided, in addition to evidence of alleged Communist "infiltration," exhaustive information on the membership, plans, and activities of specified groups.[63] Reports on the NAACP, for example, contained detailed accounts of their meetings and conventions and such activities as the preparation of a "petition directed to President Eisenhower" as well as the plans of some members to attend a "Prayer Pilgrimage" in Washington, D.C.[64]

Bureau agents also gathered information from a network of confidential sources such as "bankers, telephone company employees, and landlords."[65] On university campuses, agents recruited college deans and registrars to supply information. From these sources, the FBI gained access to private financial records, medical histories, and student files.[66] The FBI also had unlimited access to IRS tax information and searched through these supposedly confidential records for information on citizens.[67] The FBI collected this information without judicial warrant or probable cause of criminal conduct.

The FBI also used electronic surveillance in its intelligence probes. Under a 1952 executive order, President Truman *liberalized* the standard for attorney-general approval of FBI requests to conduct warrantless wiretaps. The bureau could obtain authorization in any case "vitally affecting the domestic security" and taps no longer were confined primarily to "aliens."[68] Each year the FBI placed hundreds of taps on the office and home phones of citizens and organizations.[69] Similarly, the bureau employed "bugs" or microphonic surveillance. Under existing rules, the bureau did not even need the approval of the attorney general to employ this technique to uncover "subversive activity." Employing "surreptitious entry" or trespass, FBI agents planted hundreds of bugs annually to gather information on suspected subversives.[70]

Secretly, the FBI also opened the mail of citizens without judicial warrant and in violation of United States criminal statutes. The bureau collected and opened mail under Z-coverage, its World War II program, and initiated at least one other "survey" during this period.[71] After 1958, the FBI became the chief user of an extensive CIA-operated illegal mail-opening program that intercepted the international private communications of individuals in whom they were interested.

In 1948, the FBI established an illegal burglary program directed at domestic groups. Since it was unauthorized and "clearly illegal," the FBI created a special "Do Not File" procedure for this operation. Agents trained in "lock studies" conducted hundreds of "black-bag" missions to photograph and steal confidential information belonging to domestic political organizations.[72] According to the FBI, the bureau "on numerous occasions" obtained "material held highly secret and closely guarded by subversive groups. . . ."[73]

THE OVERT WAR AGAINST DOMESTIC COMMUNISM AND DISSENT

The FBI was not content just to collect information on American citizens. From the beginning of FBI intelligence operations on the eve of World War II, J. Edgar Hoover and top bureau officials made repeated demands on the Justice Department to prosecute subversives—to take action against America's political "enemies." They wanted subversives to be prosecuted under the Smith Act for advocating revolution or under the Voorhis Act for failing to register with the government as foreign agents. The bureau also updated its lists of persons marked for arrest and detention during a national emergency.[74]

During the cold-war decade, all branches of the government aided in open war against dissent and nonconformity. The House Un-American Activities Committee and the Senate Internal Security Committee launched extensive investigations to determine the extent of Communist and subversive influence in all areas of American life. HUAC investigated communism in the arts, sciences, and professions, and in the government and entertainment industries.[75] The Senate Internal Security Committee, dominated by Senator Joseph McCarthy, investigated communism in the State and Defense departments. The committees, with staff members "on loan" from the bureau, conducted a public disruption program. Committee members read off lists of suspected Communists, lists that were often supplied by the bureau. Friendly witnesses, generally FBI undercover agents, "named names." Persons "charged" were hauled before the committees and interrogated about their beliefs and political associations. A witness who took the Fifth Amendment was presumed guilty. A witness who refused to discuss his or her political life on First Amendment grounds was subject to contempt and jailing. Individuals pilloried by the committees often lost their jobs or were blacklisted. Lives and reputations were destroyed. Political speech was "chilled" as Americans learned that to dissent was to risk public exposure and censure.[76]

The Loyalty and Security boards conducted similar inquisitions based on evidence gathered by the bureau. By 1952, the FBI had checked over 6.6 million citizens for possible "disloyalty," to determine whether they should retain their government positions or were fit to serve. Of these, 25,750 were subjected to full FBI field investigations. If the FBI uncovered evidence of possible disloyalty, an individual was given a hearing to determine whether he or she was disloyal. Thousands withdrew their applications for employment before or during these hearings. Those who went through the process were tried on the vague charge of membership or even "sympathetic association" with an organization on the Attorney General's List prepared by the FBI. Individuals were tried without being able to confront their accusers—FBI informers whose identity was a protected secret. By 1952, over 490 persons were dismissed on loyalty grounds, yet no case of espionage was ever uncovered by the investigations. The message to the public was that dissent could disqualify a person for government employment.[77]

The Justice Department entered the overt campaign against subversives in 1949. The top leadership of the Communist party was prosecuted under the Smith Act, which punished advocacy and the teaching of Communist doctrine. FBI investigations laid the basis for the prosecutions, and between 1949 and 1956, 104 members of the party were tried and convicted.[78] The judiciary sanctioned the campaign in 1951 when the Supreme Court upheld the Smith Act convictions in the *Dennis* case on the grounds that Communist "speech" had to be distinguished from other political advocacy because those who advocated the doctrine were part of an international movement. Justice Felix Frankfurter went so far as to take "judicial notice" of this "highly organized conspiracy" in rendering his decision for the Court.[79]

The only program the FBI was not able to put in motion was its plan for emergency detention in case of national emergency. Nevertheless, the bureau prepared for this eventuality throughout the cold-war decade. The bureau, often without the full knowledge of the Justice Department and under standards far broader than those laid down by Congress in 1950, maintained a number of detention lists. The Security Index had top priority in case of national crisis. This list, which included the Communist leaders, included 11,982 names. Next in line for preventive detention were members of the party, a list of 17,783 persons contained in the bureau's Communist Index. These were only the names in FBI headquarters files. FBI field offices listed over 200,000 persons considered by the FBI to constitute a danger to national security in time of crisis.[80]

SECRET WAR DECLARED

In the mid-fifties, cold-war tensions eased and the nation's political hysteria subsided. After a decade-long witch hunt, Americans paused, surveyed the constitutional wreckage, and took steps to end the government campaign against political dissent. Repressive programs were dismantled and the "McCarthy Era" came to a close.

In 1954, the United States Senate voted overwhelmingly to censure Senator Joseph McCarthy. In 1956, the United States Supreme Court drastically limited the ability of the government to prosecute under the Smith Act, and the Justice Department ended its efforts to prosecute members of the Communist party.[81] Loyalty boards withered and the Justice Department decided not to update the Attorney General's List after 1955.[82] The bureau's authority to monitor "subversive activities" was not curtailed, however. The FBI continued to gather information about the political activities of American citizens. Not unexpectedly, the FBI viewed the actions by the Congress and the Supreme Court as a serious setback in the national effort to combat subversion. J. Edgar Hoover and top bureau officials decided that drastic measures were necessary. Reasoning that the "Supreme Court rulings had rendered the Smith Act technically unenforceable" and an "ineffective" weapon in the battle against subversive elements, the bureau's top officials met to consider "something to take its place."[83] The bureau decided to set up covert action programs to wage secret war against subversives. If public bodies were no longer willing to employ FBI intelligence against citizens to "preserve" the country, the FBI was prepared to act on its own, in secret, and beyond the law.[84]

Behind a wall of secrecy, the bureau established, in August 1956, COINTELPRO in order to disrupt, expose, discredit, and otherwise neutralize the United States Communist party and related organizations.[85] FBI field offices were informed of this "top-secret" program, and special agents were assigned to develop and carry out actions to disrupt political activity. Field agents had to submit proposed actions to FBI headquarters for approval by Hoover and other top officials. Since its inception, FBI agents have taken over 2,000 actions against individuals and groups. An unknown number of similar operations—including those against the Reverend Martin Luther King, Jr., already described—were carried out under other programs not labeled COINTELPRO.

The FBI COINTELPRO against the Communist party and related organizations transformed McCarthyism into an underground operation. Under COINTELPRO, however, the FBI had even more leeway to disrupt the political activity of citizens and organizations for it could conduct its war in secret, unhindered by the law.

The FBI used press contacts to conduct campaigns to expose, discredit, and humiliate selected citizens. Derogatory information, arrest records, and other confidential bureau records were leaked to "friendly media" to form the basis for stories that could harm the reputation of citizens. Bureau-authored articles were planted in newspapers and magazines for the same purpose.

As part of its effort to neutralize the Communist party, FBI agents conducted anonymous-letter operations to have "subversives" fired from their jobs. The bureau also recruited other organizations, such as the American Legion, to launch similar actions. The bureau brought pressure on universities and schools to have professors and teachers fired and to urge other public institutions to deny Communists the right to speak or even a place to hold public meetings or assemblies. Many of these initiatives were successful.

Working through other agencies of government, the FBI took actions to disrupt the activities of the Communist party and its members. The bureau obtained the tax records of the party from the IRS and successfully encouraged IRS officials to institute "selective" tax audits of top party officials and of the Communist party itself. Other forms of official harassment included the FBI's encouragement of local police to arrest "subversives" on any pretext. When bureau informers or agents uncovered evidence of petty offenses, they immediately reported these matters to local police authorities. The FBI even placed some citizens in jeopardy of biased prosecution by approaching judges with "evidence" that persons on trial for other reasons were dangerous subversives.

The FBI infiltrated organizations and disrupted them from within. Informers were instructed to fan hostilities between members and upset plans and activities. The bureau planted so-called "snitch jackets" (false documents indicating cooperation with police) on loyal members to make it appear that they were police informers. FBI operatives established dummy chapters of the Communist party to drain off funds and then "deviate" from the party line. The FBI invaded the privacy of political associations, provoked paranoia inside groups, and destroyed their effectiveness. While this is the stock-in-trade of foreign intelligence agencies, the FBI was plying it against American citizens. As one bureau official explained:

If you have good intelligence and know what it's going to do, you can seed distrust, sow misinformation. The same technique is used in the foreign field. The same technique is used, misinformation, disruption, is used in the domestic groups. . . .[86]

The bureau's initial COINTELPRO target was the Communist party, but it soon went after "related" organizations. Over the years, the FBI commenced covert actions under the "Communist" program against the National Committee to Abolish the House Un-American Activities Committee because it believed it was "Communist-inspired"; the Reverend Martin Luther King, Jr., because the bureau believed he was under the "influence" of Communists; and the United Farmworkers Union because it allowed a Communist to speak at one of its rallies.[87]

The FBI conducted COINTELPRO by breaking the laws of the United States in addition to violating its own "charter," which gave it no authority to take such actions. The bureau violated statutes prohibiting government officials from interfering with the civil rights of citizens. It conducted its letter campaign in violation of mail fraud statutes. It leaked information in the face of a statutory prohibition against divulging information gained from wiretaps. It even acted in contravention of federal extortion laws.[88]

FBI records establish that a few high government officials were at least apprised of aspects of the anti-Com-

THE BUREAU IN WAR AND PEACE

munist COINTELPRO. Attorneys General William Rogers and Robert Kennedy were shown memoranda that described efforts by the bureau to "disrupt" the party, but without naming the program. There is a record of a cabinet briefing by Hoover in 1958, but the details are not known. Bureau records do indicate that the House Appropriations Committee knew of and approved this FBI disruptions program.[89] Except for the "captive" committee, however, members of Congress did not know the intimate details of the operation and certainly no one asked for "more" information. The FBI interpreted official silence as authority. For failing to inquire, these officials must share the blame for COINTELPRO.

Ultimately, it was a program that succeeded in hurting people and their politics, effects that cannot be measured or conveyed in a summary of its activities. Bureau action could sow dissension as well as destroy a man, as happened in the case of William Albertson after the bureau planted documents on him (a snitch jacket) to make it appear that he was a police informer.

William Albertson was a member of the American Communist party, until he was expelled in 1964. He was charged with being an FBI informer because "incriminating" evidence was found in his automobile. At that time, Albertson had been a member for almost thirty years, and had risen through the ranks of the party to become a high party official, a member of the National Committee. He had devoted his active political life to the party and the trade union movement, and had suffered the social ostracism that befell other members of the party. He was convicted under the Smith Act and although his conviction was ultimately reversed, he served time in jail for contempt for refusing to tell the court who was at a meeting he had attended. He told the court: "My wife and I have tried to raise our children in the best traditions of the American labor movement. We have given them a hatred for spies, stool pigeons, and scabs. I could not look my children in the face if I violated those traditions."

The evidence that led to his expulsion from the party

was a letter addressed "Dear Joe" and signed "Bill," a document that appeared to be in his handwriting and which offered information to an FBI agent in exchange for a "raise in expenses." Although Albertson pleaded with party officials that the letter was a fake and a forgery, he was drummed out as a "stool pigeon" and a person who had led a life of "duplicity and treachery." For the rest of his life, he tried unsuccessfully to gain reinstatement in the party. Barred from his former union because of his conviction under the Smith Act, Albertson had difficulty finding employment. Ironically, he was approached by the FBI to become a paid informer.

Albertson refused the FBI and persisted in his appeals. His family was ostracized from its former circle of friends. "Even our friends," his wife recounts, "who were sure that Bill had been framed would have nothing to do with us for fear of guilt by association." After arson threats, his home was burned. His family approached disintegration and sought therapy. The party did not answer his correspondence. "The most painful thing I ever had to experience," his widow recalls, "was watching a destroyed man trying to save himself." William Albertson was killed in an accident in 1972. He was the victim of a "snitch jacket" planted by the FBI as one of its many COINTELPRO actions.[90]

THE FBI WAR AGAINST POLITICAL DISSENT

In the 1960s, America's long tradition of political activism reasserted itself in a decade of new politics, dissent, and protest. A nonviolent civil rights movement emerged. Student activists joined in that struggle, started university-based protests aimed at "free speech" and academic reform, and established the New Left, a nonsectarian, unorganized radical movement committed to reform and "participatory democracy." Black militants called for "black power" and women started their own liberation movement. The Vietnam War molded many of these protest groups and millions of other Americans into a coalition to end the war in Vietnam. In 1972, these same Americans became delegates to the Democratic National Convention and helped to nominate the party's candidate for president of the United States.

The FBI viewed the new politics of dissent as suspicious and subversive. In part on its own, and in part in response to the demands of the White House, the FBI went after the whole spectrum of political dissent that emerged over the course of the decade. At first, the FBI monitored reform groups under the pretext of determining whether they were under the "influence" of communism. The Southern Christian Leadership Conference, the Congress of Racial Equality, Martin Luther King, Jr., and Floyd McKissick were investigated under COMINFIL and a General Racial Matters Program aimed at uncovering subversive tendencies in the civil rights movement. Similarly, the Free Speech Movement at Berkeley and the Students for a Democratic Society were monitored under COMINFIL.[91]

When the FBI could not find significant "subversive" influence, the bureau abandoned all pretense that its intelligence was directed only at organizations under the control or influence of a foreign power or dedicated to "violence." The Socialist Workers party (SWP) was placed under heavy surveillance even through the bureau conceded it was "home grown tomatoes" and in active opposition to the Communist party. The bureau took aim at the SWP because it espoused the "revolutionary principles of Marx, Lenin, and Engles (sic) as interpreted by Leon Trotsky" by "running candidates for public office."[92] The surveillance of Martin Luther King, Jr., as we have seen, was ostensibly to prevent "the rise of a 'messiah' who could unify and electrify the . . . black . . . movement,"[93] although King's criticism of the bureau may well have been the real reason.

The New Left was defined by the bureau itself as a "loosely-bound, free-wheeling, college-oriented movement." Yet it was labeled a "subversion force"[94] because it was allegedly dedicated to the destruction of America's "traditional values" and was "anti-war and anti-draft." In an earlier decade, the FBI had erased the distinction between foreign and domestic threats of subversion. In the 1960s, the FBI came to the point where it identified dissent with subversion.

THE GOVERNMENT'S POLICE

Increasingly, the FBI served as an intelligence arm of the government, on call at the whim of the president. Executive officials viewed the FBI as an agency obligated to carry out the president's wishes. Exercising "inherent power," one president after another issued sweeping orders to the FBI to collect intelligence on Americans, often for strictly political purposes. The bureau interpreted these instructions as a mandate to monitor *all* dissent.

Even when the concerns were legitimate, the orders issued to the FBI invited extensive surveillance of lawful political activity. Reacting to Klan violence in 1964, President Lyndon Johnson issued oral instructions to Hoover "to put people after the Klan and study it from one county to the next."[95] Hoover took this to justify an investigation of all members of the Klan, regardless of whether or not they were involved in violent acts. After President Johnson received word of the first ghetto disorders in 1964, he ordered the FBI to report on "their origins and extent." Hoover provided the report and started an intensive surveillance program in ghetto areas. Civil disorders reached their height in the summer of 1967 and, as a consequence, Attorney General Ramsey Clark issued a sweeping instruction to the FBI that brought countless black activists under surveillance. Clark ordered the FBI to

use the maximum resources, investigative and intelligence, to collect and report all facts bearing upon the question as to whether there has been or is a scheme or conspiracy by any group of whatever size, effectiveness or affiliation, to plan, promote or aggravate riot activity. . . .

Clark's memorandum went on to authorize the bureau

118

to take every step possible to determine whether the rioting is pre-planned or organized; and, if so, to determine the identity of the people and interests involved; and to deter this activity by prompt and vigorous legal action. As a part of the broad investigation which must necessarily be conducted . . . sources or informants in black nationalist organizations, SNCC and other less-publicized groups should be developed and expanded to determine the size and purpose of these groups and their relationship to other groups, and also to determine the whereabouts of persons who might be involved in instigating riot activity in violation of federal law. Further, we need to investigate fully allegations of conspiratorial activity that come to our attention from outside sources. . . .[96]

Executive officials frequently called on the FBI to monitor its political opposition, sometimes for purely political purposes. To uncover who was behind the sugar lobby, Attorney General Robert Kennedy ordered the FBI to place "national security" wiretaps on the lobbyists, their Washington attorneys, and their contacts at the Department of Agriculture. Concerned about the challenge of the black Mississippi Freedom Democratic party to the all-white delegation from Mississippi at the Democratic National Convention in 1964, Lyndon Johnson, we have seen, dispatched a squad of thirty agents to gather intelligence at the convention.[97]

The antiwar movement also caused the president to order the FBI into operation. Warned by the CIA that foreign countries and Communists might exploit the movement, Johnson issued instructions to Hoover in 1965 to determine the extent of subversive influence behind the antiwar protests. Johnson informed Hoover that he wanted the information to use in speeches against his critics. Hoover responded by putting the antiwar movement and the New Left under more intensive surveillance and even dispatched agents to monitor the Senate Foreign Relations Committee hearings to compare the statements of Senator Wayne Morse and other Senate war critics with the "Communist Party line."[98]

Executive branch officials did not turn just to the FBI

for intelligence on Americans. By 1968, all intelligence agencies were enlisted to spy on Americans. The CIA was ordered to investigate the foreign links of antiwar activists in 1967. Military intelligence opened up a major surveillance program aimed at Americans, to prepare for "civil disorders." The National Security Agency was brought in to monitor the international communications of black extremists and antiwar activists, and the Justice Department set up an Interdivisional Information Unit (IDIU) to collect, computerize, and evaluate reports coming primarily from the FBI and military intelligence agencies. Sharing information with all of these agencies authorized to collect information on the political activities of citizens, the bureau was at the center of a massive surveillance effort ordered by the executive.[99]

The Nixon administration gave the FBI even more latitude to conduct surveillance. The bureau was instructed by executive order to do "thumbnail" sketches (a replacement for the Attorney General's List) of the new extremist organizations as part of the government's employment security program.[100] The administration called on the FBI to help plug "security leaks" after press reports divulged the secret bombing campaign in Cambodia. This resulted in an FBI-operated "national security" wiretap program directed at seventeen government officials and newsmen.[101]

Finally, President Nixon authorized the Huston Plan in 1970, a joint FBI, CIA, NSA and military program to collect intelligence on the antiwar and black protest movements by using informers, illegal burglaries, and mail opening. When Hoover objected because its exposure might prove "embarrassing" (and also because it impinged on his turf), the operation was conducted informally. Unknown to the president, however, the FBI and other intelligence agencies of government were *already* employing these techniques against American citizens.[102] The FBI in particular had interpreted this long line of "executive orders" as a mandate to operate the most extensive, intrusive, and illegal intelligence operations in its history.

FBI INVESTIGATIONS

The FBI probed every corner of American political life to meet the "threat" of dissent. Over the course of the last decade, the FBI opened up over 500,000 headquarters files on over one million Americans.[103] The bureau's collection of information on Americans under multiple indices demonstrates that it no longer had the interest or the ability to distinguish between subversion and dissent and between political violence and lawful, if vociferous, political opinion. Under COMINFIL, General Racial Matters, Black Nationalist Hate-Type Groups, Key Extremist, and Rabble Rouser, the FBI gathered information on Martin Luther King, Jr., the Southern Christian Leadership Conference, the Black Panther party, the Nation of Islam, Stokeley Carmichael, Ralph David Abernathy, "all black student unions," and the American Indian Movement—among others. Under the Racial Matters, White Hate-Type Groups, and Rabble Rouser categories, the FBI swept up information on all members of the Klan, the John Birch Society, Gerald L. K. Smith, the Christian Nationalist Crusade, the American Nazi party, and the National States Rights party. Under COMINFIL, STUDEM, VIDEM, New Left, and Key Activist, the FBI gathered information on SDS, Tom Hayden, the Institute for Policy Studies, Jane Fonda, Sam Brown, SANE, Antioch College, "all free universities," Women Strike for Peace, the Women's Liberation movement, Clergy and Laity Concerned, the American Friends Service Committee, the Weatherpeople, the Inter-University Committee for Debate on Foreign Policy, the New Mobilization to End the War in Vietnam—virtually the entire social protest movement.[104]

Domestic intelligence became an almost fulltime occupation for the Intelligence Division of the bureau. The FBI virtually abandoned its counterintelligence operations against hostile foreign intelligence activities as it focused its effort on monitoring dissent and protecting the political order.[105] Hundreds of agents used every available technique to collect information on citizens, from scouring public source materials to committing multiple burglaries and mail openings.

Agents placed various organizations and individuals under physical surveillance, conducted extensive interviews of suspects, and plied their confidential sources for information. In addition to bank, medical, and phone toll records, the FBI had almost unlimited access to confidential tax information, especially after 1969 when the IRS, at White House request, opened its own intelligence operation designed to audit the nation's "political enemies." The FBI and IRS joined in a two-way flow of information on the political and confidential activities of thousands of American citizens.[106]

The FBI relied primarily on informers to gather intelligence. The bureau employed legions of them to penetrate political groups. At one point, the FBI had as many as 774 "sources" in the Klan[107] and over 7,402 "listening posts" in urban ghettos.[108] Informers collected all information without limit. As a one-time bureau informer inside the Vietnam Veterans against the War recalls:

I was to go to meetings, write up reports . . . on what happened, who was there . . . to try to totally identify the background of every person there, what their relationships were, who they were living with, who they were sleeping with, to try to get some sense of the local structure and the local relationships among the people in the organization.[109]

FBI informers in the Socialist Workers party managed not only to infiltrate the tiny organization but in many instances to achieve high positions. So much so that in 1975 when a federal district court judge ordered the FBI to keep its informers away from the national convention of the SWP, the government appealed the matter all the way to the Supreme Court. The FBI explained that its informants were such senior officials that if they did not attend the convention their identities would immediately become obvious.

The FBI wiretapped the telephones and bugged the offices and homes of citizens and organizations. Under authority granted by the attorney general, the FBI placed warrantless "national security" wiretaps on such domestic organizations as the Student Nonviolent Coordinating Committee, the Southern Christian Leadership Conference, the Socialist Workers party, the Students for a Democratic Society, the Jewish Defense League, and individuals such as Martin Luther King, Jr., Malcolm X., Hanson Baldwin, and Charles E. Radford, to uncover subversion, to "plug leaks," and to gather political information for the White House.[110] Acting without authority, FBI agents placed "wildcat" or "suicide" taps and bugs on antiwar groups after the United States Supreme Court held in 1972 that a warrant was required in any domestic security case.[111] The FBI also supplied a "watch list" of over 1,200 names to the National Security Agency, which intercepted the international cables and telephone communications of antiwar and black political activists watchlisted by the bureau. Neither the FBI nor the NSA obtained judicial warrants for this surveillance.[112]

The FBI conducted at least six "mail surveys" to collect and open the mail of specified citizens. At the same time, the FBI continued to supply a "watch list" to the CIA. Each year, the agency opened over 10,000 letters. Most of the information was sent to the FBI. The FBI and the CIA opened private correspondence without warrants or probable cause, and in violation of United States statutes.[113]

The FBI's illegal burglary program was also extensive throughout this period. The scope of this program may never be divulged because it is almost certain that the FBI has destroyed many of the records of this "Do Not File" operation. It is known, however, that the FBI conducted at least 239 "black-bag jobs" aimed at "fifteen domestic groups" and over ninety burglaries against the Socialist Workers party during this time.[114] In 1973 and 1974, FBI agents conducted numerous burglaries against the *families and friends* of members of the Weather Underground to look for evidence of their possible whereabouts.[115]

Each year the FBI collected intelligence and distributed it throughout the government. Public officials were kept apprised of the political opinions, plans, and activities of its citizens. The White House received FBI reports on the confidential strategies of civil rights activists and antiwar protesters, the negotiations of delegates at the Democratic National Convention in 1964, background information on the campaign staff of Barry Goldwater, Jr., the 1968 contacts of Richard Nixon's campaign with persons close to the South Vietnam government, the 1972 strategy suggestions of advisers to candidate Edmund Muskie.[116] The president and the attorney general also received an "Inlet" letter on a regular basis from the FBI designed to provide "items with an unusual twist or concerning prominent personalities which may be of special interest to the President or Attorney General.[117] FBI reports on Ralph Abernathy, Coretta King, Seymour Hersh, Sammy Davis, Jr., Cesar Chavez, and others were transmitted in thousands of dispatches sent to the Justice Department and fed into IDIU computers for storage and analysis.[118] The FBI and the Justice Department provided information to the IRS for its "enemies project." The FBI sent its information to the CIA, the Secret Service, and Military Intelligence. They, in turn, sent information to the bureau. By 1972, the intelligence agencies of the government, with the FBI at the center, had placed the political left and a large part of the Democratic party under surveillance.[119]

THE SECRET WAR

The FBI placed citizens under surveillance, surrounded them with agents, penetrated their organizations with a network of informers, wired their offices and homes, gathered confidential information on their plans and activities, and then secretly turned around and used its agents, informers, and information to "expose, disrupt, discredit, or otherwise neutralize" dissent. The FBI initiated political actions against the Socialist Workers party (1961), the Ku

Klux Klan (1964), Black Nationalist Hate-Type Groups (1967), and the New Left (1968).[120]

The FBI sowed dissension in the Klan. It conducted extensive interviewing of Klan members and infiltrated and took leadership positions in many Klaverns. It created paranoia about police surveillance and played on internal disputes. It rendered the Klan ineffective by wholesale assault.[121] FBI informers also joined in the Klan's many beatings of civil rights workers and blacks to protect their "cover." FBI agents, forewarned by informers of impending Klan violence, stood by at the scene and watched when local police did nothing to stop it.[122]

The FBI's principal effort against the Black Panther party was to provoke hostility and violent warfare between it and other militant black organizations such as Ron Karenga's United Slaves. The FBI wrote a provocative anonymous letter purporting to be from one organization to the other:

To Former [Panther] Comrade [name] . . .
  Why, I read an article in the Panther paper where a California Panther sat in his car and watched his friend get shot by Karenga's group and what did he do? He run back and write a full-page story about how tough the Panthers are and what they're going to do. Ha Ha—B—S—.
  Goodbye [name] baby—and watch out. Karenga's coming.[123]

Operating inside the Panthers, the FBI planted "snitch jackets" on militant members, inviting other Panthers to attack them for having "informed" to the police. The FBI also created dissension among the Panthers and claimed success for provoking at least four instances of assault by one militant black activist against another.[124]

The FBI worked to create violent confrontations between factions on the radical left. The bureau was prepared in this case to commit violent acts itself. In New York, agents set cars on fire with "molotov cocktails," making it appear that one faction was attacking another. FBI agents conducted at least five such bombings in 1973 and 1974.[125]

The FBI's campaign included covert acts designed to destroy the family lives of group members. The FBI sent anonymous letters to the wives of Klan and Black Panther party members accusing their husbands of infidelity. Using information gathered from its surveillance, the FBI mailed a letter to the wife of the Grand Dragon of the United Klans of America, which alleged in part:

Yes, Mrs. A., he has been committing adultery. My menfolk say they don't believe this but I think they do. I feel like crying, I saw her with my own eyes. They call her Ruby . . . and she lives in the 700 block of [deleted] Street in [deleted]. I know this. I saw her strut around at a rally with her lust-filled eyes and smart aleck figure.[126]

Written in what the bureau considered the "grammar" of typical Klan members, this type of anonymous letter was viewed by the bureau as a very successful covert tactic.

The FBI did not reserve such measures for those who might engage in violence, but also tried to provoke violence by peaceful groups. An FBI operative inside the San Diego Minutemen became a leader in a secret army organization which terrorized a Marxist professor of economics at San Diego State University who was active in the antiwar movement.[127] A former FBI agent provocateur recalls how he led the Camden Nine to conduct a raid on a local draft board that resulted in their arrest and prosecution by the FBI and the Justice Department:

I taught them everything they knew . . . how to cut glass and open windows without making any noise. . . . How to open file cabinets without a key. . . . How to climb ladders easily and walk on the edge of the roof without falling. . . . I began to feel like the Pied Piper.[128]

Under COINTELPRO and similar programs, the FBI erased the line between investigation and disruption. Informers became agents provocateurs, and surveillance methods were turned into harassment techniques. The bureau tried to convince dissenters that "there was an FBI agent behind every mailbox,"[129] and by so doing to "chill" the exercise of free speech. In one instance, it went so far as to "kidnap" an antiwar activist to scare him into stopping his protests against the war.[130]

To quell dissent, the FBI's primary efforts inevitably interfered in the political process. The thrust of the FBI campaign against the Socialist Workers party was to subvert SWP's efforts to elect candidates to public office. In 1962, the New York office of the FBI compiled an arrest and conviction record on an SWP candidate for Manhattan borough president and supplied it to a reporter for the New York *Daily News*, who published it in a column. In 1963, the San Francisco office sent an anonymous letter to a black independent candidate for mayor of the city, attacking the SWP members active in his campaign and urging him to dissociate himself from them. In 1964, the Newark office distributed leaflets attacking a New Jersey SWP candidate for the U.S. Senate for alleged antiblack political stands on issues. In 1965, the Denver office sent an anonymous letter from a "concerned mother" to the Denver School Board in which the SWP affiliations and activities of a school board candidate were detailed. The purpose of the letter was "to prevent him from being elected to the School Board." When an SWP candidate was running for mayor in 1965, the New York field office sent an anonymous letter to various newspapers and television stations revealing that the candidate had previously appeared in court in Chicago for "non-support" of his family and that his marital status could be questioned. In 1969, the New York field office sent an anonymous letter to a black SWP candidate for mayor that purported to be from white members of the SWP and attacked him for being too militant on the race issue, in order to cause dissension and hurt his campaign.[131]

The FBI moved against the New Left for similar reasons, Agents were instructed to gather "derogatory" information about the New Left activists to undercut their protest efforts. The FBI also attempted to gather data to prove that the charges of police brutality at the Chicago Democratic Convention in 1968 were false.[132]

Once again, the liberal press and the bleeding hearts and the forces on the left are taking advantage of the situation in Chicago surrounding the Democratic National Convention to attack the police and organized law enforcement. . . . We should be mindful of this situation and develop all possible evidence to expose this activity and to refute these false allegations.[133]

At one point, the bureau distributed a news article titled "Rabbi in Vietnam Says Withdrawal Not the Answer" to convince antiwar activists "of the correctness of the U.S. foreign policy in Vietnam."[134]

The FBI concentrated on those who were not convinced by the bureau's stand on the war. To undercut those who opposed *its* position on United States policy in Vietnam, the FBI instructed field agents to:

(1) prepare leaflets designed to discredit student demonstrators, using photographs of New Left leadership at the respective universities. "Naturally, the most obnoxious pictures should be used";

(2) instigat[e] "personal conflicts or animosities" between New Left leaders;

(3) creat[e] the impression that leaders are "informants for the Bureau or other law enforcement agencies";

(4) send . . . articles from student newspapers or the "underground press" which show the depravity of the New Left to university officials, donors, legislators and parents. "Articles showing advocation of the use of narcotics and free sex are ideal";

(5) hav[e] members arrested on marijuana charges;

(6) send . . . anonymous letters about a student's activities to parents, neighbors and the parents' employers. "This could have the effect of forcing the parents to take action";

(7) send . . . anonymous letters or leaflets describing the "activities and associations" of New Left faculty members and graduate assistants to university officials, legislators, Boards of Regents and the press. "These letters should be signed 'A Concerned Alumni,' or 'A Concerned Taxpayer' ";

(8) use . . . "cooperative press contacts" to emphasize that the disruptive elements constitute a "minority" of the students. "The press should demand an immediate referendum on the issue in question";

(9) exploit . . . the "hostility" among the SDS and other New

BEHIND THE GREAT WALL

COPYRIGHT 1976 BY HERBLOCK IN *THE WASHINGTON POST*

Left groups toward the SWP, YSA and Progressive Labor Party;

(10) use . . . "friendly news media" and law enforcement officials to disrupt New Left coffee houses near military bases which are attempting to "influence members of the Armed Forces";

(11) us[e] cartoons, photography and anonymous letters to "ridicule" the New Left; and

(12) us[e] "misinformation" to "confuse and disrupt" New Left activities, such as by notifying members that events have been cancelled."[135]

FBI agents faithfully carried out the instructions. They sent anonymous letters to parents, wrote leaflets, distributed handbills, and conducted campaigns to disrupt the New Left. They caused the University of Arizona to fire a college professor who had engaged in antiwar protests. They succeeded in having two other professors put on probation because they were influential in the publication of underground newspapers. They convinced institutions to deny protest groups places to meet. They sent out "disinformation" during protest demonstrations to confuse demonstrators and they blocked the efforts of university students to attend the presidential inaugural in 1969. Agents even "roughed up" radical antiwar activists to frighten them or to disrupt protest rallies. (It was bureau policy not to beat up activists too seriously so they would not go to the police and perhaps launch an investigation that would lead to the bureau.)[136]

The FBI had by the late 1960s become enmeshed in a government-wide program to disrupt dissent. As protests mounted, COINTELPRO-type operations spread to other agencies. With FBI cooperation and information, the IRS conducted selective tax audits.[137] The FBI sent information to the Secret Service, which began to take steps to "protect" the president not only from harm but from "embarassment" or from having to confront peaceful protestors.[138] The FBI and the CIA carried out a joint collection operation and the CIA became involved in disrupting demonstrations in Washington, D.C.[139] The military, also sharing information with the bureau, conducted photographic surveillance of demonstrators to let them know they were being watched.[140] After the Huston Plan was devised in 1970, America was on the verge of acquiring a full-scale secret police, with the FBI at its center.

STILL WATCHING

Today the FBI stands exposed. Many of its operations have been terminated, not by executive orders or legislation but because of the "Media Papers," the tenacity of investigative journalists, the Watergate revelations, and civil litigation. These events slowed the bureau—not the president, the Justice Department, or the Congress.

Executive officials did not approve the burglary program or COINTELPRO. These were largely secret programs. But they were secret because the FBI operated beyond accountability. Some officials even knew of aspects of COINTELPRO: the programs to disrupt the Communist party; the bureau effort to destroy King; the activities directed at the Klan. Either they approved of what the bureau was doing or did not inquire about the details.

Congress has now investigated the FBI and has uncovered an agency afraid of the subversive but even more distressed about open society and democratic government. For forty years, the FBI has operated on a theory of subversion that assumes that people cannot be trusted to choose among political ideas. The FBI has assumed the duty to protect the public by placing it under surveillance. For these long years, the FBI has watched over America's internal security threat and in the end that threat has turned out to be the democratic political process itself.

The executive and the Congress apparently share the bureau's concerns, because they have not terminated FBI intelligence operations. Today the FBI still conducts surveillance of Americans engaged in lawful political activity. Its informer network is still in place and in operation. Its field offices may still be committing burglaries and illegal wiretaps, as the Socialist Workers party suit has shown.[141] COINTELPRO has been formally ended, but other disruption programs continue. The exact scope of the bureau's activities is unknown, but its focus has not been altered. The bureau is still concerned with the opinions of men and women rather than solely with their illegal acts. The Justice Department has issued *strict* guidelines to prevent a recurrence of past "mistakes," but agents believe those guidelines authorize the bureau to continue investigating "subversive activities." The guidelines leave the matter open by permitting limited inquiries into lawful conduct. Even if that were not the case, the guidelines are only tentative rules that can be changed tomorrow by a worried executive concerned about the next political turmoil.

Only Congress can prohibit the FBI from continuing to probe political life by enacting a strict prohibition of FBI intelligence investigations. But the Congress, like the body that investigated the "Palmer Raids" after World War I, seems willing to accept the promise made by the FBI that "it won't happen again."

This wishful thinking leaves the American political process extremely vulnerable. Another crisis can trigger a new sweeping intelligence probe of American political life, a dangerous possibility in the age of sophisticated electronic surveillance and computer technology. Meanwhile, the FBI waits. As one agent stated, "Kelley [the present FBI director] said it won't be done any more, but I can assure you that it will."[142] The bureau waits . . . and watches.

THE OTHER
AGENCIES AT HOME

The American intelligence community is a far-flung conglomerate, with many agencies and groups. The bulk of its money—estimated at more than $10 billion per year in direct costs—is spent on technical intelligence-gathering operations aimed at learning about the activities of foreign governments. At least one of these organizations, the supersecret National Reconnaissance Office, which launches spy satellites, appears not to have become involved in covert operations or in surveillance of American citizens, and its activities are not discussed in these pages. But many other intelligence agencies have strayed beyond their original functions into spying on American citizens. More of the surveillance and manipulation at home was done by the FBI than by any other single agency. But the bureau was not alone. Other intelligence agencies joined in the effort, sometimes at the behest of the FBI or the president, and sometimes on their own. Some also joined the bureau in political action designed not just to gather information but to use it to interfere with the lawful exercise of political rights by Americans.

Among the agencies other than the FBI that have spied on law-abiding Americans exercising their constitutional rights are the CIA, the National Security Agency (NSA),

133

the various branches of Military Intelligence, and the Internal Revenue Service (IRS). The Justice Department has also used the grand jury to extract information and harass those whose political activities it opposed. There is a certain uniformity in the involvement of these agencies in the surveillance of Americans. Often it began as a part of their own responsibilities and then spread. The CIA was interested in potential sources of information, in potential recruits, and in those who threatened its facilities or operations. It ended gathering data on the domestic antiwar movement. Military Intelligence started with an interest in those who might threaten its ability to wage war and ended with a massive effort to gather data on many forms of dissent. The NSA puts its sophisticated information techniques at the disposal of other intelligence agencies, first to gather foreign intelligence information and then to spy on Americans. The IRS, which interested itself in those who preach opposition to the income tax, was willing to put its facilities for gathering data and harassing taxpayers at the disposal of the White House and other intelligence agencies. The grand jury was increasingly used by the Justice Department not to combat organized crime but to combat unorganized protest. In the 1960s, each agency was drawn increasingly into the White House-directed campaign against dissent. Separate programs, with names such as CHAOS and MINARET, were established as the intelligence community as a whole turned to spying on Americans and seeking to manipulate their behavior. No less than the FBI, the other agencies saw themselves as operating outside the normal constraints of the Constitution. "National security" was at stake, the people were the enemy and no holds were barred. In the chapters that follow we review briefly the contribution made by these agencies to the war at home against lawful dissent.

THE CIA

5

In a closed-door hearing on February 7, 1973, U.S. Senator Clifford Case questioned CIA Director Richard Helms on his knowledge of a 1970 White House effort to pressure the intelligence agencies into conducting surveillance of the antiwar movement in the United States:

CASE: Do you know anything about any activity on the part of the CIA in that connection? Was it asked to be involved?

HELMS: I don't recall whether we were asked, but we were not involved because to me that was a clear violation of what our charter was.

CASE: What do you do in a case like that? Suppose you were?

HELMS: I would simply go to explain to the President that didn't seem advisable.

CASE: That would end it?

HELMS: Well, I think so, normally.[1]

Helms was correct in stating that such activities would violate CIA's legislated charter, but he lied when he asserted that the CIA had not investigated the domestic antiwar movement. It had.

Responding to enormous pressure from President Johnson to uncover the foreign links to the growing unrest of the late 1960s, the CIA opened up a new division within its Counter-Intelligence Branch. Over the next seven years, the program conducted by this special staff, known as Operation CHAOS, spied on more than 7,000 American citizens and 1,000 domestic organizations.

This was the most extensive, but not the first, CIA spying operation against Americans. For years the agency had been opening mail, burglarizing homes, wiretapping phones, and secretly watching the movements of unsuspecting individuals *within* the United States, all in violation of its legislative charter.

In 1947, when Congress voted to create the CIA as part of the National Security Act, there was great concern about whether the CIA could operate in the United States and against Americans.

Congress wanted to assure the public that this agency would not lead to the growth of a secret police. Responding to these suspicions, Dr. Vannevar Bush, an administration witness, explained that the agency was concerned only with intelligence "outside this country," and not with "internal affairs."[2] To make sure, Congress wrote into the CIA's charter that the agency was prohibited from exercising "police, subpoena, or law-enforcement powers or internal security functions." Congressional debate made it clear that Congress anticipated that the CIA would simply not operate at home.

Two years later, with the passage of the Central Intelligence Agency Act of 1949, congressional apprehensions were again calmed by the assertion that the CIA had no jurisdiction within the United States, that it "has no connection with the FBI; it is not under the FBI, it does not do the same kind of work as the FBI."[3] These public assertions, however, did not coincide with the CIA's secret growth of operations within the United States and the surveillance of Americans abroad.

Because of the public uproar that would have ensued if the agency had openly expanded its domestic operations, the CIA wrote its own secret charter. Through internal directives, executive orders, and pacts with other government agencies, the CIA expanded its authority to operate at home so that it eventually encompassed activities that unquestionably violated the law, as well as its congressional charter.

From the beginning, CIA justified its involvement in domestic activities in terms of supplementing its covert operations and intelligence gathering abroad. As was discussed in Chapter Two in detail, the CIA created an intricate system of front organizations and companies to provide cover for its clandestine work. It set up its own airlines and business firms, and formed dummy foundations to funnel secret money into domestic student groups, educational publications, and labor unions. Recruiting its agents from almost every sector of the private domain, the CIA turned students, missionaries, and journalists into spies abroad. The agency also used its authority to protect its "sources and methods" to justify spying on Americans in the United States.

COLLECTING FOREIGN INTELLIGENCE AT HOME

Immediately after the passage of the 1947 act, the National Security Council issued a secret internal order for the CIA, authorizing "the exploitation, on a highly selective basis within the United States, of business concerns, other governmental organizations and individuals as sources of foreign intelligence information."[4] A year later, the CIA negotiated a "delimitation agreement" with the Federal Bureau of Investigation, which spelled out the limits of CIA activities within the United States.[5] The most effective check on CIA clandestine collection and operations in the United States was not congressional restrictions, but rather, the FBI's rigorous defense of what it regarded as its own turf. Nevertheless, the CIA got permission to deal with defectors and to gather foreign intelligence against selected persons and enterprises.

During the cold war, émigrés from the Eastern European countries became prime sources of information for the agency within the United States. Later, in its war against Fidel Castro, the CIA heavily infiltrated the Cuban community based in Miami, and created its own network of spies. For over a decade, beginning in 1960, Cuban refugees were paid by the agency to spy on their neighbors, and report their findings to the CIA. While on the CIA payroll, and reportedly at CIA direction, Cuban exiles even launched a campaign to boycott products manufactured by countries trading with Castro's government, and organized picket lines in front of foreign embassies. One Cuban explained the operation as originally a counterintelligence effort, "but it soon became domestic snooping plain and simple."[6] He added, "As far as I know they haven't discovered a single Castro spy here, but they sure made many detailed reports, including gossip, about personal lives of prominent Cubans, if anything usurping the functions of the FBI."[7]

By 1963, the CIA had become so intimately involved with briefing and debriefing its agents, and coordinating their activities within the United States, it created an extremely secret Domestic Operations Division. Explained in a classified document, the division was to "exercise centralized responsibility for the direction, support, and coordination of clandestine operational activities of the Clandestine Services conducted within the United States against foreign targets."[8] Among its activities was the burglarizing of foreign embassies at the request of the National Security Agency.

Not all CIA foreign-intelligence-gathering efforts on the domestic front were so clearly in violation of the law. Perhaps the one legitimate domestic network established within the country was the Domestic Contact Service (DCS). Authorized in a secret directive, the service set up field offices around the country to gather foreign intelligence from willing and open sources. CIA agents would normally interview American businessmen, scholars, or even tourists after their return from travels abroad. Sometimes, however, when the agency learned of a trip to a certain country beforehand, it would approach the traveler in advance to request specific information to be investigated.

When the CIA as a whole began to conduct surveillance of Americans, the Domestic Contact Service was drawn into the process. In early 1969, the service began to receive an increasing volume of reports on "black militant activity," and opened a new case on the subject. Since some of the material was related to foreign contacts, the DCS routed it to Operation CHAOS, the CIA's major program for spying on dissident groups. The ball was set in motion, and a few months later, Operation CHAOS requested DCS to expand its coverage to include all black militants, radical youth groups, radical underground newspapers, and deserter and draft resistance organizations.[9] CHAOS also requested specific information from the DCS, such as background information on twenty-eight co-conspirators indicted in the Chicago riots, and full coverage of the legal proceedings of the trial.[10] For four years, the Contact Service provided both Operation CHAOS and the FBI with hundreds of reports on domestic political activity, further adding to their already bulging files. In light of its newfound capabilities, the Domestic Contact Service was transferred from the Intelligence Directorate to the Operations Directorate in 1973.[11]

COLLECTION FROM AMERICANS ABROAD

While expanding its operations against Americans at home, the CIA sought to keep the FBI from increasing its operations abroad. In order to accomplish this, the agency was prepared to spy on Americans to meet not only its own needs, but those of the FBI as well. At least by 1963, the FBI manual authorized requests to CIA to investigate Americans abroad, and by 1966, the CIA and the bureau negotiated another secret agreement further to coordinate their activities. Among other duties, it confirmed the CIA's right to continue to "handle" its foreign assets within the United States, in return for providing the FBI with information "bearing on 'internal security matters.' "[12] As part of the new contract, the CIA reported on the foreign activities of "domestic dissidents" by passing on information from its own agents to the bureau.

Purportedly only interested in Americans believed to be foreign agents, the CIA reported on a vast range of traveling United States citizens with no apparent foreign intelligence value. Perhaps at the request of the FBI, the CIA put black entertainer Eartha Kitt under surveillance, beginning as far back as 1956. According to documents in her file, Kitt had danced briefly with a group whose leader allegedly sponsored a number of "communist-front activities" in 1948. The file also noted that she had signed an advertisement supporting Dr. Martin Luther King's civil rights drive in the South. Certainly of interest to both the CIA and the FBI for these reasons, she was put under surveillance, and "confidential" sources reported on her activities from Paris to New York.[13]

THE MAIL-OPENING PROGRAM

In its search for every available source of potential intelligence concerning America's foreign enemies, the CIA began a massive mail-opening program that lasted for twenty years. In 1952, first at LaGuardia airport and later at Kennedy International, the agency intercepted mail being sent to and from the Soviet Union. Postal authorities were told that the CIA only wanted to copy the names and addresses on correspondence sent between the Soviet Union and the United States, but agency employees secretly opened and photographed the letters. A postal clerk was given a yearly bonus of $500 just to deliver the bulging mailbags to a secret room at the airport, where he even helped the CIA agents sort the letters.[14] Eventually, a special laboratory was set up to examine the contents for secret codes, or invisible ink messages.

In the hope of gathering intelligence on Soviet intentions, a number of former agents, defectors, suspected agents, and foreigners were placed on a "watch list" of those whose mail would be opened. This limited focus was soon broadened, however, at the request of the FBI and other components of the CIA, to include Americans having no connection with a foreign power.

The mail-opening program was recognized as a clear violation of law by those who ran it. "This thing is illegal as hell,"[15] confirmed CIA's director of security, Howard Osborn, in 1969. In response to possible exposure of its illegal activities, or "flap potential" as it is called, the agency wrote a number of cover stories in the event the word would get out. A memo written in 1962 exemplifies CIA's arrogance toward the law:

. . . since no good purpose can be served by an official admission of the violation, and existing federal statutes preclude the concoction of any legal excuse for the violation . . . it is important that all federal law enforcement and U.S. intelligence agencies vigorously deny any association, direct or indirect, with any such activity as charged.[16]

The memorandum also suggested that it might be necessary "to find a scapegoat to blame for the unauthorized tampering with the mails."

Because of its obvious illegality, the mail-opening program was one of CIA's most tightly held secrets. The FBI found out about it only when bureau officials approached postal authorities to start their own mail cover program, only to be informed that the CIA already had one. (The bureau, however, decided not to inform the agency of *its* ongoing mail-opening program at the time.) Two CIA directors, John McCone and Admiral Raborn were never even informed of the project. The only attorney general briefed on it was John Mitchell. Postmasters general were repeatedly deceived, and no president—with the possible exception of Lyndon Johnson—was let in on the secret that the CIA was systematically reading the mail of American citizens.

The results of the mail intercept gave little insight into

the inner workings of the Soviet bureaucracy, and produced almost no leads on foreign agents working in the United States. In 1976, James Angleton, the CIA chief of Counter-Intelligence, explained why he thought the mail-opening program would produce useful information. The Russians, he reported, thought we abided by the Constitution and therefore would never open first-class mail. But a 1961 inspector general memo reported that "no tangible operation benefits had accrued to the SR Division as a result of this project."[17] Its importance lay in the accumulation of domestic intelligence, however, and in 1956, it was transferred to the Counter-Intelligence Branch. By the early 1960s, the CIA was opening the mail of Americans who had no conceivable connection with Soviet intelligence.

The CIA's mail-opening project took on an increasingly domestic tinge as early as 1958, when the FBI learned of its existence. The bureau, realizing the program's potential in terms of its own operations against the civil rights movement, placed specific individuals and groups on the "watch list." Later, the bureau added domestic peace groups to the CIA watch list, and continued to share in the wealth of domestic information produced by the program until its termination in 1973. By then the FBI had contributed almost 300 names,[18] and in return, received over 50,000 items of intercepted mail.[19] In addition to supplying the mail project with specific names of peace organizations, antiwar leaders, and black activists, the FBI submitted general categories of people to be pursued. These ranged from "all correspondence of a suspicious nature" to "persons sympathetic to the Soviet Union, North Korea, North Vietnam, and Red China."[20] The CIA didn't just passively receive FBI names for the watch list, but in 1969, as part of Operation CHAOS, solicited them. The CIA also had its own watch list, including the American Friends Service Committee, Federation of American Scientists, authors like Edward Albee and John Steinbeck, congressmen and senators, and Americans traveling abroad, including a member of the Rockefeller family.[21]

Over three-quarters of the mail opened was not determined by the "watch list" at all, but by random selection. "It might be according to individual taste, if you will, your own reading of current events,"[22] explained one CIA interceptor. By this time, mail was being intercepted not only from the Soviet Union, but between Asian and Latin American countries as well. In 1971, the mail of U.S. Senator Frank Church, who was later to head the Senate Select Committee on Intelligence, was opened. Instead of issuing a general rule that the mail of American elected officials should not be opened, an internal memo provided that all such correspondence be placed in a separate file called "Special Category Items."[23] As usual, the CIA dealt with obviously potential "flaps" by making them more secret. Eventually, mail to or from Senators Church and Edward Kennedy, Richard Nixon, a congressman, and a governor were included in this special file.[24]

Results of the mail opening were disseminated to the White House as well as to other intelligence agencies. According to a March 1971 CIA memorandum, the project boasted of supplying the president with "coverage of overseas contacts and activities of persons within the United States who are critical concern from the viewpoint of internal security, including bombing and terrorism."[25] It is difficult to imagine a clearer violation of the CIA's charter, which specifically prohibited it from engaging in "internal security functions." The mail-opening program came to an end only in 1973 when Chief Postal Inspector William Cotter told the agency to secure presidential approval or end the operation. By then, the CIA had reviewed over 28 million pieces of mail, photographed over 2 million, and opened over 215,000 letters.[26]

PROTECTING THE CIA AT HOME

Another justification for CIA operations directed at Americans was the need to protect its operations and secrets from outside exposure or penetration. CIA's Office of Security routinely conducts security checks on its employees and those it is considering for recruitment, and investigates individuals who are perceived as posing a threat to the agency's facilities or personnel. But within this broadly defined area of operations, which may appear legitimate on the surface, the CIA has almost unlimited authority to investigate almost anyone either as a potential source, a potential employee, or a potential spy.

One CIA employee, suspected of involvement in the Communist party in the 1930s, was investigated for eight years in the late 1940s and early 1950s, because of the suspicion he might leak classified documents. In the process, he was spied on, his phone was tapped, his room bugged and burglarized.[27] Another employee, under investigation

"I'M HERE TO PROTECT YOU, SWEETIE"

COPYRIGHT 1976 BY HERBLOCK IN *THE WASHINGTON POST*

for attending meetings of an organization thought to be "left wing," was put under surveillance for a year. Seven microphones were placed throughout his apartment, and his mail was read.[28] But the Office of Security did not limit itself to investigations of its own people. Although former CIA Director Richard Helms testified that the CIA had no authority to conduct such investigations against people not working for the agency, the CIA physically and electronically spied on three newsmen in the 1950s and early 1960s.[29] Almost a decade later, it investigated Jack Anderson, Les Whitten, and *Washington Post* reporter Michael Gelter.[30] In 1971, the agency put six individuals under heavy surveillance as a result of a report they planned to assassinate the director of CIA and kidnap the vice president. Nothing was uncovered.[31]

The Rockefeller Commission report confirmed that the Office of Security conducted "special coverage" investigations against its own personnel as well as people who had no relationship to the agency. "Special coverage" is simply a euphemism for physical and electronic surveillance, burglary, mail opening, and reviewing tax returns.[32]

In 1967, as protest activity spread, the CIA set up two programs ostensibly aimed at protecting its employees and facilities from demonstrators. Project RESISTANCE was established to provide protection to CIA recruiters visiting college campuses. Soon the project was responsible for protecting all government recruiters, and instead of receiving information only from obvious sources such as college newspapers, the CIA began soliciting intelligence from college administrators and local police. Soon so much information on antiwar activists and their organizations was being collected that a special Targets Analysts Branch was formed to deal with the mounting influx. RESISTANCE agents produced "situation reports," including the minutes of police department meetings, all of which were sent to the Domestic Operations Division. By the end, this one operation had produced over 600 files, and had indexed thousands of names of American students and campus "radicals."[33]

Project MERRIMAC, also originating within the Office of Security, represented an extreme deviation into domestic lawlessness. Designed to provide advance warning of demonstrations that might threaten CIA's personnel or facilities in Washington, D.C., MERRIMAC agents infiltrated over ten activist organizations, ranging from the Washington Ethical Society to the Black Panthers, from the War Resisters League to the Congress for Racial Equality.[34] CIA infiltrators followed prominent leaders home, took pictures of participants in demonstrations, and jotted down license-plate numbers. Attitudes of individuals within the organizations, their relationships with other groups, and even their sources of income, were all reported. As one of the directors of the project begrudgingly admitted, "I think it started out legitimately concerned with the physical security of installations . . . it just kind of grew in areas that it perhaps shouldn't have."[35]

Women Strike for Peace (WSP), one of the organizations CIA chose to infiltrate in 1967, had been the focus of CIA attention for many years. Founded by Dagmar Wilson in 1961, WSP rallied a growing number of women around the issues of nuclear disarmament and an end to the arms race with the Soviet Union, and thus came under suspicion as promoting "Moscow's aims." Within a few months of its first meeting, Ms. Wilson and her fledgling organization became the subject of CIA memoranda. In January 1962, a short history of the WSP, biographical sketches of its leaders, and summaries of its countless demonstrations were compiled for the CIA's Office of Security. The memorandum also noted that the New York Police Department, as well as the FBI, was investigating Women Strike for Peace. That same year, Ms. Wilson was called before the House Un-American Activities Committee.

Three years later, the CIA became even more intrigued with WSP. A number of its women traveled to Djakarta, Indonesia, where they participated in a meeting with Vietnamese women representing the liberation forces of North and South Vietnam. On their return, the women held a meeting at American University to discuss the trip. A CIA agent, sitting in the audience, took almost verbatim notes on the different reports and commentaries given by the travelers, and wrote down each person's political analysis of the Vietnam War.

Surveillance of WSP increased, and finally, in February 1967, the CIA sent an infiltrator into their D.C. headquarters. WSP had become one of the ten select targets of Project MERRIMAC. Previously considered a Communist front for the Soviets, now the organization was under investigation for being potentially "violent" and a threat to CIA installations and personnel. The rationale changed, and so did the tactics.

The infiltrator not only attended the meetings, but photographed women demonstrators, and confiscated confidential steering committee meeting records and lists of women attending conferences within the United States and overseas. Countless leaflets, announcements, and newsletters were amassed in the CIA's file on WSP, and on almost every sheet of paper, names, addresses and phone numbers were diligently circled or underlined. CIA's infiltration of the group was terminated in December 1968, but surveillance continued until 1971—at least that was the date of the last sheet of paper dropped into the WSP file. During that decade of spying and collecting material, the CIA unearthed no paid foreign connection, no evidence of any illegal activities, and certainly no history of violence.[36]

In seeking ostensibly to protect its facilities and recruiters from demonstrations, the CIA worked closely with local police forces. Advanced "police training" was one skill that the CIA acquired as part of its foreign operations abroad, and shared with federal and local police. Police departments from Washington to Los Angeles sent representatives to the agency training courses, to learn such skills as detonating explosives, lockpicking, and surreptitious entry.[37] The CIA also provided the Washington Metropolitan Police Department with radio-equipped automobiles to monitor antiwar demonstrations, as well as cameras, gasmasks, tear-gas grenades, and protective flack jackets.[38] In return, state and local police shared their arrest records with the agency—which might explain why the CIA had in its possession the names of 300,000 people arrested for homosexual acts.[39] Local police also provided badges and other forms of local identification for CIA operatives to use as cover. In one instance, police officers of the Fairfax (Virginia) City Police Department accompanied CIA's Office of Security personnel while they burglarized a business establishment in Fairfax, without a warrant, to photograph some papers.[40] The CIA shared not only its special techniques, but also its total disregard for the law.

Thus by 1967, when President Johnson turned to the CIA for proof that the American antiwar movement was directed from abroad, the agency had a long tradition of operations against United States citizens. Although CIA Director Helms told the Senate Foreign Relations Committee, under oath, that he could not recall if there was presidential pressure on the CIA to conduct surveillance of American citizens, he and others later recounted that Johnson complained that not enough evidence of "foreign money and foreign influence" was being found. "It's got to be there" the president would reportedly yell at the CIA director.[41] Helms agreed to try to find it.

OPERATION CHAOS

In August 1967, the CIA created the Special Operations Groups within the Counter-Intelligence Division. Richard Ober, chosen to head the new project known as Operation CHAOS, was uniquely suited to the job. In early 1967, *Ramparts* magazine had exposed CIA secret funding of the National Student Association, causing acute embarrassment to the agency. In response, Ober was assigned to investigate members of the staff of the magazine and their friends, in an effort to discover any connection with hostile foreign intelligence agencies. (CIA also urged the IRS to open an investigation on the magazine's tax-exempt status.)[42] By the time Ober began work at Operation CHAOS headquarters, he had already proved his credentials by indexing several hundred names of American citizens, and creating almost fifty files.[43]

From the beginning, the program was predicated on the belief that the foreign connection existed, and it was just a matter of finding it. CHAOS agents were to watch antiwar activists in their travels abroad for this purpose. The first action taken by the new Special Operations Group was to cable all CIA field offices abroad, outlining the need to keep tabs on "radical students and U.S. negro expatriots," in order to find the extent to which "Soviet, Chicoms [Chinese Communists] and Cubans are exploiting our domestic problems in terms of espionage and subversion."[44]

The agency thus monitored the overseas movements of countless antiwar activists as they traveled around the world, as well as ex-patriots. The CIA burglarized their hotel rooms and their homes, eavesdropped on their conversations,[45] and bugged their phones. The internal directives issued to provide "guidance" regarding who should be the targets for intelligence collection abroad reflected the confusion and frustration of the government effort as a whole. Field offices were instructed to look for connections between United States groups and "communist, communist front, or other anti-American foreign elements abroad."[46] A November 1967 memo called on agents overseas to report on foreign relationships, which "might range from casual contacts based on mutual interest to clearly controlled channels for party directives."[47] Two years later, a directive from Tom Huston, a White House assistant, explained that "support should be liberally construed to include all activities by foreign communists designed to *encourage*"[48] (emphasis added) domestic groups in any way. The White House and the agency were grasping at straws. Enormous amounts of useless information were gathered because it was not clear when and how the intelligence might be used. Ober directed his agents to collect "any material, regardless of how innocuous the information may appear."[49]

To deal with this massive influx of material, from other agencies as well from as the CIA, the agency set up a highly mechanized system. Whenever the name of an individual or organization showed up as a result of these efforts, it was analyzed, indexed, and filed in the CHAOS computer system known as HYDRA. By programming a specific name, an agent could instantly retrieve all cables, documents, or memoranda that even mentioned the target.

Due to pressure from President Nixon, the CHAOS staff was increased to over fifty,[50] and by 1959, CHAOS began to develop its own agents abroad who would focus entirely on the task at hand. In order to track political activists abroad, these agents went through a process of establishing their "credentials" within the radical movement in this country. During their training period, they would be extensively debriefed by their advisers, and CIA gained purely domestic information. In fact, so much reporting went on that one agent was likened to a "vacuum cleaner."[51] Another actually became an officer within his organization, while yet another became an adviser in a United States congressional campaign, and furnished CHAOS reports on behind-the-scenes activity of the campaign. In one instance, a CHAOS agent, on leave from his spying activities abroad, rejoined his unwitting friends in the radical community and reported extensively on their private lives and personal relationships.

Spying on radicals in this country was also an incidental result of agents being trained by the CIA to penetrate foreign intelligence agencies, as part of a program called "Project 2." After a period of basic training, these agents would enroll at a university and feign involvement in some activist group. Although the trainees were told by their case officers not to gather domestic information, one agent, for example, submitted a sixty-page report over a three-week period, including information on a planned demonstration, groups meetings, and activities relating to the women's movement.[52] While abroad, these agents, although not specifically assigned to CHAOS, were valuable assets to the overall collection effort.

Throughout the CHAOS operation, the FBI was not only the major recipient of the massive flow of memos, reports, and clippings from the CIA, but also the most generous donor. By June 1970, the FBI was sending in reports to the CIA at the rate of 1,000 a month.[53] In addition, the two agencies extensively briefed and debriefed each other's agents, with the bureau submitting specific questions to be answered by CHAOS infiltrators. By 1972, some twenty FBI informants were actually working abroad under CIA direction and control.[54]

As the purported expert on foreign ties to the American peace movement, the CIA prepared a number of major studies on the subject. One report, known as "Restless Youth," was a thick volume analyzing the international student movement, including a long section on the Students for a Democratic Society. Another study's very title, "Definition and Assessment of Existing Internal Security Threat—Foreign," exemplifies the extent to which the CIA was operating outside its congressional charter. The Domestic Contact Service also produced a series of reports, including one on the background of certain individuals who had accused the CIA of involvement in the assassination of the black leader Malcolm X. Ironically, all these studies concluded that the domestic dissent was a product of social and political conditions in this country, and not the result of an international conspiracy. As late as 1971, when Operation CHAOS had grown to grand proportions, a report was issued confirming "there is no evidence . . . that foreign governments, organizations or intelligence services control U.S. new left movements."[55] The program continued to expand its scope, not because its activities provided any leads, but in order to prove the opposite. Richard Ober explained the phenomenon:

. . . to respond with any degree of knowledge as to whether there is significant foreign involvement in a group . . . one has to know whether each and every one of these persons has any connection . . . having checked many, many names, and coming up with no significant directions, one can say with some degree of confidence that there is no significant involvement.[56]

In its continuing search for that illusive connection, the CIA worked in concert with every intelligence agency of the federal government. The Justice Department gave the CIA thousands of names to be put on file, while army intelligence officers briefed CIA agents on domestic radicals. Other federal agencies submitted names to be placed on the "watch list" for CIA's mail-opening program, while the CIA submitted its targets for the National Security Agency's program of intercepting cable traffic. Even friendly intelligence agencies of other countries were asked to assist. At times, the agencies even put pressure on each other to step up their activities against the peace movement. In a letter from CIA Director Helms to FBI Director Hoover in 1970, Helms encouraged the FBI to reinstate its domestic mail-opening program, which had been discontinued in 1966. Helms, stressing the need for expanded coverage of the Soviet bloc, the New Left, and foreign agents, urged continued cooperation in gathering intelligence on "bombings, hijackings, assassination, and the demeaning of law enforcement officers."[57]

The CIA was well aware that it had violated its charter by becoming so intimately involved in the internal security apparatus of America. A cover letter from Helms to Henry Kissinger, accompanying the Operation CHAOS report "Restless Youth," warned that "this is an area not within the charter of this Agency, and I need not emphasize how extremely sensitive this makes the paper."[58] As domestic operations expanded, there was increasing discomfort among those being asked to carry them out. Some area division chiefs wanted nothing to do with Operation CHAOS. In fact, the reaction was so negative at times that CIA Director Helms was forced to send out a memo in 1969 calling for full support of the program, and assuring the stations that this was within the statutory authority of the agency. An inspector general's report on CHAOS written in 1972 reflects the growing uneasiness:

We also encountered general concern over what appeared to constitute a monitoring of the political views and activities of Americans not known to be or suspected of being involved in espionage. . . . stations were asked to report on the whereabouts and activities of prominent persons . . . whose comings and goings were not only in the public domain, but for whom allegations of subversion seemed sufficiently nebulous to raise renewed doubts as to the nature and legitimacy of the CHAOS program.[59]

Agency officials, however, refused to acknowledge illegality either to the public or to their own personnel. In a speech to the American Society of Newspaper Editors in April 1971, CIA Director Helms totally denied rumors that the CIA was involved in domestic spying. Referring to the 1947 ban on the exercise of police and law enforcement powers, Helms declared, "We do not have any such powers and functions; we have never sought any; we do not exercise any; . . . in short, we do not target on American citizens."[60] Helms was later to refer to this public assertion in a talk given to his own employees, when he added, ". . . you can rely on these denials."[61] Helms's statements dramatically demonstrate how breaking the law forces endless lying, deceit, and coverup.

Before it came to an end, Project CHAOS compiled what the Rockefeller Commission described as a veritable mountain of material. It had created personality files on over 13,000 people, including some 7,000 American citizens, and subject files on 1,000 domestic organizations.[62] The CIA spied on the whole spectrum of peace activist and civil rights groups. CHAOS agents followed the activities of the organizations' leaders abroad, spied on their meetings, broke into their hotel rooms, and sent thousands of cables back to headquarters detailing their activities. Three hundred thousand names of American citizens were cross-indexed within agency files,[63] and thousands of Americans were placed on "watch lists" to have their mail opened and their telegrams read.

Operation CHAOS finally came to an end in 1974, as part of the winding down of the massive surveillance programs of the late 1960s and early 1970s. In general, specific programs were ended either because public dissent was in fact subsiding, or out of fear that the programs would be exposed. There was never a reevaluation of the CIA's domestic role, and in fact, the agency continues its operations at home and against Americans abroad. On February 17, 1976, President Gerald Ford issued an executive order that claims to place restraints on the intelligence agencies' illegal activities, but in fact authorizes and ratifies their continuation.

In that order, the CIA is authorized to conduct clandestine operations to gather foreign intelligence information from foreigners in the United States, as well as Americans believed to be acting on behalf of a "foreign power." The order reaffirms CIA's broad mandate to conduct investigations of Americans who are potential recruits, or whose activities pose a threat to agency security. The most alarming charter given to CIA is the power to infiltrate, "for the purpose of reporting on or influencing activities," organizations primarily composed of foreign nationals.[64] The obvious targets for such disruption are immigrant groups and foreign student organizations. Here for the first time, CIA is officially allowed to conduct covert operations in America. The agency still spies on Americans abroad, still accepts requests from the FBI to put traveling citizens under surveillance, and claims the right to wiretap and burglarize American homes and apartments overseas.

The 1947 ban on domestic involvement remains inoperative.

MILITARY
INTELLIGENCE

6

In July 1969, the Department of Defense opened a new war room in the basement of the Pentagon. Staffed by some 180 people and packed with all the latest equipment —data processing machines, closed circuit television, teletype networks, elaborate situation maps—the new operation was a marvel of military technology. The most striking aspect, however, was not the imposing technology, but the purposes that were being served. This was not a regular command center but a very special operation—a "domestic war room," the headquarters of the Directorate for Civil Disturbance Planning and Operations. It was the coordinating center for the Pentagon's domestic war operations.

The office, now known as the Division of Military Services, played a central role in the military's widespread intelligence operations against the American people, a sweeping campaign of civilian surveillance which ultimately affected more than 100,000 citizens. In the fall of 1968, there were more Army Counter-Intelligence Analysis Branch personnel assigned to monitor domestic citizen protests than were assigned to any other counter-intelligence operation in the world, including Southeast Asia and the Vietnam War.[1] In the later part of the 1960s and early 1970s, 1,500 army plainclothes intelligence agents with the services of more than 350 separate offices and record centers watched and infiltrated thousands of legitimate civilian political organizations.[2] Data banks with as many as 100,000 entries each were maintained at intelligence headquarters at Fort Holabird, Maryland, and at Fourth Army headquarters at Fort Sam Houston, Texas.

As with the FBI and other intelligence agencies, citizens and organizations singled out by military surveillance were those who exercised their right to speak out: the oppressed minorities, advocates of reform, and those on the political "left." The growth of the army intelligence bureaucracy paralleled the growth of dissident protest movements through the 1960s. Military intelligence undercover agents focused on the civil rights movement of the early 1960s, and then moved to the New Left anti-Vietnam War coalitions of later years. No political gathering, no matter how small, was considered insignificant. No distinction was made between groups preaching violent action and those advocating peaceful dissent. Even the most established and nonviolent groups such as the NAACP and the American Friends Service Committee became targets of military surveillance.

With the exception of the FBI, the military intelligence services collected more information on American politics in the sixties than any other federal agency. The army conducted a full-scale Pentagon operation within the United States, and the figures and attitudes reflect this approach. Where a civilian agency might have opened a hundred files, the military created a thousand; the army established CONUS and CONARC intelligence commands, and then reorganized and reinitiated them as USAINTC, the Directorate of Civil Disturbance Planning, and the Division of Military Support. They ran operations with such code names as GARDEN PLOT, ROSE BUSH, PUNCH BLOCK, STEEP HILL, LANTERN SPIKE, QUIET TOWN, GRAM METRIC, and CABLE SPLICER; and they developed intelligence "compendiums," a "mug book," daily, weekly and monthly intelligence summaries, special reports, "city packets," contingency and alternative contingency plans, computerized filing systems, and crossover index files to information. All were based on agent spot reports, radio intercepts, incident and personality files, newspaper clippings and data from numerous civilian sources. Each level of the military hierarchy tried to placate its superiors by collecting as much or more information than the task required, whether it was of any importance or not. The attitude pervading these army operations was best stated by Robert E. Jordan III, general counsel to the army: "the people on the other side were essentially the enemy."[3] The army conducted a de facto war against all citizen protest, legitimate and illegitimate, violent and peaceful, white and black.

EARLY MILITARY SURVEILLANCE

Historically, the United States military preceded even the Federal Bureau of Investigation and the Justice Department in initiating surveillance of law-abiding American civilians. With the outbreak of World War I, military agents and volunteers of the American Protective League investigated civilian labor disputes, families who associated with soldiers, women friends, and antiwar protesters. Pacifists opposed to the American war policy, individuals considered "left wing," and members of the Russian-Jewish, German, Japanese, and Italian ethnic populations were investigated as potential spies, saboteurs and subversives. By the end of the war, over $2 million had been spent on military intelligence assignments aimed at American citizens.[4]

After the war, in March 1923, the adjutant general issued explicit orders to terminate covert military collection of information on citizen politics.[5] Despite this order, the Military Intelligence Division, renamed G-2, continued to collect intelligence in order to forecast disorders involving labor and racial minorities. Inquiries were made into groups labeled "subversive" in questionnaires distributed to "loyal Americans," many of whom were veterans of the American Protective League. Information was also collected through local police offices, state officials, and the newly formed FBI. This G-2 intelligence collection was conducted secretly until terminated in the late 1920s.

The increase of protest accompanying the Great Depression brought the armed forces once again into the fray to defend the status quo. In May 1932, World War I veterans marched into Washington demanding a war bonus. Fearing the spectacle of unemployed veteran soldiers protesting in the nation's capital, the War Department directed local intelligence officers to investigate the bonus marchers and report on their preparations, which were described as "Communist-inspired." The chief of army intelligence, in a coded radio message, requested information:

With reference to any movement of veteran bonus marchers to Washington originating or passing through your corps area, it is desired that a brief radio report in secret code be made to the War Department indicating presence, if any, of communistic elements and names of leaders of known communistic leanings.[6]

Some of the responses were as confused as the request. One report from an intelligence officer in the Eighth Corps stationed in Houston, Texas, noted that the bonus marchers from California were affiliated with Jewish Communists financed by Metro-Goldwyn-Mayer and supported by the Soviet Union.[7] Possibly influenced by these overblown reports, Herbert Hoover's administration overreacted and called in federal troops to deal with the marchers.

Military officials continued to investigate civilian political groups without authorization or approval throughout the 1930s. In areas of the Midwest, where isolationist views and labor organizing were widespread, the Sixth Army Corps developed a plan for gathering information on several thousand groups, including pacifists and civil libertarians. The military independently selected the targets for their monitoring operations, without civilian oversight. Although the supposed objective was to parry threats to the military and the government, most of the groups selected were legitimate and nonviolent in character. Two targets were the American Federation of Labor (AFL), and the Congress of Industrial Organizations (CIO).[8]

As the armed forces geared up for war abroad in the late 1930s and early 1940s, military surveillance of citizens at home began to expand as well. Intelligence activities included spying on dissident or antiwar groups, loyalty investigations of suspect citizens, and attempts to counter spying by Axis agents and sympathizers, including the rounding-up of Japanese-American citizens for internment in West Coast concentration camps.[9] During this time, a delimination agreement between the FBI and the military sought to impose civilian control and other limitations on army domestic intelligence.[10] Nevertheless, the military continued its own covert surveillance of civilian politics, although on a slightly reduced scale.

The disregard for civilian-imposed limitations on military surveillance continued into the period after World War II. Throughout the late 1940s and the 1950s, the military collected information on diverse personalities and used it, in part, for political reasons—including gathering information on political campaign activity at the specific request of elected officials.[11] G-2 Tokyo, at General Douglas MacArthur's command, illegally released intelligence information to right-wing American publicists, which was subsequently used to undermine the policies of the Democratic party in office.[12] Fort Holabird became a central records facility within the United States for collecting and collating domestic intelligence from both civilian and military sources.

THE 1960s INTELLIGENCE CAMPAIGN

With the rise of citizen protest and the involvement of federal troops to control demonstrations during the 1960s—especially in the area of civil rights—the scope and focus of the military's domestic intelligence operations expanded greatly. Often justified as necessary to enforce federal desegregation laws, these intelligence activities were in fact directed primarily against one side of the conflict: the black civil rights protesters whom the military had ostensibly been called in to protect. Neither white segregationists nor local law enforcement plans or tactics interested the military as much as did black civil rights groups and their leaders.

When federal troops were deployed to Oxford, Mississippi, in 1962 and 1963, intelligence agents began collecting information on individuals and groups involved in the demonstrations.[13] This information supplemented data files from southern police departments and the FBI, which the army had begun assembling in 1961 when it seemed probable federal troops would be employed to quell mass protests in Montgomery, Alabama.[14] Army agents operated with a clearly distorted view of their mission: the information they gathered was of little or no relevance to the needs of military commanders in the field. Instead of accumulating city maps, data on local police, likely targets for rioters, and exit and approach routes for deploying troops, army agents gathered political and personal information on local citizens and groups.

As more troops were committed to control racial disturbances and enforce desegregation orders, military officials took measures to anticipate further problems. In 1963, the Joint Chiefs of Staff designated the chief of staff of the army as its executive agent for civil disturbance matters, and the Continental Army Command was given primary responsibility for selecting and deploying troops in emergency situations. As part of these preparations, the investigative and counter-intelligence units of the Continental

Armies (CONUS) were expected to provide briefings to the command, and were to serve the information needs of the task force commanders.

In 1963, responding to an obvious lack of information in Birmingham, Alabama, Creighton Abrams (later army chief of staff) sent a memorandum to Chief of Staff General Earle G. Wheeler detailing a greatly expanded role for military intelligence collection. Claiming that there was an "inhibiting effect" in not allowing army intelligence preparation prior to the deployment of federal troops in racial situations, Abrams recommended that "We in the Army should launch a major intelligence project without delay, to identify personalities, both black and white, develop analyses of the various civil rights situation in which they *may* become involved, and establish a civil rights intelligence center" (emphasis added).[15] The proposal was not approved, but it foreshadowed unbridled expansion of military intelligence activities five years later. At that time, the army was assigned to gather intelligence *prior to* and in anticipation of the involvement of federal troops, a directive which provided virtually unlimited scope to military intelligence activities.

Despite regulations restricting the covert use of military intelligence agents to select instances approved by the commander of the Continental Army Command, after coordination with the FBI,[16] army agents regularly collected and maintained information on domestic organizations and unaffiliated civilians. The 113th Intelligence Corps (presently the 113 MI Group) began to compile records on Minneapolis residents as early as 1962, despite the lack of potential civil disturbance.[17] Similarly, in 1963, army agents infiltrated the March on Washington for Freedom and Jobs.[18] In Oklahoma City, agents of the 112th MI Group photographed and reported on early anti-Vietnam War protests near that city's federal courthouse in 1965.[19] In 1966, agents of the 11th MI Group rented a truck and followed James Meredith on his "walk against fear" through Mississippi.[20] In all of these instances, the army acted on its own, without coordination with the FBI and often without higher-level military or civilian DOD (Department of Defense) approval.

The Army set out to learn everything it could about participants in civil disturbances, including not only demonstrators but also the president. One technique to learn what the president was up to was to listen in on his phone conversations. Since presidents often use military communications channels this was easy to do. Whenever a president made use of military communications, his conversations would be recorded. Thus when President Kennedy talked with Deputy Attorney General Nicholas Katzenbach while he was in the South, military commanders in the Pentagon listened in to learn what was going on.

The major turning point in military surveillance did not come, however, until 1967. Following the Detroit riots, Cyrus Vance visited the troubled city as President Johnson's personal representative to study and report on how the executive could deal with future urban disorders. Vance's report focused on the need for greater "physical intelligence" and planning for potential federal deployments. Indeed, the failure of military intelligence to provide needed strategic information was clear: despite prior intelligence activity in the city, General John Throckmorton arrived in Detroit in the summer of 1967 in the midst of riots with only an oil company map to use in directing his troops.[21] Vance recommended:

In order to overcome the initial unfamiliarity of the federal troops with the area of operations, it would be desirable if the several continental armies were tasked with reconnoitering the major cities of the U.S. in which it appears possible that riots may occur. Folders could then be prepared for those cities listing bivouac areas and possible headquarters locations, and provide police data, and other information needed to make intelligence assessment of optimum employment of federal troops when committed.[22]

In response, the army issued comprehensive plans for the collection of intelligence. These plans turned the army loose, but the surveillance and intelligence activities that occurred were not responsive to the problems Vance had found. Military surveillance evolved instead into a massive nationwide program to monitor civilian politics. Vance's proposals unleashed the military intelligence apparatus; they did little to control it. The campaign to monitor political expression became more and more overt. For example, the North American desk of the Counter-Intelligence Analysis Branch comprised three divisions: "left-wing," "right-wing," and "racial." These sections were sometimes referred to as the "counterespionage/countersubversion section."[23] The targets of the army's intelligence mission became those who exercised their constitutional right to dissent and challenge the public policies.

By the late 1960s, the direct political nature of military intelligence operations was quite explicit. A telling indication of this was the February 1968 annex to the army's Civil Disturbance Plan, where "dissident elements" and "subversives" were clearly identified as primary targets of surveillance. The activities of the peace movement were judged "detrimental" to the United States, and American antiwar activists were viewed as possible conspirators manipulated by foreign agents.[24] This search for foreign influence within the antiwar and civil rights movements was equally evident in an October 1967 request to the National Security Agency by General William Yarborough seeking "Indications that foreign governments or organizations acting as agents of foreign governments are controlling or attempting to control or influence the activities of U.S. 'peace' groups and 'Black power' organizations."[25] Yarborough also requested available information on identities of United States individuals and organizations in contact with foreign agents, and advice given by agents of foreign governments to groups and foreign agencies seeking to control or influence United States organizations. Yarborough and the army were certain that dissent could not occur without foreign orchestration.

No evidence linking these movements to foreign powers was found, but this did not prevent army officials from continuing to amass files on civilian groups. Military officials viewed civil rights protests and antiwar movements as programs to overthrow the government rather than legitimate expressions of popular opposition. Like the Vance request for tactical information, the search for foreign agents served as an excuse for massive political surveillance.

Military intelligence activity accelerated during 1968, particularly after the April 4 assassination of Dr. Martin Luther King, Jr. As black rebellion swept through cities in the aftermath of the murder of King, army troops were called into the District of Columbia, Baltimore, Chicago, and numerous other locations. With military involvement in urban areas expanding rapidly, a permanent task force was created to direct military operations. The Directorate for Civil Disturbance Planning and Operation established a massive round-the-clock operation to monitor civil disturbance developments. In July 1969, this new directorate moved into the "domestic war room" in the Pentagon, where it reviewed contingency plans for using over 250,000 troops against domestic protests and riots. The Intelligence Branch of the new directorate regularly published a computerized survey of recent and expected political protests.[26] These surveys contained data on the location of the event, the sponsors and leaders involved, and a short narrative account of what transpired. All types of activities, no matter how peaceful or legal, were covered.

During this peak period of domestic unrest, the White House, the Department of Justice, the FBI, and the Defense Department also applied pressure to designate and watch *particular* individuals and groups involved in "domestic dissent."[27] The growing demands for information on specific targets encouraged lower-ranking intelligence officers to collect information by practically any means available. There developed, as former Assistant Secretary of Defense Robert Froehlke defined it before a Senate committee, "a practical inconsistency between the level of demand for information imposed and the methods of collection authorized."[28] This information, he asserted, "couldn't conceivably be collected unless you got it through covert means."[29] While much information in the extensive military intelligence files was obtained from the FBI and local police, massive amounts were collected through illegal means by army intelligence agents across the country.

As army intelligence operations multiplied, military agencies accumulated vast amounts of information, much of it, according to one analysis, "sketchy, subjective, and of little practical value."[30] The Senate Judiciary Committee reported, "Comments about the financial affairs, sex lives, and psychiatric histories of persons unaffiliated with the armed forces appear throughout the various records systems."[31] The army applied the term "domestic unrest" to the activities of "all groups that sought to change government policy."[32] Intelligence units were told to obtain information on the presence of "militant outside agitators," known leaders, purposes and objectives of dissident groups, the source and extent of funds, and how funds were distributed.[33] Selected groups included Americans for Democratic Action, the Urban League, the American Civil Liberties Union, the Klu Klux Klan, and the Communist party.[34] Army agents infiltrated Resurrection City during the 1968 Poor People's March on Washington.[35] Agents also posed as students to monitor classes in Black Studies at New York University.[36] The army infiltrated the October and November 1969 moratorium marches around the country. Military personnel even posed as newspaper reporters and television newsmen during the 1968 Democratic National Convention in Chicago to tape interviews with demonstration leaders.[37]

The files compiled by army units were massive. At Fort Holabird, the computerized Spot Report Index, started in 1968, received as many as 1,200 reports a month during 1969 and, according to the Senate Subcommittee on Constitutional Rights, may have been "one of the most extraordinary chronicles of domestic political activity ever compiled."[38] The Incident File possessed coding and cross-references to a "subversive file," which, as of December 31, 1971, held 211,243 dossiers on organizations and 80,731 biographical files.[39] At Fort Monroe, Virginia, a separate computerized file was established in May 1968, which in one year of operation indexed 4,398 incident reports of army intelligence agents. One four-week computerized printout from the Fort Monroe data bank (for the period December 15, 1969 to January 11, 1970) listed incidents of which eighty-five were antiwar and fifty were racial. In addition to these two major sites, more than 300 military intelligence offices throughout the country maintained their own files, some of which were forwarded to national filing systems while others were retained at the local level.[40]

Military surveillance operations were an integral part of the broader intelligence network. Political information was disseminated throughout the intelligence community. Information flowed from agency to agency along a two-way street. Data collected by the army were disseminated to a wide variety of agencies. Local police agencies and the Federal Bureau of Investigation provided the bulk of information used in many key army reports.[41] For example, a two-volume *Compendium* published by the Counter-Intelligence Analysis Branch of the army identified more than 100 organizations and approximately 350 activist leaders, and was drawn "primarily" from the FBI.[42] The *Compendium* was in turn distributed to the Department of Justice, the FBI, the CIA, the State Department, the Secret Service, and eight United States defense attachés overseas.[43]

More important than the dissemination of intelligence was the role the military played in coordinating activities with the FBI and other state and federal agencies, and in teaching civilian representatives the army's philosophy and techniques on civil-disorder control. In violation of federal statutes, a representative of army intelligence sat on the interagency Intelligence Evaluation Committee, and the army's general counsel served on the Law Enforcement Policy Committee.[44] The army also created a

master plan, known as GARDEN PLOT, which provided
an outline for standardized procedures to be used for handling civil disturbances by the National Guard, regular
armed forces, *and civilian authorities*.[45] Based on preparations for future disturbances, GARDEN PLOT trained
troops for possible deployment, and taught military and
civilian leaders how to control these activities in a "war-
room" setting. The DOD's domestic war room and
twenty-four-hour-per-day monitoring of civilian disturbances were central aspects of GARDEN PLOT.

Military management training was brought to the local
level and involved the FBI and other civilian officials. As
far back as 1962, J. Edgar Hoover gave the army complete access to FBI files without charges for clerical or
computer time, in exchange for the army's agreement to
conduct biannual seminars in the philosophy and use of
riot-control techniques for more than 200 FBI agents and
officials.[46] War games were held to practice coordination.
In the U.S. Sixth Army area—including California,
Washington, Oregon, Nevada, and Arizona—Cable
Splicer III, a GARDEN PLOT operation, simulated demonstrations by radical "leftist" groups on imaginary campuses and high schools along the Pacific Coast. The names
selected for the mock groups in these war games indicate
the usual targets of military intelligence: "the Scholars
Democratic League, on the campuses; the International
Brotherhood of Labor Reform, among the blue collar
workers; and the International Fraternity of Progress of
Non-Caucasian, among the minority groups."[47]

Just twenty-one days after federal troops killed four
Kent State students during an anti-Vietnam War demon-
stration, 1,700 military, civilian, and corporate officials
met to discuss an after-action report on the war game.
Major corporations represented included the Bank of
America, Lockheed, Boeing, Sylvania, Pacific Gas and
Electric, Pacific Telephone and Telegraph, Standard Oil
of California, Jet Propulsion Laboratories, SCM, Dic-
taphone, and the John Hancock Mutual Life Insurance
Co.[48]

EXPOSURE AND CURRENT ACTIVITIES

As with CIA Operation CHAOS and other illegal secret intelligence programs, only public exposure and the threat of congressional action led to the termination of military surveillance activities. Christopher Pyle, a former army intelligence officer, revealed the scope of the military's domestic intelligence activities in the January 1970 issue of the *Washington Monthly*, charging that "the Army had assembled the essential apparatus of a police state."[49] Several earlier evaluations within the army had expressed "reservations" about the programs or judged them unnecessary and out of control, but it took the Pyle article and widespread public pressure to curb the growth of army spying on American citizens.

Once the wide scope of military domestic activities became clear, it was evident that they had violated both specific statues and the long-standing Anglo-Saxon tradition separating civil law enforcement and the military. The Posse Comitatus Act, originally enacted in 1878, makes it illegal for anyone to use "any part of the Army" to enforce civil laws without a presidential proclamation, and then only as a "last resort," where state and local officials are unable to maintain order.[50] Whether the president and high-level civilian leadership were aware of the widespread military activity throughout the 1960s remains unclear. After examining the matter in as much detail as documents then (and now) available make possible, the Senate Subcommittee on Constitutional Rights was able to conclude only that "the highest levels of the Departments of Defense and Justice were or should have been informed."[51]

Professor Morris Janowitz told the Senate Subcommittee on Constitutional Rights: "The type of surveillance conducted by the Military is not only at odds with civil-military traditions, but also irrelevant to the underlying causes of said unrest . . . that reflect underlying social and economic conditions. . . ."[52] Robert Lynch, acting adjutant general of the army, ordered on June 9, 1970, that the collection plan of May 1968, under which the expansion of army activities had occurred, be altered: "Under no circumstances will the Army acquire, report, process, or store civil disturbance information on civilian individuals or organizations whose activities cannot, in a reasonably direct manner, be related to a distinct threat of civil disturbance exceeding the law enforcement capabilities of local and state authorities."[53] The army thus confessed its guilt, and publicly began to dismantle the massive apparatus that had been constructed.

Yet despite this public cleansing, the measures that the army took, in fact, did not establish adequate safeguards to prevent future recurrences. The initial internal directive issued on March 1, 1971, to limit the military's collection practices possessed, as Senator Sam Ervin of North Carolina stated, "qualifications, exceptions, and ambiguities which permit surveillance even within the confines of an otherwise restrictive policy."[54] The DOD directive permitted intelligence collection on civilians who constitute a "threat" to DOD property or persons, although no definition of what such a threat might involve was provided. The directive allowed surveillance of demonstrators at or near military installations (which were broadly defined to include induction centers and recruitment offices), including civilian political activists involved in soldier affairs, such as GI counseling organizations.[55] And finally, the directive may be altered by the secretary of defense whenever he wishes.[56]

Senator Ervin proved prophetic; in practice as well as theory, the 1971 directive was no obstacle to military intelligence operations deemed "necessary" by the army. Since the date of the directive, the army has continued its intelligence activities, though on a much restricted scale. In particular, the Senate Intelligence Committee cites nine formal requests for approval of covert surveillance activities made by the military services to the newly formed Defense Investigative Review Council (DIRC). Between 1971 and 1975, eight of these requests were routinely approved and were aimed at civilian groups.[57]

Moreover, although many data banks were destroyed during 1970 and 1971, a considerable amount of information is still maintained on the political activities of United States citizens. Investigations by the DIRC, conducted from September 1971 to July 1973, found intelligence files on American political activity at bases around the country.[58] The investigations also disclosed continued covert agent operations and close liaison with civilian law enforcement agencies. Among the operations documented during the Ervin Committee's 1974 investigation were surveillance of protesters at the Democratic and Republican national conventions in Miami,[59] as well as a special liaison operation at Wounded Knee, South Dakota, in the spring of 1973.[60]

It thus seems clear that military intelligence operations against American citizens did not end with the 1971 revelations. The practices have continued—though reduced—and the bureaucratic structure remains in place. The current DOD directive governing "Acquisition of Information Concerning Persons and Organizations Not Affiliated with the Department of Defense," issued on December 8, 1975, still contains the same loopholes as previous directives.[61] For example, with the specific approval of the secretary of defense, information may be "acquired which is essential to operational requirements flowing from the mission . . . to assist civil authorities in dealing with civil disturbances."[62] As the Senate Judiciary Committee reported in 1976.

. . . similar imprecise language in earlier directives was in large part responsible for the abuses of the past. The "threat" exception is a loophole that has the potential to nullify the general restrictions embodied in the directive.[63]

In the past, the military has regularly been called in to control civil disturbances and monitor the political activities of American citizens. Despite recent disclosures and guidelines, the potential for rebuilding the domestic war room has been preserved. The teletypes and data processing machines, silent now, may be readied to whir into action at the first sign of domestic protest.

THE
NATIONAL SECURITY
AGENCY

7

Until the recent intelligence investigations, Americans were virtually unaware of the existence of the National Security Agency. As the NSA's programs have come to light, we see yet another intelligence agency that expanded its activities in the mid-1960s as part of the campaign against political activity and that systematically flouted the Constitution and the law.

What is extraordinary about the NSA is its capacity for collecting information, and the tool that this gives the government for intruding upon the lives of its citizens. Referring to the NSA, Senator Frank Church viewed the problem in this way:

The U.S. government has perfected a technological capability that enables us to monitor messages that go through the air . . . between ships at sea, between military units in the field. We have a very extensive capability of intercepting messages wherever they may be in the air waves. That is necessary and important as we look abroad at potential enemies. At the same time, that same capability at any time could be turned around on the American people. And no American would have any privacy left, such is the capability to monitor everything—telephone conversations, telegrams, it doesn't matter. There would be no place to hide.[1]

The NSA has a greater potential for gathering information than any police state has ever had. The FBI can merely dream of putting an agent behind every mailbox; the NSA literally has the capacity to intercept all communications. As far as the record shows, it has so far limited itself to eavesdropping on communications that have at least one terminal in a foreign country—although this "restriction" allows it to intercept *all* international messages of Americans.[2]

The NSA has not developed its own covert action programs to disrupt and neutralize selected political groups. It did carry out several burglaries during the 1950s, installed a few bugs to maintain its own security, and inspired the CIA[3] and FBI[4] to commit burglaries in foreign embassies on its behalf. More important, the NSA has complemented the programs of the other intelligence agencies by servicing their requests for information. Using its own "watch list" and those provided by the CIA, the FBI, the Secret Service, and the BNDD (Bureau of Narcotics and Dangerous Drugs), the NSA has used its special technology to run a program of information collection and dissemination. The watch lists determined what messages were targeted and to which agencies—in addition to its own Office of Security—the information was passed.

NSA'S MISSION

From what is known of it, the mission for which the NSA was originally created is code-making and code-breaking. World War II proved the critical value of having such a capacity. In 1952, President Truman issued a top-secret directive, "Communications Intelligence Activities," which established the NSA.[6]

National Security Council Intelligence Directives (NSCIDs) and Director of Central Intelligence Directives (DCIDs) set up the operating structure of the NSA.

The code-making arm of the NSA is the COMSEC (Communications Security) program; its mission is to protect United States government messages by developing codes and the equipment used to transmit them. The code-breaki.g part of the NSA's mission is called SIGINT (Signals Intelligence), which is itself divided into two branches. ELINT (Electronic Intelligence) monitors and interprets electronic signals such as radars, missiles, etc. COMINT (Communications Intelligence) monitors electronic signals which are intended as messages. It is under the COMINT program that the NSA's abuses of power have occurred.

NSA SURVEILLANCE PROGRAMS

The public record now provides information about three of the NSA's COMINT programs that affected the rights of Americans. The oldest program is SHAMROCK, which involved the interception of all private cables leaving the United States. Overlapping this is the watch-list program, ultimately labeled MINARET, which involved checking all electronic messages that had at least one terminal outside the United States for names on watch lists provided by other agencies. And finally, there were the files of NSA's Office of Security, which contained the information that its surveillances had collected on Americans.

The SHAMROCK program had its beginnings in August 1945, when the Army Signals Security Agency asked the three cable companies (RCA Global, ITT, and Western Union) that government access to international cables be continued after the war. The companies' lawyers advised that it was illegal in time of peace under the Communications Act of 1934 (47 U.S.C. 605), which reads:

No person receiving, assisting in receiving, transmitting, or assisting in transmitting, any interstate or foreign communication by wire or radio shall divulge or publish the existence, contents, substance, purport, effect, or meaning thereof. . . .

After some hesitation, the cable companies nevertheless agreed, provided that the attorney general would assure them that he would protect them from criminal liability and lawsuits. The government apparently never informed the cable companies that its activity was not limited to foreign targets but also analyzed and disseminated the telegrams of Americans. The companies never asked what was done with the fruits of their cable surveillance.

The companies did, however, continue to seek assurances that they would not be prosecuted, and the record shows that in 1947 Secretary of Defense James Forrestal told them that the program was vital and that both the president and the attorney general approved; they would be protected during the Truman administration. The following year, however, the secretary of defense was unable to get Congress to relax the 1934 act in order to allow the government access to the radio and wire communications of foreign powers, which would have made the program legal as it was originally conceived. The promise of protection was reiterated in 1949 by Secretary of Defense Louis Johnson, and the companies apparently never sought assurances again.[7]

In 1952, when the NSA took over from its precursor, the Army Security Agency, the cable interception program continued uninterrupted, even though NSCID-6, a National Security Council directive,[8] was apparently intended to limit the NSA's processing to the *coded* messages of spies and foreign governments, and to prohibit intercepting the ordinary telegrams of everyone else. The NSA has since claimed, however, that this limitation was really meant to apply only to uncoded *mail* (which was FBI or CIA turf, in any case) and not to any electronically transmitted messages, including telegrams. The NSA claims that SHAMROCK did not exceed its executive charter, and that it is an embarrassment only because it induced cable company employees to violate the Federal Communications Act.

SHAMROCK continued unabated until the scandals involving the intelligence community began to break. Dr. Louis Tordella, the NASA's deputy director from 1958 to 1974 and the official in charge of the program, stated that to the best of his knowledge, no president since Truman has known about SHAMROCK.[9]

In its early and technologically primitive years, the information gleaned from SHAMROCK was processed against a small NSA watch list, which had been geared primarily to foreign rather than domestic intelligence. But with the technological developments of the 1960s, the scope of NSA surveillance mushroomed. With the evolution of magnetic tapes for transmitting telegrams and computer scanning for selecting particular kinds of messages, the NSA was ready to plug the watch lists of its client intelligence agencies into SHAMROCK. By the late 1960s, when the surveillance of domestic groups had got into full swing, the NSA was intercepting some 150,000 messages per month in the SHAMROCK program alone, dwarfing the CIA's mail-opening program.[10]

Since at least 1962, in addition to SHAMROCK, the NSA has run—without the benefit of judicial warrants—a program for selecting, intercepting, reviewing, and disseminating the international radio and phone communications of specific American organizations and individuals on watch lists. The lists were initially established in order to monitor travel to Communist countries and to protect the president and other high officials. The fact that, in the latter case, the NSA would end up picking up not only calls about the officials, but the calls of the officials themselves[11] is a measure of the electronic surveillance problem. As with the other intelligence agencies, there was apparently no serious effort to minimize what their vacuum cleaner sucked in. And the NSA's technology produces a tremendous "multiplier effect"—if an organization is selected, so are all its members. If an individual is on the watch list, then all conversations to, from, or about him or her are also intercepted. Anyone mentioning one of the magic words, in any context, has his or her message selected and examined for personal, political, and economic information.

The watch-list program for pinpointing American dissent began in earnest in the fall of 1969, as the NSA's contribution to the intelligence community's search for the ever elusive foreign involvement behind the civil rights and antiwar movements. The names included on the watch lists were a mix of people and organizations involved in protest politics. They ranged from radical political groups, to celebrities, to ordinary citizens taking an active interest in the political controversies of the time. As we have come to expect from the intelligence agencies, the names on the list included the peaceful, nonviolent, and totally legal. And there was, of course, a great deal of overlap in the watch lists submitted by the various agencies.[12]

From 1965 to its end as an organized program in 1973, the watch list encompassed some 1,650 names, which had been supplied by the CIA, the FBI, the Secret Service, the BNDD, and the DOD, as well as some which the NSA itself contributed. Figures available for the 1967-73 period indicate that the list then held some 1,200 American names; 950 had been submitted by the FBI, 180 by the Secret Service, 50 to 75 by NSA, 30 by the CIA, and 20 by the DIA. And although the links to foreign support were never found, the NSA nevertheless found reason to disseminate to these client agencies some 2,000 reports—mostly containing information which was personal and politically innocuous—during the 1969-73 period.[13]

In July, 1969, the NSA decided to formalize the watch-list program by issuing itself a charter creating Project MINARET. This formalization had two functions. First, it imposed secrecy procedures on the program that were even stricter than those the NSA ordinarily used, and second, it imposed procedures to disguise the NSA's participation in the program. In short, the NSA's MINARET employed virtually all the bureaucratic techniques available for preventing leaks about illegal activities and for eliminating a "paper trail." And although the NSA officially contends that this watch-list operation was a legitimate part of its foreign intelligence mission, the fact remains that the MINARET intelligence product was subjected to special security controls that were not applied to the NSA's legitimate intelligence information.[14]

Before the advent of MINARET, only the intercepted communications between two Americans were subject to special secrecy procedures; after MINARET, all communications to, from, or about United States citizens were classified top secret, "For Background Use Only." In addition, the information was not serialized in order to be absorbed into the regular NSA record-keeping systems, and none of the reports disseminated carried any markings that would identify the NSA as the original source. These extraordinary procedures indicate that, internally, the NSA could not have actually considered MINARET an extension of its normal intelligence mission.

The Senate Select Committee's report offers a fairly detailed discussion of one NSA operation performed at the request of the Bureau of Narcotics and Dangerous Drugs. The BNDD arrangement with the NSA provides a case study of both an enterprising use of the NSA technology for creating a loophole in the protections of the Fourth Amendment, and of the confusion involved in trying to determine precisely what clandestine agencies have done, and why.[15]

In 1970, the BNDD concluded that under the Supreme Court wiretap decision in a case known as *Katz*[16] it could not legally wiretap public telephone booths in order to monitor suspected drug traffic between New York and South America. While the BNDD noted that *Katz* had specifically placed Fourth Amendment restrictions on wiretaps of public phones, it ignored the Court's holding that the Fourth Amendment "protects people, not places." The bureau evidently concluded that it had found a loophole by getting the NSA to tap into the international communications links rather than into a specific phone, and it asked the NSA to monitor the international links carrying these phone conversations.[17]

In late 1972, as part of an NSA effort to increase secrecy around its drug traffic surveillance, the CIA was asked to contribute the intercept operators for the BNDD program. The CIA agreed and monitored the operation from a station located on the East Coast. But by February

1973, the CIA general counsel, Lawrence Houston, concluded that the BNDD watch list was actually a law enforcement procedure, and therefore went beyond the CIA's statutory charter.[18]

The BNDD operation gives some indication of the difficulty in trying to determine just what kind of reasoning lies behind the decisions of clandestine government agencies. NSA officials have stated that the CIA had apparently not been troubled by the "law enforcement" function, and that the reason given for pulling out of the program was the fact that the CIA's intercept station was located within the United States.

At any rate, when the CIA bowed out, the NSA reconsidered its role in the BNDD surveillances and decided that "supporting an agency with a law enforcement responsibility" was outside the normal scope of its mission.[19]

The NSA terminated the drug surveillance program in June 1973, and, in August or September, the NSA destroyed the program's paper trail—all the records relating to the product, internal memoranda, and administrative documents. Actually, however, this changed very little; falling back on its established label of "foreign intelligence," the NSA continued (by no small coincidence) to monitor some of the *same* links until July 9, 1975, well after the heat of the first congressional investigation of its activities had begun. This is another clear example of how, once a program is found to be of questionable legality, the internal housecleaning consists largely of shuffling the same activity into another file with a more legitimate-sounding name.

TERMINATION OF PROGRAMS
AIMED AT AMERICANS

The watch lists were a self-authorized program—one of the NSA's prerogatives, stemming from having no legislative charter or congressional review of its activities. And while many of the COMINT interceptions took place with one terminal in the United States—with an estimated 10 percent taking place between *two* Americans, i.e., having no foreign link other than mere geography—it was not until the Watergate furor and the threat of possible exposure that the NSA gave any serious consideration to the legality of its programs. Once the legality of these programs was reviewed, the conclusion was that they could not pass muster. For at least a decade, all the participating agencies, at least two attorneys general (John Mitchell and Richard Kleindienst), and two secretaries of defense (Melvin Laird and James Schlesinger) were aware of the watch-list activities, yet none of these agencies or officials had taken steps to review the legality (with the single exception of the BNDD program). Nor had the United States Intelligence Board (USIB)—which ordinarily sets the intelligence requirements for NSA—ever given formal approval to the operations.[20]

In 1972, the Supreme Court handed down the decision in *U.S.* v. *U.S. District Court* (better known as the *Keith* case),[21] which held that wiretapping Americans who did not have a significant connection with a foreign power could only be done with a warrant. But it was apparently not *Keith* itself which ultimately stopped the watch-list activity, because the program in fact peaked early in 1973; at that time there were some 600 American and 6,000 foreign names on the watch list.[22] Rather, it was evidently a combination of the *Keith* decision, a new director for the NSA, and the first round of Watergate revelations that led to a review of MINARET and to its termination. Watergate was beginning to erode the sense of official invulnerability when General Lew Allen, Jr. became the NSA director in August 1973. Allen became concerned about MINARET and suspended its activities; in September, he asked the client agencies to reaffirm both their requirements and the "appropriateness" of the program.[23]

As a result, the watch lists got their first serious review from within the attorney general's office, and the record shows some of the problems involved in trying to determine what exactly goes on in secret programs. When Assistant Attorney General Henry Petersen asked FBI Director Clarence Kelley about the bureau's link to the NSA and MINARET, Kelley's response consisted of what might be called, at best, an active misrepresentation of the facts.

Kelley wrote that the FBI had requested information "concerning organizations and individuals who are known to be involved in illegal and violent activities aimed at the destruction and overthrow of the United States Government."[24] Considering that the watch lists contained the names of totally peaceful and nonviolent organizations and people, the statement is unjustified.

Kelley went on, however, to deny that the NSA/FBI operations were, in effect, based on a watch list designed to snare particular individuals. The bureau did not consider the NSA watch list an electronic surveillance within the meaning of the *Keith* decision:

We do not believe that the NSA actually participates in any electronic surveillance per se of the defendants for any other agency of the government, since under the procedures used by that agency they are unaware of the identity of any group or individual which might be included in the recovery of national security intelligence information.[25]

The Kelley memorandum is remarkable on two counts. First, it clearly misrepresents the facts to Petersen, an official who was in a position ultimately to determine the situation for himself. Second, it tries to create a legal loophole by asserting that it is permissible to violate the Fourth Amendment rights of Americans as long as the victims are found at random—scarcely a probable cause standard for a search and seizure. The bureau response, in other words, was a bold-faced untruth, followed by an equally bold-faced assertion that it could determine by itself what the Bill of Rights permitted.

In October, Assistant Attorney General Henry Petersen and Acting Attorney General Elliot Richardson advised NSA that MINARET was of "questionable legality."[26]

And the NSA, like the FBI, responded by resorting to paradox rather than logic: since the communications had been collected "as an incidental and unintended act in the conduct of the interception of foreign communications," the fact that the watch list was used to pick out particular people somehow didn't count. Under this reasoning, government power to intrude on all aspects of its citizens' lives continues to be authorized as long as it is asserted that the surveillance is conducted accidentally-on-purpose. The NSA terminated Project MINARET (but did not stop intercepting the communications of Americans) in the fall of 1973 because of the legal problems.[27]

The SHAMROCK interception of cables—with the help of the cable companies—was longer-lived. It did not end until May 15, 1975, when Secretary of Defense James Schlesinger ordered its termination. The reasons given were that it was no longer a valuable source of foreign intelligence (had it ever been?) and that there was an increased risk of exposure.[28] Indeed, the exposure was soon to come.

SHAMROCK had surfaced in the documents given to the Rockefeller Commission in May 1975. In June and July, the Senate Select Committee on Intelligence, drawing on a shy reference in the published commission report, asked for more information about that agency's program. They were told that the subject was so sensitive that only Senators Frank Church and John Tower (the committee's chairman and vice chairman) could be briefed. No meetings, however, were immediately arranged.

In July and August, a series of news stories appeared which leaked all the major points of the SHAMROCK program into the press. As a result, the full committee was briefed in September. A report was prepared, and the NSA objected not to the substance of the report but to the fact that its material was classified. The report was ultimately read into the record, however.

Although SHAMROCK and MINARET are both officially ended, the same programs are still going on in only slightly modified form. Since telegrams are now sent by airwaves, the NSA no longer needs the cooperation of the cable companies to get access to their magnetic tapes. And given the predictability of the watch lists and the NSA's experience with them, the agency's analysts know what kinds of information its client agencies have an interest in.

The NSA is still free to disseminate in any fashion that it chooses the information it collects. The current operating principle for dissemination procedures is that "relevant information acquired by [NSA] in the routine pursuit of the collection of foreign intelligence information may continue to be furnished to appropriate government agencies."[29]

The current situation, then, is that the NSA *still* scans all messages, its computers *still* select messages for the analysts' attention according to whatever criteria are chosen, and the analysts *still* decide for themselves if the information meets a "legitimate" requirement. According to the Senate Select Committee's final report,[30] the names of Americans are usually—but not always—deleted before the information is disseminated. The fact that there is no longer an *official* watch list (as far as is known) is merely a formality. More important, there are still no legislative controls on the NSA; a new executive order is all it would take to reactivate an explicit and itemized watch-list program, and plug it back into the computers.

THE NASA'S OFFICE OF SECURITY

The NSA's Office of Security also was part of the surveillance game. With the ostensible purpose of keeping the NSA sources and methods secure, the Office of Security compiled files on some 75,000 American citizens during the years 1952 to 1974. The mere mention of a name in any NSA intercept was the criterion for opening a file, which meant that the Office of Security contained the distillate of the vast electronic surveillance system.

In addition to its contribution to the NSA's watch lists,

the CIA had access to these Office of Security files for thirteen years. As the Senate Select Committee report concluded, we may assume that this information went into Operation CHAOS, but without having to go through the inconvenience of leaving a watch list's paper trail. This access perhaps explains why the CIA watch list totaled only thirty names.

The files on Americans in the Office of Security were destroyed in 1974. The official reason given was that a reorganization of intelligence community files led to the conclusion that the value of these files on Americans did not justify the costs in time, money, and storage space. It is just as likely that the timing of this housecleaning operation was determined when the NSA calculated the costs in embarrassment if the files were subpoenaed for a congressional investigation.

THE ABSENCE OF LEGISLATED CONTROLS

For all its awesome technological power, the NSA has never really been out of control; it has simply never been subject to any explicit limitations on its operations. While the CIA had been created by statutes that had intended, however unsuccessfully, to put limits on its activities, the NSA has never been subject to a similar embarrassment. It had been created by executive fiat, and was regarded as too secret to require or to need statutes to back it up. Its enormous capabilities have been developed and operated without any substantial congressional authorization; its budget appropriation has been carefully camouflaged within the huge Defense Department budget, and because of its supersecret status it has, until now, enjoyed an isolation from controversy that the CIA might envy. At the same time, it has been able to fall back on a statute—P.L. 86-39—that exempts the NSA from disclosure laws, including the Freedom of Information Act.[31]

Although the NSA has been running, at a cost of $4

billion per year, the largest and most sophisticated surveillance operation in history, it has been shrouded in secrecy. The House investigations marked the first time that a director of the NSA has been required to appear publicly before a committee of Congress. Only two months earlier, the president's Rockefeller Commission report had found it politic to leave the National Security Agency discreetly unnamed. Its discussion of the CIA CHAOS/NSA connection only alluded to the NSA as "another agency of the government," which carried on "international communications activity."[32]

The NSA has also made every effort to stay out of court: the government has dropped prosecutions rather than open the NSA's surveillance program to judicial scrutiny. As a result, no court has yet been in a position to hand down a decision expressly affirming that the Constitution and the laws apply to the NSA.[33]

Until this happens, the NSA's official position is that the Fourth Amendment,[34] which requires the government to get a court order in order to listen in on someone's phone calls, does not apply to that agency. In his first public testimony, NSA Director General Lew Allen, Jr., asserted that the NSA's authority to eavesdrop on the international communications of Americans comes from the president's power as commander in chief, and apparently, as long as it claims that the interception is for "foreign intelligence" purposes, NSA can listen in on any and all international communications.[35] The only restriction to which the NSA has adhered is apparently contained in the top-secret directive which established the agency in 1952. The NSA limits itself to tapping into only international communications for "foreign intelligence" purposes—but this means that one terminal can be inside the United States, and that one or both subjects can be United States citizens.

In addition, the executive branch still backs up the NSA's claim. Executive order 11905, issued by President Ford as an intelligence "reform" package, authorizes

Parade of Disclosures

NSA to continue its massive warrantless surveillance. The executive order imposes no restrictions on the NSA's operations; it makes no mention of safeguards, guidelines, or limitations, such as explicitly prohibiting watch lists or minimizing eavesdropping to cover only legitimate targets.[36]

Congressional investigations have now revealed enough about NSA to make it clear that something must be done. The agency's potential power is staggering, and must be brought into line with the basic civil liberties of Americans. In its final report, the Senate Select Committee on Intelligence viewed the problem this way:

The [NSA] watch list activities and the sophisticated technological capabilities that they highlight present some of the most crucial privacy issues facing this nation. Space age technology has outpaced the law. The secrecy that has surrounded much of NSA's activities and the lack of Congressional oversight have prevented, in the past, bringing statutes in line with NSA's capabilities.[37]

THE
INTERNAL REVENUE
SERVICE

8

PRESIDENT NIXON: Do you need any IRS (unintelligible) stuff?

JOHN DEAN: Uh—Not at the— . . . Uh, there is no need at this hour for anything from IRS, and we have a couple of sources over there that I can go to. I don't have to fool around with Johnnie Walters [IRS commissioner] or anybody, we can get right in and get what we need.

Excerpts from a transcript of a tape recording of a conversation among President Richard Nixon, John Dean, and H. R. Haldeman, March 13, 1972.[1]

No agency of the United States federal government retains more information on American citizens than the Internal Revenue Service, and no other agency is given more arbitrary powers to compile this information than the IRS. Tax files are a virtually endless repository of financial records for all working Americans, corporations, private associations, and political groups. To determine that a fair and equitable tax is paid, citizens are required to entrust a yearly accounting of financial worth to the Internal Revenue Service detailing the earning and expenses of their daily lives, charitable and political organizations they support, medical information and other tangible records covering travel, residence, and education. Businesses and organizations file similar types of information with the IRS, including complete lists of employees and earnings; and tax-exempt organizations are held accountable for the programs and "political" positions which they hold.

By law, the IRS maintains far-reaching investigative powers to enforce tax statutes. Unlike the FBI and other law enforcement agencies, the Internal Revenue Service may *legally* investigate *any* American without a judicial warrant and without reason to believe a crime has been committed. Moreover, it can demand the production of records entirely on its own authority. When marshaled for purposes above and beyond the collection of revenue taxes, the Internal Revenue Service is an ominous weapon of the government. It can endlessly harass all who cross its path, and at the same time gather information otherwise unobtainable through legal means.

Like the CIA and the FBI, the IRS was used as an instrument of the government's war against dissent in the 1960s. The IRS was a valuable component of the overall mechanism: it coordinated with the FBI and the Justice Department to harass dissidents, provided information to the FBI and the CIA (which in some cases was used to disrupt domestic dissent), and was asked to serve as the president's "hired gun" against various administration opponents. The IRS divulged its trusted records to the White House and to the intelligence agencies without following legal procedures to protect the privacy rights of innocent taxpayers. Yet, unlike the FBI and the CIA, the IRS acted at the behest of others, like a programmed robot. There was no J. Edgar Hoover or Richard Helms to direct the IRS on its campaign against dissent. Instead, it operated on general orders from congressional subcommittees and the White House and executed special "hits" against priority targets.

Although the IRS has often been characterized by political corruption, it does not run deep to the lower levels of the bureaucracy. With its curious mix of central control and local autonomy, only a few specially placed officials are needed to marshal the resources of the IRS against

THE INTERNAL REVENUE SERVICE

political targets. Richard Nixon, for example, could not persuade IRS Commissioner Johnnie Walters to accept John Caulfield, head of security for the president's office, as the head of a political task force within IRS,[2] but Assistant IRS Commissioner Vernon Acree gained access to the tax returns for some of those on Nixon's "enemies list" and sent them to the White House, ultimately accomplishing the same objectives.[3] The Special Services Staff (SSS), which acted from 1969 to 1973 as the IRS watchdog on political activism, had only nine staff members in the basement of the Washington national office, yet because they could trigger an audit on a political opponent by the local IRS offices, their actual power extended well beyond their size. Moreover, the actions that the SSS initiated were legitimate functions of the IRS. An IRS local agent could act with complete innocence when conducting an audit ordered by the Special Services Staff or by the White House—and indeed he might uncover tax improprieties—yet the very fact that the audit was conducted or the tax laws strictly enforced for political reasons constituted an administrative COINTELPRO as arbitrary and capricious as the covert trickery of the FBI.

GROWTH OF THE STRIKE-FORCE MENTALITY

The selective enforcement of tax laws has occurred consistently over the past two decades, but it did not begin as a means to attack political dissent. Money is central to any criminal conspiracy, and executive officials attempting to control organized crime quickly discovered that the pen of a certified public accountant was as effective a weapon as a sheriff's handgun. While it was often impossible to follow the trail between the numbers runner and the racketeering boss, the high-flying spender could be held to account by the Internal Revenue Service for wealth beyond that listed on his tax returns. It is thus not surprising that under the direction of various attorneys general and congressional committees, the IRS has played an important role in governmentwide strike forces pursuing racketeers and organized crime figures. In January 1952, almost 2,300 IRS investigators conducted investigations of 12,879 racketeers.[4] At the peak of the organized crime drive during the Kennedy years, the use of IRS agents was central to the plan of attack on mob figures. Al Capone, who successfully avoided prosecution and conviction on numerous possible charges, could not avoid imprisonment on charges of tax fraud—and he was only one among many.

"Selective enforcement" brought with it a set of investigative techniques different from those used in tax fraud cases and balanced enforcement programs. The approach is the opposite of that used to develop greater tax compliance: rather than select cases on the probability that they will return a greater tax yield, the strategy was to bring the full investigative powers of the IRS to bear on an individual singled out for other purposes. IRS officials and agents began to develop contacts with the Justice Department and the Federal Bureau of Investigation; undercover agents, informants, and wiretap specialists began to frequent the IRS offices. Later, in 1969, the Special Services Staff would build on these preestablished channels of communication with the FBI and Justice.

Although the use of the taxing power to succor friends and harass opponents no doubt comprises an interesting side-history of federal tax-collection agencies dating back to the Revolution, IRS participation in the governmentwide campaign against political targets can be traced back only to the mid-1950s. Most likely under pressure from the FBI, the IRS focused its selective enforcement capabilities throughout the 1950s on dissident organizations and individuals under attack by J. Edgar Hoover's FBI, Senator Joseph McCarthy, and the House Internal Security Committee. For example, from 1955 through 1958, the Internal Revenue Service went to enormous lengths to audit the tax returns of Reuben G. Lenske, an alleged member of the Communist party and an affiliate of the National Lawyers Guild.[5] The IRS devoted two investigators full time to the audit, despite the relatively slight prospects that the investigation would return a proportionally equivalent tax assessment. The special agents interviewed between 500 and 1,500 witnesses, covering Lenske's political and private affairs, as well as his financial matters. They made assessments on Lenske's property which were many times their real worth, and attempted to impose liability above and beyond his ability to pay. Indeed, the IRS prosecution of the case was so egregious that a federal court, in reversing the IRS ruling that Lenske owed money to the government, charged the IRS with conducting "a crusade . . . to rid our society of unorthodox thinkers and actors by using federal income tax laws and federal courts to put them in the penitentiary."[6]

In a similar case, the IRS conducted, from 1954 to 1964, a ten-year crusade against the Communist party of the United States through a jeopardy tax assessment for the year 1951. The IRS first made the assessment in 1956, following an extensive audit two years earlier, and then let the matter lie dormant for five years while the party appealed. In the early 1960s, for reasons unknown, the government resumed prosecution of the case and, in a novel decision, a lower-level tax court denied the party's request for review because the attorney who signed the appeal petition for the party was not formally authorized to act on its behalf. In 1964, a United States Court of Appeals, after examining the record, finally ordered the appeal, finding that the Communist party could not be "thrown out of court, for the reasons and under the circumstances obtaining, without verging too closely towards the wholly unacceptable proposition that the rules of the game vary with the players."[7]

THE ADVENT OF POLITICAL STRIKE FORCES

The first organized political "strike force" was formed within the IRS in 1961, and was directed against right-wing political groups. The action was stimulated by two November 1961 speeches and one press conference of

President John F. Kennedy attacking "right-wing extremism" and charging that tax-exempt funds of "right-wing" organizations were being diverted for non-tax-exempt purposes.[8] The next day Attorney General Robert Kennedy and John Seigenthaler, his special assistant, called on the IRS to investigate the tax status of these groups.[9] The initial target list was drawn up by Mitchell Rogovin, attorney adviser to the IRS commissioner (and in fact the CIA's secret liaison in the IRS), on the basis of political criteria. Eighteen "right-wing groups were selected for investigation, and one left-wing group (the Fair Play for Cuba Committee) was [later] added to the list."[10] Although the groups were clearly selected for political reasons and at White House direction, the IRS was careful to justify its action with the pretense of impartial administration of tax laws. In a March 9, 1963, memorandum, reminiscent of "potential flap" memos circulating throughout the CIA and the FBI, the director of the Audit Division wrote:

[We] have used the term "political action organizations" rather than "right-wing organizations" throughout this discussion. This has been done to avoid *giving the impression* that the Service is giving special attention to returns filed by taxpayers or organizations with a particular political ideology.[11] [emphasis added]

Clearly the concern was with the reputation of the IRS, not the legitimacy of its conduct.

Five months after the initial effort against "right-wing" groups, a list of nineteen "left-of-center" organizations was sent to the IRS Audit Division compiled, perhaps, by the FBI.[12] The accompanying memorandum again warned of potential "flaps": although the primary effort was directed against the right-wing groups, the façade of balanced enforcement would be maintained by also auditing a number of left-wing organizations.

White House interest in the tax standing of "extremist" organizations increased as IRS status reports detailed findings on right- and left-wing organizations. On July 23, 1963, President Kennedy called IRS Commissioner Mortimer Chaplin to urge development of a second phase of the program and "proceed with an aggressive program on both sides of center."[13] In response, the IRS drew up a plan to conduct "10,000 examinations of exempt organizations of all types, including extremist groups." Unlike the first, smaller program, which had triggered audits of these groups at the local and district levels, the plan called for a national office to gather information sent from the audit centers and then rule on exempt standing. IRS officials met twice with White House representatives and once with the attorney general to shape the coming strategy.[14] Lists of left-wing and right-wing organizations were to be compiled, with initial action directed at the tax-exempt status and activities of right-wing groups. The initial list of targets was in essence a Kennedy "enemies list." Mitchell Rogovin, now a permanent IRS liaison with the White House and Justice Department, tailored the list to White House specifications. He met on August 20, 1963, with Myer Feldman at the White House, and on Feldman's suggestion dropped two organizations and added three others to the "hit" list. Of the initially proposed twenty-four groups, the IRS revoked the tax-exempt standing for three right-wing and one left-wing group.[15]

Despite this early success, the massive Ideological Organizations Project to examine 10,000 exempt organizations never materialized. Reduced White House interest in the project following John Kennedy's assassination was in large part responsible. Beyond this, the project conflicted with the bureaucratic objectives of the IRS. IRS commissioners justified their budgets to Congress on the promise of returning more taxes for each dollar of allocation, and therefore viewed the project as a waste of resources, particularly in the absence of continual presidential pressure. In a July 11, 1963, memorandum to the president's deputy counsel, the commissioner of IRS stated this problem:

In the past, examinations of exempt organizations were held to a minimum since these difficult and time-consuming audits were rarely productive of revenue. Also, for every man year spent on such examinations there is a potential loss of approximately $175,000 otherwise produced from income tax audits.[16]

With the White House no longer so interested in right- or left-wing political groups, the smaller program was phased out of development and formally terminated in 1967 under Lyndon Johnson.[17]

THE ILLEGAL DISCLOSURE OF IRS FILES

Although this concentrated effort to annoy dissident organizations was never fully implemented, the IRS responded in different ways throughout the 1960s to those prosecuting the war against dissent. The IRS frequently fed the FBI material for its COINTELPRO operations. The transmittal procedure for tax information was a semi-formal link between the FBI and the IRS Intelligence Division, circumventing the regular IRS Disclosure Branch and the procedures established to protect the integrity of IRS information. In practice, the IRS gave the FBI access to any of the files, from tax returns to the results of tax investigations.

In one instance, FBI officials requested tax returns on the Ku Klux Klan. They asked the IRS for tax information, which they planned to use for "discrediting or embarrassing the United Klans of America."[18] The bureau wanted tax information for two reasons: first, to determine whether a known Klansman had reported income from the Klan, and to confront him with this; and second, to make public illegally the information linking the Klansman with the organization. Although it is unclear from FBI documents whether either of these two plans was implemented, the IRS readily released the returns of the particular Klansman for the years 1959 through 1963, and for the Klan organization for 1961 and 1963, without requiring so much as a formal statement of what these returns were to be used for.[19]

In 1968 the informal tie between the FBI and the Intelligence Division of IRS was discovered and termed "illegal" by the head of the IRS Disclosure Branch, and control of all information sent to the FBI was shifted to official channels. Yet this new procedure had no effect on the quantity and quality of the tax information made available for nontax purposes; the sole difference was a greater flow of paper between the two agencies. New procedures, which required that the FBI give the purpose and intended uses of tax information requested, proved but a semantic hurdle for the bureaucrats. At the request of the FBI, it became common practice for the Internal Security Division of the Justice Department to process a form letter asking for returns, reciting the conclusion that the regulatory criteria for use had been met. Invocation of the phrase "necessary in connection with an official matter before this office involving the internal security . . ." was judged sufficient by the Disclosure Branch to make returns available. Between 1966 and 1974, the Federal Bureau of Investigation received full cooperation on approximately 200 requests to the IRS, usually involving the names of more than one taxpayer per request. Of the 200 requests, about 20 percent involved foreign intelligence matters, 15 percent were used in criminal investigations, and the great majority—approximately 65 percent—were for domestic intelligence or COINTELPRO purposes.[20]

The Senate Select Committee on Intelligence reports that most of the tax information received from the IRS for the FBI's COINTELPRO operations was used to disrupt and "neutralize" the political thrust of the New Left and Key Activists within that movement. Within two weeks of initiating the Key Activist project in May 1968, the FBI had turned to the IRS for help. They requested tax returns for sixteen Key Activists, and before the end of the year another nineteen were added to the list. Although the letters requesting the information asserted that the information was needed for "reasons involving internal security . . . in connection with the official duties" of the office, the intended use was harassment. A February 3, 1969, internal memorandum of the FBI noted that the IRS had initiated tax-related investigations on the political dissidents, and "anticipated the IRS inquiry will cause these individuals considerable consternation, possibly jail sentences eventually." It went on to assert that "this action is consistent with our efforts to obtain prosecution of any kind against Key Activists to remove them from the movement."[21]

This was not the sole FBI plan to employ tax information as an instrument of political "neutralization." Of the ninety black leaders selected by the "Key Black Extremist" COINTELPRO, the tax files on seventy-two were released to the FBI.[22] In one instance, highlighted by the Senate Intelligence Committee, an FBI local office investigated information from an individual's tax returns and sent an allegation of impropriety to a local IRS office, triggering an audit. The hope was again that an audit would prove "difficult and embarrassing," and would result in financial loss. Most important, however, the bureau anticipated that the timing of the audit would be "a source of distraction during the critical period when he is engaged in meetings and plans for disrupting of the Democratic National Convention." Any drain upon the time taken up by the audit "can only accrue to the benefit of the Government and general public."[23] That this program was highly illegal was noted by another FBI internal "flap" memorandum, which suggested agents be "cautioned that the nature of this new endeavor is such that under no circumstances should the existence of the program be made known outside the Bureau."[24]

During the 1960s, the IRS also released contributor lists for tax-exempt and nonexempt organizations involved in political activity. The FBI used these lists in COINTELPRO. One target was the Southern Christian Leadership Conference, which the FBI classified as a "Black-Nationalist Hate-Type Organization," and its leader, the Reverend Martin Luther King, Jr., perhaps the favorite target of the government's domestic intelligence programs. The IRS forwarded the tax returns of Dr. King and SCLC, and its complete investigative files, to the FBI in response to a general request for "all available information" concerning them.[25] The FBI, prior to the request, had drawn up plans to send a phony letter to all organization donors under the signature of Dr. King, advising them that SCLC was under tax investigation. The FBI hoped that this letter would raise doubts among donors and reduce contributions. While this plan was never implemented, records show that the FBI had access to contributor lists of other organizations spied on by COINTELPRO, including the left-wing Students for a Democratic Society.

The Central Intelligence Agency also had access to the supposedly confidential records of the IRS. CIA dealings with the IRS were, however, on a totally unofficial basis through contacts initially established within the IRS to prevent tax investigations of CIA proprietary companies.[26] Usually tax returns traveling through these informal channels were for CIA investigations of its own employees or potential intelligence sources, but on two occasions, once in 1967 and a second time in 1972, the CIA attempted to use the IRS to attack its political opponents. In 1972, in the spirit of extralegal cooperation between the two agencies, the CIA obtained the tax returns of Victor Marchetti, an ex-CIA employee, who was preparing a book for publication which was highly critical of CIA operations. CIA records show that an IRS "Confidential Informant" was used to trigger tax audits on Marchetti.[27] Another earlier case involved *Ramparts* magazine, following its publication of an article exposing CIA use of the National Student Association. A February 2, 1967, CIA internal memorandum recording contacts between the two agencies indicated an IRS willingness to tailor its treatment of *Ramparts* to meet CIA concerns, but reflects doubts within the IRS about whether it could produce profitable information. The IRS also recognized the "political sensitivity," and indeed illegality, of the requested action, and in an unusual move asked CIA officials to make a formal record of the request to cover themselves in case of inquiry by a "member of Congress or other competent authority."[28] The IRS did not, however, refuse the request.

THE SPECIAL SERVICES STAFF:
AN ADMINISTRATIVE COINTELPRO

In 1969, following the inauguration of Richard M. Nixon, the IRS was pressured into playing an even larger role in the secret government campaign against activist organizations and individuals. Yielding to the White House and Congress, the IRS created an institutional strike force against political dissent. Like the attacks on organized crime in the 1950s and 1960s, the Special Services Staff was designed to trigger the government's tax-enforcement apparatus on the basis of political criteria.

The first call for the Internal Revenue Service to begin an enforcement program based upon political criteria came from White House aide Thomas Huston, acting on a request from President Nixon "for the IRS to move against leftist organizations taking advantage of tax shelters."[29] This request followed a series of meetings of White House staffers over a period of six months concerned with such problems as organizations "abusing their tax-exempt status by engaging in political activities that opposed the administration."[30] On June 16, 1969, Huston and Dr. Arthur Burns, a top domestic adviser to the president, conveyed this interest to IRS Commissioner Randolph Thrower, at a meeting during which Burns reportedly put pressure on the IRS chief, stressing the president's "great concern over the fact that tax-exempt funds may be supporting activist groups engaged in stimulating riots both on the campus and within our inner cities."[31] Huston suggested several specific organizations to hit, and later followed up his suggestions with memoranda and phone conversations.

Nine days later, a congressional voice called independently for the IRS to enter a campaign of politically based enforcement. At a June 25, 1969, hearing of the Permanent Subcommittee on Investigations of the Senate Committee on Government Operations, IRS Deputy Assistant Commissioner for Compliance Leon C. Green was "raked over the coals" for the lack of IRS prosecution of "ideological and activist organizations." At the time, the subcommittee was investigating organizations whose vocal opposition to the Vietnam War and struggle against racial discrimination had sharpened the level of political debate within the country. In the executive session hearing, committee members called for the IRS to cooperate with committee staff members in these investigations.[32]

On July 2, 1969, officials of the Compliance Division of the IRS first met to discuss the creation of a group inside the IRS to examine "ideological organizations" and to collect intelligence on dissident groups through a "strike force" approach.[33] Later that month, the Special Service Staff was established "to coordinate activities in all Compliance Divisions involving ideological, militant, subversive, radical and similar type organizations; to collect basic intelligence data, and to insure that the requirements of the Internal Revenue Code concerning such organizations have been complied with."[34] The Special Service Staff was a mechanism to take advantage of the decentralized character of the IRS. Its purpose was to gather information on political groups and individuals throughout the government, and to stimulate audits by local and district IRS offices based upon this information. It remains unclear how instrumental White House and congressional pressure had been in establishing the SSS. Although influenced by outside pressures, which led IRS officials to believe they had made a "commitment" to the White House to follow up on the administration's initial interest,[35] officials within the IRS assumed responsibility for forming the special unit. As with the FBI and military intelligence programs, interest from the higher levels of the White House triggered a bureaucratic reaction that may have exceeded the expectations of the president and his aides.

Once in operation, the SSS became a political tool responsive to the FBI, the Internal Security Division of the Justice Department, and other government agencies monitoring political dissent. Paul Wright, who headed the SSS, felt, like J. Edgar Hoover, "that he was participating in an effort to save the country from dissidents and extremists," and identified the smaller operations of SSS with the larger campaign conducted by the FBI.[36] In one instance where he pressed the Detroit District Office to reopen an audit case on a group of political activists, he gave as primary reason that "they are notorious campus and anti-draft activists having records under anti-riot laws. They are the principal officers in the Radical Education Project, an offshoot of the Students for a Democratic Society, and have been identified as members of certain Communist front organizations. . . . while revenue potential might not be large in some cases, *there are instances where enforcement against flagrant law violaters would have some salutary effect in this overall battle against persons bent on destruction of this government*"[37] [emphasis added]. These were hardly tax-related criteria. As the July 24, 1969, memorandum creating the SSS had asserted, "from a strictly revenue standpoint, we may have little reason for establishing this committee or for expending the time and effort which may be necessary." Nevertheless, political considerations dictate that "We must do it."[38]

Indeed, those in the executive agencies who had initially pressured the IRS to initiate action against dissident organizations, saw the Special Service Staff as an important complement to other methods of harassing political dissidents. The ability to stimulate an audit of an organization or individual created a legitimate "administrative" COINTELPRO operation—one which was particularly effective against those tax-exempt organizations involved in political activity that had proved difficult to reach. Tom Huston, assessing the value of the SSS, asserted in a September 21, 1970 memorandum:

What we cannot do in a court room via criminal prosecutions to curtail the activities of some of these groups, IRS could do by administrative action. Moreover, valuable intelligence-type information could be turned up by the IRS as a result of their field audits.[39]

The FBI, in a similar vein, perceived that the SSS would "deal a blow to dissident elements."[40]

In pursuing their non-tax-related objectives, the SSS operated on a slim web of perceived authority and internal justification for its mission. It aimed at "extremist groups and their principals, who, by their stated attitudes and actions, could be expected to ignore or willfully violate federal tax statutes."[41] Yet, as with other illegal intelligence programs, this provided only a paper rationale to justify examining the positions and politics of politically active groups. The IRS recognized the impropriety of its own program, and erected a structure of secrecy to protect those responsible. Staff memoranda circulated within the IRS strictly on a "need-to-know" basis, excluding those who might have revealed its purposes. Throughout, despite the bureaucratic growth of SSS, which had expanded beyond the scope of original White House and congressional interest, the Special Service Staff saw itself as directly accountable to the White House. As one IRS internal "talking paper" asserted, widespread notoriety would embarrass "the Administration or any elected official," not the IRS itself.[42]

For the most part, the SSS did not even make the decision about which groups or individuals were to be watched. Unlike every other special compliance group within the IRS, in which target selection is based solely on tax criteria, the SSS initiated investigations in response to information reports from outside agencies. The FBI was the single largest source of targets for the Special Service Staff. In its four years of operation, the SSS received 11,818 separate reports from the FBI, over 6,000 of them classified, including FBI COINTELPRO reports, and an FBI list of over 2,300 organizations categorized as "Old Left," "New Left," and "Right Wing."[43] If the subject of an FBI report had not already been under examination, the SSS would sometimes begin a file on that person or group. Information from the FBI comprised 43 percent of the data gathered by the SSS, and in its first year of operation more than four of every five SSS referrals to the

THE LAWLESS STATE

field for audit noted the FBI as an important source of information.[44] The Inter-Divisional Information Unit (IDIU) of the Department of Justice also provided leads for SSS investigations, including lists of 10,000 and 16,000 persons and organizations that might *potentially* engage in civil disturbances, and the Internal Security Committees of the Congress also provided the SSS with a list of target groups and individuals.[45] Beyond these sources, the SSS had access to the army's Counter-Intelligence *Compendium* which listed "dissident individuals and organizations," and made contact with the air force's Counter-Intelligence unit as well.[46]

Except in one select instance, the Special Service Staff had no capability to gather independently its own information on political activity. The office essentially became a clearinghouse for political information from other government agencies and from published sources. The Special Service Staff did, however, establish secret "drop boxes" and two pseudonyms to subscribe to over thirty publications, from which information on individuals and organizations was developed.[47] And in its one actual intelligence operation, an informant located in Washington, D.C., provided a biweekly "intelligence digest" on demonstrations and other antiwar activities.[48]

Out of this information, the SSS developed files on all ranges of political groups and individuals, at times triggering audits by other divisions of the IRS. The SSS requested 225 field audits of persons and organizations, and resulted in tax assessments totaling $622,000 ($82,000 against organizations, $580,000 against individuals), although $501,000 of this assessment was attributable to only four cases.[49] Files compiled by the SSS on an individual would typically contain information on political activities and affiliation, an FBI report, as well as tax information and returns.[50] Dossiers on tax-exempt organizations were of a similar character.[51] By 1973, the IRS had political and tax intelligence files on 8,585 individuals and 2,873 organizations. The preponderance of these files (41 percent) were on black and ethnic targets, while antiwar and New Left individuals and organizations formed 18 percent and 11 percent respectively. Fifteen percent of the files were on right-wing racist and extremist targets.[52] Included among this mass of information were files on such political figures as Senator Charles Goodell (R-N.Y.), New York Mayor John Lindsay, columnist Joseph Alsop, and Nobel Prize winner Linus Pauling.[53] Organizations examined by the SSS also ranged across the political spectrum and included the Student Non-Violent Coordinating Committee, the Minutemen, the Ku Klux Klan, the Americans for Democratic Action, the Communist party, the National Student Association, the Urban League, the California Migrant Ministry, and the Church League of America.[54]

The Special Service Staff never reached peak efficiency before its operations received wide publicity, which resulted in the decision to end the operation. An August 6, 1973, *Time* magazine revealed a November 1972 internal IRS memorandum stating that the SSS "was gathering information about 'violent groups' advocating such things as arson, firebombing, etc., and 'nonviolent groups' who participated in activities such as peaceful demonstrations, burning of draft cards, and the organization and attendance of rock festivals."[55] Labeling the memorandum "antithetical to the proper conduct of . . . tax administration," IRS Commissioner Donald Alexander abolished the functions of the SSS on August 13, only a week after the first *Time* story.

Ironically, when shut down in August 1973, the SSS was precariously close to putting its files on computers, a move which would have made the SSS more efficient and better able to cooperate with the other agencies in the intelligence apparatus. Computer files would no doubt have provided potential interlock with the FBI criminal index, military intelligence files, CIA CHAOS data, and other computer data systems on political activity. A special study within the IRS determined that an automated index of information on political activists and organizations with a programmed monitoring and triggering mechanism could be developed at relatively low cost.[56] On March 12, 1973, Commissioner Johnnie Walters had approved plans to proceed with installation of the system. However, no progress was made before the entire SSS operation had to be terminated.

THE INTELLIGENCE GATHERING AND RETRIEVAL SYSTEM (IGRS): COMPUTERIZED ABUSE

During the entire period of time the SSS was in operation, the IRS was also considering the establishment of a nationwide automated system of gathering and disseminating intelligence-type information which could have interlocked the SSS with the rest of the intelligence network. The Intelligence Gathering and Retrieval System, was "to provide an effective, uniform means of gathering, evaluating, cross-indexing, retrieving and coordinating data relating to the individuals and entities involved in *illegal activities* and having potential tax violations on a district and individual basis" [emphasis added].[57] As with the "strike force" plan of selective political enforcement, the proposal had its origins in plans to move against organized crime. In 1964, a Central Index of Racketeering and Wagering Investigations (CIRWI) was formed as a prototype for a nationwide retrieval network. Several years later, a national system was considered, to extend beyond the organized crime area.[58]

The potential for the IGR System to monitor political activities was apparent even in the early study-group meetings on the proposal. A June 25, 1969, "Report of Task Force on Intelligence Gathering and Retrieval System" noted:

In recent years the growing menace of organized crime, racketeering and corruption has been recognized as a critical national problem. . . . The techniques used by syndicated crime to infiltrate legitimate business and to corrupt public officials have reached new heights of sophistication. *Some of the same techniques are also being adopted by various major subversive and radical elements to further breakdown [sic] the basic fibers of our society.* . . . The Intelligence Division has reached the point where it can no longer rely on haphazard, outdated method to identify those of the criminal element who are evading taxes [emphasis added].[59]

The IGRS was initiated in May 1973 and suspended on January 22, 1975, amid public charges that the system was an IRS "hit list" containing information on the personal lives of Americans and part of a vast data bank with unlimited access given to federal agencies, such as the FBI. In practice, the IGRS never did prove effective at handling massive amounts of information. However, examination of the files accumulated during its short period of existence shows its potential for becoming an ominous index of American political activity. "Politically motivated intelligence" was fed into the system in at least one district.[60] In Los Angeles, IRS agents had gathered intelligence on activists and militants, particularly black militants under a code for "illegal activity," which carried the designations "subversives" and "sabotage."[61] Reportedly, targets designated under the IGRS were primarily "liberals, anti-war activists, ghetto leaders and the like,"[62] including Los Angeles Mayor Thomas Bradley, former Attorney General Ramsey Clark, Congressman Augustus Hawkins, and groups such as the American Civil Liberties Union, the Communist party, the Baptist Foundation of America, and the Medical Committee for Human Rights.[63]

The decentralized nature of the IGRS made it almost impossible for the national office to control information entering the system, or the techniques used to gather it. Many abuses occurred. For example, in April 1972, one special agent working with the Justice Department Organized Crime Strike Force in Miami, Florida, initiated Operation LEPRECHAUN to collect evidence of political corruption among local Florida officials. Over a period of approximately three years the project accumulated information on the sex and drinking activities of prominent

Miami individuals. In gathering this information, the IRS special agent employed forty-one informers (twenty-nine paid and twelve unpaid).[64] Two of these informants— allegedly without the knowledge of the IRS specal agent —burglarized the office of Evelio Estrella, a candidate for the U.S. Congress.[65] Another informant was involved in unauthorized electronic eavesdropping at the direction of the Miami Police Department and the IRS special agent. Although the Miami operation created what was clearly the most far-reaching covert intelligence net of all the IGRS units, this was far from the only example of illegal methods used to gather information for the IGRS.

THE PRESIDENT'S HIT SQUAD

Perhaps more successful than the Special Services Staff and the Intelligence Gathering and Retrieval System, were instances where the IRS made "specific hits" on political opponents at the request of the White House and other government officials. At various times from 1969 through 1973, President Nixon, acting through his White House staff, applied pressure on the IRS to use its powers against selected targets. We know, for instance, of the 1972 effort to have the IRS audit key persons on the White House "enemies list," which included such people as Democratic National Committee Chairman Lawrence O'Brien,[66] Harold Gibbons of the Teamsters Union,[67] and members of Senator George McGovern's presidential campaign staff.[68] Although IRS officials have claimed that they re- sisted these efforts—a claim substantiated in part by White House staff memoranda accusing the IRS of "lack of guts and effort"[69]—some enforcement actions were taken.

Another instance involved revoking tax-exempt status for public-interest law firms. After an August 1970 IRS report on the Special Service Staff, which Tom Huston termed "long on words and short on substance,"[70] the IRS announced that it would stop granting tax-exempt status to the public-interest firms, pending a study. For the most part, public-interest law firms represented consumer and environmental interests, as well as other under-represented causes, and used the courts to challenge the policies and practices of the administration and the large corporations. The immediate effect of the IRS move was to halt the funding flow to these groups, since tax-exempt status was necessary for gaining the support of wealthy private donors and the larger tax-exempt foundations such as the Ford Foundation. No public record conclusively demonstrates that the White House *forced* the IRS to initiate this action, but based on the ongoing administration contacts with the service and the timing of events, it seems probable that White House influence played a crucial role in the decision. One month later, following widespread public and congressional charges of bias, the IRS decision was reversed.

A further example of White House influence concerns the two-and-one-half-year refusal of the IRS to consider the application for tax-exempt standing of the Center for Corporate Responsibility, a Washington, D.C., public interest group started by Ralph Nader. On May 2, 1973, the group filed suit claiming that it had been unlawfully denied tax-exempt status as a result of selective treatment for political, ideological, and other reasons having no basis in statute or regulation. Included in the IRS file on the Nader group was a handwritten memo indicating "perhaps White House pressure." On December 11, 1973, U.S. District Court Judge Charles R. Richey held that the tax exemption had been unlawfully denied and that the center had been singled out for "selective treatment for political, ideological or other improper reason."[71]

In almost every case of IRS intelligence-type activity, the service operated under pressure from the White House or the Congress. Yet in one instance, the IRS developed a COINTELPRO-type operation of its own, aimed at an "enemy" of unique interest to the IRS: those individuals attacking the constitutional validity of internal revenue taxes. In 1973, the IRS began to examine and infiltrate tax-protest groups through undercover agents. These agents, often posing as husband and wife, attended meetings of tax protestors, took down names, license plates, and telephone numbers of people present, and recorded events and plans that took place. Agent memoranda included the political and other opinions expressed at the meetings.[72] In one case, an agent gained sufficient trust to be elected group treasurer, and he released the entire organizational mailing list to IRS headquarters.[73] Presumably, these lists of tax protestors were used to trigger selective audits of their tax returns.

The infiltration of tax-protest groups resulted in the presence of an IRS agent at a meeting to decide legal strategy for the defense of individuals indicted for tax-code violations.[74] In one especially reprehensible action, a national office agent gained access to a draft legal brief for a protester's defense against willful failure to file tax returns. This brief eventually reached the Los Angeles office of the U.S. attorneys prosecuting the case.[75]

Given the history of the IRS, the prospects that it will not remain involved in politically motivated tax enforcement, or that information given the IRS will not circulate freely through the government, seem remote. Nothing has been done to change the laws governing release of tax information—although the IRS has stated its intention to follow the regulations more closely in the future. No IRS official has been prosecuted for any offense committed during the 1960s or throughout the Nixon years—indeed, Vernon Acree, the Nixon contact at the IRS, was promoted to commissioner of U.S. Customs, presumably as a reward for his obedience to the administration, and he remains in that office to this day. It is still possible to use the administrative processes of tax collection for political reasons. Unless reforms occur in law, the old adage that "nothing is inevitable but birth, death and taxes" may again, as it was in the 1960s, be better stated that, for political activists, "nothing is inevitable but birth, death, taxes and an audit."

THE
GRAND JURIES

9

The federal grand jury, a body of twenty-three citizens who decide whether there is sufficient evidence to hold another citizen for trial, seems an unlikely weapon for the executive branch to use against dissent. Yet its purported investigatory powers, its protected secrecy, its appearance of independence, and its legality have made the grand jury one of the most powerful instruments for intelligence gathering and political disruption in use today.

A sitting grand jury has enormous legal powers. A federal prosecutor can subpoena anyone to appear before a grand jury anywhere without explanation. Subpoenas can be issued for any records, correspondence, documents, fingerprints, hair samples, handwriting exemplars, or other items of interest.[1] There is no limit to the number of witnesses who can be called, and no restrictions on the nature or number of questions that can be put to them. There are no rules about the kinds of evidence that can be used—rumors, hearsay, results of illegal searches or warrantless wiretaps, irrelevant or prejudicial information—all inadmissible in open court.[2] The government may use informants without exposing their identity, for their cover is protected by the grand jury's secrecy. In theory, some of these powers are subject to review by the courts, but in practice, the courts rubber stamp the prosecutor's whim. The witness enters the chamber alone, losing the right to remain silent and having no right to have a lawyer present —rights the witness would have even in a police interrogation. No witness need be informed of the purpose of the investigation, or even if he or she is its target; no witness has a right even to be warned that whatever he or she says could be used to bring charges against him or her.[3] A grant of partial immunity is often used to coerce testimony from a witness who invokes Fifth Amendment protection; a witness can be jailed without trial for contempt of court for up to eighteen months for continuing to assert that right after immunity is granted. Upon release, the same witness may be called before a new grand jury, asked the same questions and jailed again for an additional eighteen months. Witnesses have no right to a transcript of even their own testimony; in fact, the prosecutor controls what, if anything, is recorded.[4]

Historically, the grand jury was to be a "people's panel" that would protect suspects against overreaching prosecutors and unwarranted prosecutions. The grand jury's primary function was to determine whether an indictment should be brought against the accused; it sat in judgment on the evidence presented by a prosecutor and acted as a check on his discretion. The eminent British legal theorist John Somers once wrote, "Grand juries are our only security, inasmuch as our lives cannot be drawn into jeopardy by all the malicious crafts of the Devil unless such a number of our honest countrymen shall be satisfied with the truth of the accusation."[5] Thus the framers of the American Constitution included a grand jury indictment as a right guaranteed by the Fifth Amendment.

In addition to its charging function, the grand jury has been accruing an independent investigatory role. It constitutes, as the Supreme Court has said, "a grand inquest, the scope . . . [not limited narrowly] . . . by questions of propriety or forecasts of the probable results of the investigation."[6] Its investigatory function was designed to insure that criminal activities that the police might be reluctant to investigate—the misconduct of the rich or powerful —could be pursued by citizens meeting together. The Supreme Court has thus consistently refused to limit the grand jury's authority and powers, "because the task is to inquire into the existence of possible criminal conduct, . . . its investigative powers are necessarily broad."[7]

It was the Justice Department of the Nixon administration that first turned the powers of this people's tribunal against political dissent and transformed the grand jury into an intelligence agency. Its motivation was similar to that which led the FBI to begin COINTELPRO. HUAC congressional investigations were no longer useful instruments to discredit political dissenters. The search for a weapon led the FBI to COINTELPRO and the Justice Department to the grand jury. The Nixon Justice Department recognized what had been true for decades: in operation, the grand jury was not so much a proud and independent people's panel as a pliant instrument of the prosecutor. As federal district court judge William Campbell concluded, "Today, [the grand jury] is but a convenient tool for the prosecutor. . . . Any experienced prosecutor will admit that he can indict anybody at anytime for almost anything."[8] Indeed, if one jury panel refuses to indict, a prosecutor may present the same evidence to another and another, until one agrees to return an indictment.

In 1969 and 1970, the Nixon Justice Department assembled the other elements necessary for a political grand jury network. Robert Mardian was named head of a revitalized Internal Security Division (ISD) in the Justice Department, which had been inactive since the McCarthy era. Its staff was increased from seven to sixty lawyers, and Mardian appointed Guy Goodwin, a forty-four-year-old prosecutor, to serve as head of a special litigation section within the ISD. Goodwin would serve as the field marshal, organizing a network of grand juries throughout the nation to locate "enemies" and gather evidence against them using grand jury investigations.

The last pieces were supplied by the Organized Crime Control Act of 1970, the Nixon administration's draconian police legislation. The act expanded the powers of federal grand juries, empowering the Justice Department to convene special investigative grand juries for eighteen months (with an extension of an additional eighteen months if desired) and by creating a more limited form of immunity for witnesses, called "use immunity."[9] Under "forced immunity," which was first developed in 1954, if a witness refuses to testify, claiming his or her Fifth Amendment right against self-incrimination, a prosecutor can force immunity upon the witness, and thus "waive" any Fifth Amendment right to silence. Before 1970, only "transactional immunity" was available and limited to specified offenses, generally those associated with organized crime. ("Transactional immunity" meant that a witness could not be prosecuted for anything related to the transactions about which he was forced to testify.) The new use immunity was not limited to specific crimes and provided protection only from evidence gained from the testimony; if "independent sources" provided other evidence against the witness, a prosecution could still be brought for the same transaction. A recalcitrant witness could now be given immunity and jailed for contempt if he or she refused to testify. If he or she chose to testify, he or she might yet be prosecuted with "independent sources of evidence."

The Nixon administration argued that the use-immunity provision of the 1970 Organized Crime Control Act was needed to aid grand jury investigations of organized crime, but forced immunity has proved to be of little use in such cases. Informers in crime syndicates are killed; thus subpoenaed gangsters are often grateful for the opportunity to prove their loyalty by spending several months in jail for contempt. Use immunity is occasionally useful when forced upon peripheral movement people to gather intelligence, but its true value is as a weapon to put uncooperative witnesses in jail and to frighten others who are politically involved.

Using forced immunity to punish witnesses who refuse to cooperate is a fairly recent prosecutorial tool, and was first developed in an attempt to break up an organized crime syndicate. In 1965, two relatively unknown assistant U.S. attorneys in Chicago, Sam Betar and David Schippers subpoenaed Sam Giancana, later famed as the Mafia contact in the CIA's assassination plots against Castro. Giancana was granted forced immunity and jailed for contempt of court when he refused to testify. Betar said, "Giancana went to prison. And jailing him created a state of chaos and fear in the minds of associates. At first they had thought we were just trying to grab some headlines with the grand jury. But once the lesser lights learned that we'd found a way to put the head of the whole show in jail, they didn't know how to cope."[10] Later Betar said, "I don't want to brag but I know we laid the groundwork for the way immunity provisions have been used in the past few years."[11]

By 1970, all the pieces were in place; all that was required was a Justice Department willing to abuse its prosecutorial responsibility. The Nixon administration supplied that ingredient. From 1970 to 1973, the ISD conducted over 100 Guy Goodwin-supervised grand juries in eighty-four cities of thirty-six states, calling some 1,000 to 2,000 witnesses by subpoena, returning some 400 indictments.[12] The indictments were often merely *pro forma*, to cover the real investigative purposes of the grand juries. The normal conviction rate on grand jury indictments is 65 percent; less than 15 percent of the 400 ISD indictments were convictions or pleas to lesser charges.[13] Targets included the Black Panther party, Vietnam Veterans against the War, Daniel Ellsberg, the Los Angeles antidraft movement, the Catholic Left, Mayday, the Puerto Rican independence movement, the American Indian movement, the Movimiento Chicano, the women's movement, Irish unification supporters, labor unions, radical lawyers, and legal workers. Senator Edward Kennedy, reviewing the campaign in 1973, summarized the situation:

The use of "political" grand juries by the present administration is unprecedented. In a sense, of course, the practice is a throwback to the worst excesses of the legislative investigating committees of the 1950's. In this respect, the Internal Security Division of the Justice Department represents the Second Coming of Joe McCarthy and the House Unamerican Activities Committee. But the abuses of power of the Department's overzealous prosecutors do not even know the bounds of a Joe McCarthy, because their insidious contemporary activities are carried out in the dark and secret corners of the grand jury, free from public scrutiny. . . .[14]

The political grand juries used the pretense of investigating crimes to collect massive amounts of information on radicals throughout the country. One of the first major Guy Goodwin panels was convened in Tucson, Arizona, in October 1970. Goodwin subpoenaed five young activists from Venice, California, to testify about an alleged purchase of dynamite, *after* an indictment had already been returned against the man who allegedly bought the dynamite. The grand jury was used to develop in-depth information about radical activities in southern California. Goodwin asked questions such as: "Tell the grand jury every place you went after you returned to your apartment from Cuba, every city you visited, with whom and by what means of transportation and whom you visited during the time of your travels after you left your apartment in Ann Arbor, Michigan, in May of 1970."[15] The five witnesses at first refused to testify and spent five months in jail for contempt of court. As they left the jail, Goodwin subpoenaed them again before a new grand jury. At that point, three faltered and testified.

Since their purpose is to collect information, political grand jury investigations are characterized by the sweeping questions asked regarding memberships in political organizations, names of other members, and the activities of the groups. Guy Goodwin has become famous for asking such questions as:

Seattle—May, 1972: "Tell the grand jury every place you have lived for the last two years prior to this date, advising the grand jury the period of time you lived at each location, with whom, if anyone, you resided, and what occupation or employment you had during each period."

Tucson—November, 1970: "I would like to ask at this time if you have ever been a member of any of the following organizations, and if so, to tell the grand jury during what period of time you belonged to any of these organizations, with whom you associated in connection with your membership in any of these organizations, what activities you engaged in and what meetings you attended, giving the grand jury the dates and conversations which occurred: The Save Our Soldiers Association, the Coalition, the Los Angeles Reserve Association, the Peace and Freedom Party, the Humanistic and Educational Needs of the Academic Community Organization?"

Detroit—June, 1971: "I would like to know if you were in Ann Arbor in the early part of February, 1971, and if you met any people in Ann Arbor who lived in Washington, or who you later found out lived in Washington; and if so, who were they, where did you meet, and what conversations were had?"[16]

Goodwin subpoenaed Leslie Bacon from Washington, D.C., to testify before a Seattle grand jury as a material witness in the bombing of the nation's Capitol. Goodwin questioned her primarily about upcoming Mayday activities and her political activities in the previous two to three years. Ms. Bacon was later indicted on perjury and conspiracy in New York, but all charges were dropped by the government. Recently an FBI official, who had direct knowledge of the investigation, admitted, "We didn't know a damn thing. Leslie Bacon was the only thing we had and that was just a fishing expedition. She was called before a grand jury in Seattle because we thought we were more likely to get an indictment out there."[17]

Grand juries have also been used effectively to disrupt legitimate political activities, a sort of quasi-judicial

COINTELPRO. For example, in 1972, the Vietnam Veterans against the War (VVAW) planned a series of demonstrations at the Democratic and Republican political conventions, scheduled to be held in Miami in July and August. Three days before the Democratic convention opened, Guy Goodwin issued a first batch of twenty-three subpoenas to members of the VVAW, almost all either national, regional, state, or chapter organizers throughout the South. They were called to a grand jury in Tallahassee, 500 miles from Miami, on the very day their demonstration was scheduled to take place in Miami. Many were held a week, asked a few desultory questions and released. Five were jailed for up to forty days until their contempt citations were reversed. Eight veterans were ultimately indicted for conspiracy to engage in violence at the Republican convention in August. All defendants were acquitted by the trial jury on all counts. But VVAW's activities were totally disrupted, the organization severely weakened, and falsely branded as terrorist. On July 13, the Democratic convention passed a resolution condemning "this blatantly political abuse of the grand jury to intimidate and discredit a group whose opposition to the war has been particularly moving and effective."[18] A recent Fifth Circuit Court decision in a related case said the VVAW grand jury proceedings were "part of an overall governmental tactic directed against disfavored persons and groups . . . to chill their expressions and associations."[9]

The use of the grand jury for political purposes, perfected during the Nixon administration, is described by Moore's *Federal Practice:*

[W]hen technical and theoretical distinctions are put aside, the true nature of the grand jury emerges—i.e., it is 'basically . . . a law enforcement agency.' Nowhere is this characterization more apt than in considering the use of grand jury proceedings by the Nixon Administration. In Nixon's war against the press, the intellectual community and the peace movement generally, the federal grand jury has become the battleground.[20]

The grand jury continues as a major battleground. Although the use of political grand juries temporarily ceased during the Watergate investigation, there has been a resurgence of grand jury abuse under Attorney General Edward Levi.

When the Watergate scandal broke, disclosing illegalities committed by the highest officials of the Justice Department (Mitchell, Kleindienst, and Mardian), the Internal Security Division was disbanded and subsumed into the Criminal Division of the Justice Department. However, spokesmen for the Justice Department assert that the shift indicates no change in policy, and the new head of the ISD, Kevin Maroney, has confirmed that the ISD will continue to investigate "politically motivated crimes" and to use grand juries as it has in the past.[21] Guy Goodwin remains an employee of the Criminal Division of the Justice Department.

The same pattern of abuse of grand juries as intelligence-gathering operations with COINTELPRO objectives has reemerged with the FBI giving more decisive direction. FBI agents increasingly threaten with grand jury subpoenas citizens who refuse to answer their questions. Subpoenas bear the signature of a U.S. attorney, but agents have filled in blank subpoenas when people would not talk freely, and in one known case, have subpoenaed a witness to appear before a nonexistent grand jury.[22] Ralph Guy, a U.S. attorney in Detroit, has admitted that FBI agents are often sent out to question witnesses with grand jury subpoenas in their pockets.[23] Congress has repeatedly refused to delegate subpoena power to the FBI, feeling that no executive agency should possess what was essentially a judicial power.

In 1975, FBI agents descended upon the women's community in Lexington, Kentucky, and New Haven, Connecticut, allegedly pursuing a tip about Susan Saxe and Katharine Powers, wanted for a bank robbery in Boston. Hundreds of people were interviewed and asked detailed personal questions. Six refused to talk to the FBI in Lexington and were promptly subpoenaed before a grand jury purportedly investigating the "harboring of fugitives." FBI agents visited the families of some of the witnesses, urging them to pressure their children to cooperate with the bureau. In one case an eighty-four-year-old grandmother was visited by agents and told that her granddaughter was a lesbian. Six people were jailed for contempt after refusing to testify in Lexington. Five ultimately testified. The investigation was never pursued further, although one witness, Jill Raymond, spent fourteen months in the county jail. The exact pattern was repeated in New Haven where Ellen Grusse and Terry Turgeon refused to testify and spent a month in prison. Both were then subpoenaed upon release and spent an additional six months in prison until the prosecutor withdrew their subpoenas. No indictments were handed down in either community; none of the women was charged or tried for any offense, except refusing to cooperate in the dragnet. For the witnesses the choices were all unpalatable. To cooperate was to assist the government's surveillance of the women's movement and protected political activity; to refuse was to face contempt-of-court citations and jail. In either case, the grand jury created suspicion and divisions among friends; it invaded individuals' privacy and disrupted their political activities.

In New York City and Puerto Rico, people identifiable in some way with the Puerto Rican independence movement, the Puerto Rican Socialist party or the Puerto Rican Nationalist party, have been subpoenaed to grand jury investigations under the guise of "bombing and explosives" investigations. In New York City, the FBI questioned the Puerto Rican community extensively, threatening to subpoena those who wouldn't answer questions about political activities and associates dating back many years. The court accepted the government's proposition that merely being associated in the Puerto Rican Socialist party was sufficient basis to justify a subpoena. Citiens attending court hearings were photographed and became objects of later FBI interrogations. Two witnesses,

Lureida Torres of New York City and Edgar Maury Santiago in Puerto Rico, have already been jailed. The grand jury subpoena, receiving almost automatic judicial approval, served to brand Puerto Rican activists and organizations with a terrorist label without a shred of evidence, just as grand jury subpoenas had earlier stigmatized members of VVAW as violent in 1972.

To date, no restraints have been imposed upon the use of grand juries as a weapon against political dissent. In 1975, a second wave of "political" grand juries began, starting with the Lexington and New Haven probes mentioned above. Other political grand juries have recently been convened against labor unions in Washington, D.C., and Florida, the American Indian movement at Wounded Knee, South Dakota, Oklahoma, and Iowa, and the Chicano movement in Colorado. There have been grand jury proceedings in the Symbionese Liberation Army/Patty Hearst case in Pennsylvania and in California, and in the filming of a movie made on Weather Underground in Los Angeles. In addition, radical defense lawyers and legal workers are now being subpoenaed in political cases across the country and asked for their records and/or information about their clients.[24]

Shirley Hufstedler, a judge on the Ninth Circuit Court of Appeals, observed recently:

Today, courts across this country are faced with an increasing flow of cases arising out of grand jury proceedings concerned with the possible punishment of political dissidents. It would be a cruel twist of history to allow the institution of the grand jury that was designed at least partially to protect political dissent to become an instrument of political suppression.[25]

The "cruel twist" continues as yet unchecked.

THE
LAWLESS STATE

10

Like the impeachment hearings and the Pentagon Papers, the investigations of the intelligence agencies have provided a glimpse behind the mask of state. The revelations—richly documented in a detailed, if sadly incomplete, record—teach different lessons to each who reviews them. The preceding chapters have reviewed the central text: the shocking range of routine, illegal, destructive acts undertaken by these agencies at home and abroad, which endangered the lives and trampled on the rights of so many. What can also be drawn from the record is a fairly complete overview of the operating principles of the secret realm of government.

BASIS OF AUTHORITY:
PRESIDENTIAL ASSERTION

The clandestine bureaus are the true progeny of the post-war presidency, tracing their legal birthright not to legislation but to presidential assertions of "inherent power." According to bureau spokesmen, the FBI's "authority" to spy on Americans rests upon the "constitutional powers and responsibilities vested in the President." Similarly, the

CIA's covert intervention abroad is based not on its legislated charter, but on the president's "inherent foreign policy powers." The National Security Agency and the National Reconnaissance Office, bureaus charged with communications and satellite intelligence respectively, were created entirely by secret executive directive, and annually consume over $4 billion without a statute to define their duties. What is true for programs is also true for techniques: the Justice Department has asserted a presidential power to order warrantless wiretaps, bugs, and "surreptitious entries" (break-ins) against American citizens for intelligence purposes. Even the secrecy that cloaks the intelligence bureaus is based upon a classification system established by executive order, without statutory basis.

The intelligence agencies are assigned the responsibility for routine spying and political policing at home and abroad. Secrecy is necessary, for the primary function of the agencies is to undertake disreputable activities that presidents do not wish to reveal to the public or expose to congressional debate. The agencies also collect secret intelligence information, which helps to justify presidential power by providing it with a claim of special knowledge. The "mysteries of government" do much to still criticism of activities apparently beyond the comprehension of mere citizens or legislators.

Perhaps the most important function of secrecy is to insulate the clandestine agencies from the civil society and government. Wrapped in a secrecy system fastened by security clearances, lie-detector tests, and classification markings, the officials of the secret bureaus develop a unique loyalty and allegiance to the agency. The Senate Intelligence Committee found that the intelligence agencies were a "sector of American government set apart. Employees' loyalties to their organizations have been conditioned by the closed, compartmented and secretive circumstances of their agencies."[1] The Senate report compared intelligence service with monastic life, with similar rituals, disciplines, and personal sacrifices. In the intelligence bureau, however, the monastic training prepared officials not for saintliness, but for crime, for acts transgressing the limits of accepted law and morality.

Secrecy also insulates the civil society from the secret realm of intelligence. It protects the innocence of the citizenry, producing reactions like that of Senator Philip Hart of Michigan, a gentle and honest man, who, when faced with the truth about the FBI, blurted,

I have been told for years by, among others, some of my own family, that this is exactly what the Bureau was doing all of the time, and in my great wisdom and high office, I assured them that they were wrong—it just wasn't true, it couldn't happen. They wouldn't do it.[2]

Because of the secrecy, the "vicious and unsavory" tactics that are part of the daily routine of the secret agent are hidden from the citizenry, preserving their own sense of decency.

The secret agencies of the president operated for some twenty-five years with few questioning their operations. The national consensus, founded on anti-communism and developed by periodic crises, supported a bipartisan foreign policy and a strong, active presidency. The president's authority to defend the national security was generally accepted, and his instruments went unquestioned. Few reporters, legislators, or citizens even attempted to strip away the veil of secrecy to expose the spy bureaus to review, and the few that tried, failed. In this, the intelligence agencies enjoyed the license of the secret police in a dictatorship: they could spy on others without concern for others reviewing them.

The national consensus, secrecy, and the mantle of the presidency enabled the covert bureaus to operate outside the normal checks and balances of the constitutional system, and above the law itself. For over twenty-five years, Congress simply abdicated its legislative and oversight functions. Perhaps the best example was provided by the late Senator Allen Ellender, a longtime member of the Senate Appropriations Committee, which appropriated money to the CIA. When asked in 1971 if the committee had approved financing for the CIA's 36,000-person secret army in Laos, Ellender replied: "I did not know anything about it. . . . I never asked to begin with, whether there were any funds to carry on the war. . . . It never dawned on me to ask about it."[3]

For the most part, the congressional ignorance was voluntary. Senator Leverett Saltonstall, for many years ranking Republican on the oversight subcommittee, summarized the widespread feelings on the Hill: "It is not a question of reluctance on the part of CIA officials to speak to us. Instead it is a question of our reluctance, if you will, to seek information and knowledge on subjects which I personally, as a member of Congress and as a citizen, would rather not have."[4] The Saltonstall attitude was not entirely irresponsible. It may be preferable for legislators to remain ignorant of activities that they dare not control, for in this way they avoid complicity in them. In any case, the Congress operated for twenty-five years in blissful ignorance, appropriating secret funds of untold amounts to the intelligence agencies without even knowing where the money was hidden in the general budget.

Certainly at the height of the cold war, legislative approval for virtually any activity was available if requested. The fact that the agencies did not seek legislation to legitimate their activities indicates both their disdain for congressional authority and the desire of executive officials to claim exclusive monopoly over national security activities.

The courts were no different from the Congress, for secret activities seldom came before them. No criminal prosecutions were brought, simply because no attorney general even considered trying to control the secret bureaus. Indeed, for twenty years, the CIA and the Justice Department had a formal agreement that Justice would refer all cases involving CIA personnel or operations to the agency's general counsel for review. If the counsel decided that CIA sources or methods would be endangered, the Justice Department would drop the case.[5] Needless to say, the vast majority of cases involving CIA personnel were not prosecuted. The formal agreement of the CIA was the informal practice with the FBI. No attorney general dared cross J. Edgar Hoover and investigate the bureau.

When the courts did receive a rare case involving the covert agencies, they usually accorded the bureaus extreme deference. Thus, the Supreme Court refused to allow a citizen to bring suit against the CIA's secret budget, even though the Constitution explicitly requires a regular accounting of expenditures.[6] Similarly, an appellate court invented a cause of action for the CIA so that it could enjoin Victor Marchetti, a former employee, from publishing a book revealing agency secrets; the Supreme Court refused to review this unprecedented prior restraint of political speech.[7] The Supreme Court affirmed the right of the government to use informers without restriction, and appellate courts carved out an area for warrantless "foreign intelligence wiretaps" from the protection of the Fourth Amendment.[8] In dicta, the Supreme Court also recognized a presidential privilege to withhold national security information.[9]

AGAINST THE LAW

Not surprisingly, modern presidents claimed the right to order secret agencies to operate against the laws in the name of national security. Richard Nixon, the most vocal proponent of presidential powers, believed that "it is quite obvious that there are inherently governmental actions which if undertaken *by the sovereign* in protection of the interest of the nation's security are lawful, but which if undertaken by private persons are not . . ." [emphasis added].[10] The characteristic Nixon assumption that the president is "sovereign" neatly inverts the constitutional principle that only the people are sovereign, governed under the law, and that "all offices of the government—from the highest to the lowest, are creatures of the law and are bound to obey it. . . ."[11]

Nixon's claim, however bald, was far from unique, as

demonstrated by the extraordinary number of intelligence agency programs that routinely violated the laws, criminal or otherwise. It was far from exceptional that a middle-level CIA official disobeyed Nixon's own order to destroy all toxic poisons in accordance with a treaty passed by the Senate and signed by the president. Asked about the violation, former CIA Counter-Intelligence Staff Chief James Angleton, a veteran of the agency known as "Mother" to his colleagues, stated, "I find it inconceivable that a covert agency is expected to obey all the overt orders of the government."[12] By overt orders, Angleton was referring to the laws and treaties of the United States, as well as to presidential directives.

Within the executive branch, it was widely assumed that a president could sanction otherwise illegal acts. J. Edward Day, postmaster general during the Kennedy administration, was so astonished to learn that even the CIA's general counsel considered the agency's mail-opening program to be illegal, that he wrote a letter to the Senate Intelligence Committee:

If the CIA's lawyers concluded that the CIA could not open mail to and from communist countries in the early 1960's without violating the law, I think the CIA needs better lawyers. . . .

In my opinion, the statutes relating to opening of mail must have read into them an exception for opening mail to and from communist countries by the CIA in time of cold war. . . .[13]

Day's opinion was widely shared. CIA covert action abroad routinely violates United States treaties, which are part of the "laws of the land," yet agency officials are stupefied when anyone suggests that covert action is therefore illegal. Mail opening itself is not greatly different from the warrantless wiretaps and microphone placements for which the Justice Department claims a national security exemption from the Fourth Amendment. Only three weeks after the Supreme Court denounced the use of a microphone in the bedroom of a criminal defendant, Eisenhower's attorney general, Herbert Brownell, gave the bureau sweeping new authority to engage in bugging for intelligence purposes. For the FBI, Brownell's order superseded the Supreme Court's ruling as effective law.

In day-to-day operations in the secret realm, the law was simply "not at issue," as William Sullivan, former assistant director of the FBI for intelligence, testified. Questions of legality were seldom raised, perhaps the best evidence of the wide internal acceptance of a national security prerogative above the law. Indeed, the secret bureaus were intended to violate "hitherto accepted norms of human conduct"; mere illegality was a sandlot concern in comparison. COINTELPRO was begun because bureau officials agreed that "existing law did not suffice"; it is hardly surprising that FBI officials testify they "never gave it a thought" that COINTELPRO flagrantly violated the laws and the Constitution. Sullivan's conclusion, drawn from ten years' service on the U.S. Intelligence Board, was that he had never heard legal issues raised at all, "because we were just naturally pragmatists. . . . As far as legality is concerned, morals or ethics, [it] was never raised by myself or anybody else."[14]

If questions of "ethics" were raised, national security provided absolution. If it were effective, it was justified. Thus CIA memoranda repeatedly drew attention to the illegality of the CIA's twenty-year mail-opening program, but Richard Helms testified he was never seriously concerned, since the program seemed to provide useful information "from time to time." "Surreptitious entries" were, according to FBI memoes, "clearly illegal," but continued, for they were allegedly "invaluable in combatting subversive activities."[15]

No programs were ended because they violated the law or the Constitution. Yet in an obscure, backhanded fashion, the records reveal a strong undercurrent of concern for law, an almost subterranean sense of criminality. Like a gang of thieves, intelligence officials showed respect for the law by acting in stealth, fearing exposure. Again and again, concern for legality was expressed in concern for greater secrecy, better cover stories. Officials might act against the law, but they would not advertise it in public. Thus CIA Director Richard Helms wrote a cover memo to Henry Kissinger over "Restless Youth," the CIA's study of the youth movement at home and abroad:

> This is an area not within the charter of the agency so I need not emphasize how extremely sensitive this makes the paper. Should anyone learn of its existence it would prove most embarrassing to all concerned. . . .[16]

When army officers decided to ignore the opinion of the attorney general and conduct illegal radio monitoring, the agents were instructed to wear disguises to avoid detection.[17] Hoovers's abiding concern with "embarrassment to the Bureau," led to the notorious "Do Not File" file, for memoranda about illegal or outrageous activities. Do Not File memos were destroyed annually. If asked about any specific incident, bureau officials would state truthfully that there were no records in their files.

Yet despite the consensus, their mandate, their isolation, and their authority from the president, the secret bureaus had some difficulty convincing even their own employees that national security totally revoked the law. In May 1973, former Director of the CIA James Schlesinger asked CIA employees to forward to him any activities *which they considered* to be illegal or improper; the response totaled over 700 pages of memoes, which came to be known as the "family jewels." On the other hand, when the "family jewels" were requested under the Freedom of Information Act, agency officials refused to release a single word, explaining that making them public would reveal "intelligence sources and methods."

The residual feeling of unease accounts for the tendency of officials to terminate programs that were threatened with exposure. The CIA's mail-opening and drug-testing programs, NSA's cable interceptions, military surveillance of citizens—all were terminated or limited because of public exposure. Indeed, in 1966, J. Edgar Hoover even ended the FBI's Washington program of warrantless wiretaps, "garbage covers," and "black-bag jobs." But Hoover was simply seeking a better cover story. He transferred management of most of the FBI's illegal programs from the

"Seat of Government" to field offices. When the FBI was involved in litigation, Hoover could state honestly that no records of illegal activity existed at FBI headquarters. If the field office programs were discovered, Hoover—like his successor, Clarence Kelley—could claim that he had no idea anything like that was going on.

PARALEGAL DISORDER

Instead of having their functions defined by legal charters and limited by law, the clandestine bureaus operate on a principle of higher orders. Authority and limits are provided by presidential executive orders, national security decision memoranda, bureaucratic directives, even news releases and public speeches. These pronouncements might best be termed paralegal, for they are legal in effect, but based purely on executive assertion. They define the missions, functions, and operating procedures of the covert bureaus. They are often accompanied by detailed "delimitation agreements," sensitive treaties between agencies which divide up the turf, understandings as complex and as fragile as disarmament accords between nations or territorial arrangements between Chicago gangs.

The primary paralegal documents are issued by the president or his cabinet officers, and can be revoked or altered at will, even on a case-to-case basis. Thus any presidential order that violates a national security directive will generally be viewed as an exception to the directive, rather than an illegal order.

Paralegal documents are not simply creations of the president. As a rule, they are broad and general and have meaning only as the bureaucracy interprets them. Moreover, the orders themselves are often directly or indirectly the product of the agencies, gaining presidential authority for pet projects or missions. Conventional wisdom in Washington understands that administrations come and go, but the bureaucracy remains forever. Over a period of time, agencies can often get authority for their favorite projects, using political officials as foils for their own purposes. Hoover, for example, used Franklin Roosevelt's curiosity about possible Nazi sabotage in 1936 to present a blood-curdling portrayal of subversion from both right and left, gaining the president's approval for a massive domestic surveillance program.

Perhaps the best example of the ability of the intelligence agencies to write their own charters is provided by the Huston Plan—the Nixon White House plan to coordinate and intensify domestic intelligence operations. Representatives of all of the major intelligence agencies met patiently with the president's young, ambitious aide, Tom Charles Huston, to discuss what might be done to increase spying on domestic organizations. The proposals forwarded to the president for his approval gave the agencies authority for mail openings, interception of international calls, and surreptitious entries. None of the agency representatives informed Huston that they were already engaged in such activities without presidential authority. The Huston Plan was their way of gaining approval for what they were already doing. When the plan was rescinded, the activities continued without pause, and without authority.

The Senate Intelligence Committee found that the "intelligence agencies have often undertaken programs without authorization, with insufficient authorization, or in defiance of express orders."[18] The FBI's various COINTELPRO, for example, were never revealed to Justice Department or White House authorities. Aspects—what the Senate Committee called "hints and partial obscured disclosures"—were slipped by presidents and attorneys general for approval. Former Attorney General Nicholas Katzenbach noted:

As far as Mr. Hoover was concerned, it was sufficient for the Bureau if at any time an Attorney General had authorized [a particular] activity in any circumstances. In fact, it was often sufficient if any Attorney General had written something which could be considered to authorize it or had been informed in some one of hundreds of memoranda of some facts.[19]

Just as COINTELPRO lacked higher authorization, so

did the CIA's twenty-five-year mail-opening program, the FBI's "black-bag jobs," the military's massive surveillance program, NSA's cable intercept operations.

To some degree, such initiatives were expected of the secret agencies, which were responsible for inventing ideas and programs. Since the clandestine agencies played a "new game," which violated all the prior rules, they were expected to develop an expertise in the "unsavory and vicious." In an internal memo, CIA General Counsel Lawrence Houston noted that the CIA had to take the initiative in planning covert operations because "the average person, both in government and outside, is *thinking along normal lines*."[20]

Additionally, the political officials formally charged with limiting the bureaus often preferred not to know what was being done, particularly the criminal details. Repeatedly, high civilian officials avoided responsibility, refused to inquire, never expressed the slightest curiosity or doubt. When Allen Dulles went to see J. Edward Day, Kennedy's postmaster general, about the CIA's mail-opening program, Day testified that he asked Dulles, "Do I have to know about it?" Dulles did not volunteer the information.[21]

The CIA developed a formal doctrine, "plausible denial," which rationalized the "need not to know." Initially referring to measures designed to hide the hand of the United States in a covert action abroad, "plausible denial" came to be used internally "to mask decisions from the President and his senior staff members."[22] One common technique was the use of Aesopian language in conversation. Assassination was gingerly referred to as the need to "eliminate Castro," or "neutralize Lumumba," or "remove Schneider." The CIA's special assassination capability was called "executive action." Civilian officials could protest their innocence and agency officials claim their approval from the same conversation. The logical extension of the doctrine, according to the Senate Intelligence Committee, was that "subordinates, in an effort to permit their superiors to 'plausibly deny' operations, fail to inform them about those operations."[23]

The need not to know was practiced throughout the covert apparatus. When J. Edgar Hoover showed Attorney General Robert Kennedy his scandalous report on Martin Luther King, Jr., Kennedy's main concern was apparently for his political reputation. (Lyndon Johnson's was apparently to order Bill Moyers to distribute the document.) Katzenbach's complaint about Hoover's use of partial authorization is matched by the universal unwillingness of any attorney general, including Katzenbach himself, to inquire further when suspicious pieces of paper passed by for signature.

Within each agency, the desire for "plausible denial" had a similar effect. Within the CIA, for example, informal procedures frequently supplanted formal ones, a sort of Gresham's law for secret bureaucracy. CIA officials

THE TROUBLE WITH CUTTING CORNERS

LAWS OF THE UNITED STATES ON USE OF POLICE AND INTELLIGENCE AGENCIES

COPYRIGHT 1975 BY HERBLOCK IN *THE WASHINGTON POST*

transmitted orders orally, or passed written orders along with a wink that effectively revoked them. As one anonymous official testified, "I don't think that you are going to find a piece of paper for everything that this Agency or any other Agency has done. There are lots of things that get done by word of mouth."[24] Written orders often provide merely a misleading "paper trail," designed to cover responsibility, a fact which severely hampered the congressional investigations. Shown a damaging memorandum composed by another official, General Marshall S. Carter, a former deputy director of the CIA in 1962, commented that "mumorandums [sic] for the record have very little validity in fact."[25]

One incident portrays the atmosphere best. In October 1960, Michael Mulroney, part of an "extremely secret" unit within the CIA, was asked by Richard Bissell, the director of the Clandestine Services, to assassinate Lumumba. Mulroney testified that he refused the assignment. After a second discussion with the persistent Bissell, Mulroney walked into the office of Richard Helms, Bissell's deputy, and told Helms that he was refusing the assignment. Mulroney testified, "In the Agency since you don't have documents you have to be awfully canny and you have to get things on the record." The oral exchange was to protect Mulroney, but in what way? Mulroney later went to the Congo. Was the discussion with Helms merely a cover story for his assignment? Helms knew not to ask any questions, and the Senate Committee could not find out.[26]

THE RULE BY NOBODY

In sum, the secret bureaus have been far from mere instruments of presidential whim, but have operated on a complex interrelationship, divorced from law. Hannah Arendt has described it as "the rule of an intricate system of bureaus in which no men, neither one nor the best, neither the few nor the many, can be held responsible and which could properly be called the Rule by Nobody."[27]

Intelligence officials operated on what Senator Howard Baker described aptly as a "common web of perceived authority."[28] The perceived authority developed within each bureau, according to its culture and its activities. A kind of common law of unauthorized activity evolved to chart plausible limits of authority. If the agency was engaged in warrantless wiretaps and bugs, it was a short step to mail openings and break-ins. This kind of logic was frequently found in the record. For example, when an anonymous CIA agent, who wanted guns shipped to the Dominican Republic in the diplomatic pouch, found the agency initially reluctant, he wired back that pistols had already been shipped in the diplomatic pouch in his previous two assignments. There was indeed precedent for his request; the guns were pouched, and Rafael Trujillo was eventually assassinated.[29]

The limits on the agencies were basically self-imposed. "Self-discipline," former Assistant Attorney General and current Supreme Court Justice William Rehnquist testified, "on the part of the executive branch will provide an answer to virtually all of the legitimate complaints against the excess of information gathering."[30] Richard Helms once said, "The nation must to a degree take it on faith that we too are honorable men devoted to her service."[31]

THE CRIMES OF STATE

The threat of a covert national security apparatus becomes clear from its operating principles. "National security," "internal security," "foreign intelligence," "in the national interest"—these are empty receptacles into which virtually any substance can be poured. Most important, they are inescapably political terms, requiring subjective political definition. Like all political decisions, the definition of the terms must be done publicly, with open discussion and debate.

When the president and undercover bureaus are left to define the terms in secret, predictable abuses occur. Inevitably, presidents tend to equate dissent with subversion, and opposition to the president with opposition to the national security. As Tom Charles Huston testified:

The risk was that you would get people who . . . would construe political considerations to be national security considerations, to move from the kid with the bomb, to the kid with the picket sign and from the kid with the picket sign to the kid with the bumper sticker of the opposition candidate.[32]

Thus, every postwar president used the clandestine bureaus to collect political as well as "internal security" data. The temptation was simply too great to ignore. Needless to say, the worst corruption came with the Nixon administration, when "national security" became part of the cover-up of the crimes of the president and his aides. The Nixon tapes provide the spectacle of the president, John Dean, and H. R. "Bob" Haldeman inventing a "national security justification" for the break-in at the office of Dr. Lewis Fielding, the psychiatrist of Daniel Ellsberg, the man who released the Pentagon Papers. When the president asked what could be done if the break-in were revealed publicly, Dean suggested, "You might put it on a national security basis." Later Nixon said, "With the bombing thing coming out, and everything coming out, the whole thing was national security." Dean replied, "I think we could get by on that."[33]

The presidential abuses are paralleled by similar bureaucratic excesses. Like the presidents, each bureau tended to equate criticism of it with criticism of the nation's security. Each secret bureau used its surveillance techniques to watch or harass its domestic critics. The IRS automatically institutes an audit of any public critic of the income tax, and sends informers to attend antitax meetings and take down names. Military intelligence agents were particularly concerned with critics of the military. Hoover was constantly directing the attention of his agents to critics of the bureau; name checks, field investigations, and often more would result.

The bureaucratic corruption was the use of secret political intelligence for institutional or personal purposes. Hoover, for example, was the master of the implied blackmail. He kept in his private office hundreds of "OC" (Official and Confidential) files, which reputedly detailed the private lives of politicians and federal officials. One can envision the scene at which Hoover informed Attorney General Robert F. Kennedy that a bureau wiretap on Sam "Momo" Giancana, the reputed Chicago Mafia capo, had picked up calls between the White House and Judith Campbell, "friend" to both Giancana and John F. Kennedy. Hoover no doubt reassured the young attorney general that not one word about the existence of these tapes need come out, as long as he, Hoover, remained in office. No doubt Kennedy complimented the director on his long and valuable service to his country, and assured him that his position was secure.

Far more serious than these "routine corruptions" is the conflict that occurs over who shall define "threats" to the national security. The secret bureaus consider themselves the repositories of expertise on subversion at home and abroad; it becomes their duty to protect Americans—even against themselves—in a world far crueler than any citizen could imagine. As time goes on, the bureaus thus become less and less responsive to outsiders, whether legislators, cabinet officials, or citizens. Inevitably a gap widens between the practices of the covert bureaus and the beliefs of the citizenry. When the consensus supporting the old policy dissipates—as it did in the jungles of Vietnam and the suites of the Watergate—a crisis ensues.

Thus, when the intelligence investigations started, the bureaus resisted, using every tactic of delay, obstruction, and obfuscation possible. The House Intelligence Committee, chaired by Congressman Otis Pike, concluded in its final report that "if this Committee's recent experience is any test, intelligence agencies that are to be controlled by Congressional lawmaking are, today, beyond the lawmakers' scrutiny."[34] Ironically, this conclusion was penned before the administration and the CIA managed to convince the House to suppress its own committee's report.

The House committee was not alone. FBI Director Clarence Kelley was deeply embarrassed when his sworn testimony that the bureau had terminated all illegal break-ins in 1966 was proved wrong, and break-ins were occurring during his own tenure as director. It seems clear that veteran bureau officials were continuing the activities they considered necessary, without telling even their own director. Similarly, career CIA officials didn't bother to inform CIA directors John McCone and Admiral Raborn—both outsiders to the agency—that the CIA was involved in assassination attempts against Castro, and was maintaining an illegal mail-opening program in the United States. Clearly as outsiders, the two might not recognize the need for such programs as well as intelligence veterans. It is this attitude, slowly built up over years of lawless activity in the nation's "interest," that can indeed threaten the entire notion of a government ruled by law and accountable to people.

"We become lawless in a struggle for the rule of law—semi-outlaws who risk their lives to put down the savagery of others," says Peter Ward, the CIA agent in a novel by E. Howard Hunt. Hunt would probably not understand the irony.

In the 1950s we were told that Communists used Aesopian language, infiltrated and disrupted political groups, subverted the free press and democratic process, and used "fronts" to mask their activities. Afraid of them, we have inevitably come to mirror our own image of them. To protect ourselves from the tyrannous, we have slowly built our own tyranny.

James Madison wrote: "At the foundation of our civil liberties lies the principle which denies to government officials an exceptional position before the law and which subjects them to the same rules of conduct that are commands to the citizen." In the end, the sides of the dual state, military and civil, secret and open, arbitrary and legal stand, in Edmund Burke's phrase, in "dreadful enmity." Now may be our last opportunity to decide against the nether side of the state.

CONTROLLING
THE INTELLIGENCE
AGENCIES

HAVE THE
CRIMES STOPPED?

11

There is a danger, now that Watergate is over and the official investigations of the intelligence agencies are concluded, that the country will be lulled into believing that the mere cataloguing of the abuses of the past has solved the problem for the future. It has not; revelations are not the same as reforms.

We still have what amounts to a clandestine branch of government: no safeguards have been installed, no new legislation has been enacted to restore the balance of power and define the proper functions of the intelligence agencies, and there is still no sign that the laws already on the books are going to be enforced against government officials. Nor does the record give any indication that the agencies have any internal braking system to keep their programs under control; their housecleaning gestures—such as they are—have come from a desire to short-circuit the possibility of reforms being imposed from the outside rather than from any change in attitudes. FBI Director Clarence Kelley reportedly wrote a private letter concerning his public "apology" for the bureau's COINTELPRO activities, explaining that it was made in the hope that it "might well prevent or at least somewhat retard the proliferation of highly restrictive legislation. . . . I want to

THE LAWLESS STATE

renew my pledge to all ex-agents to do my best to maintain the pre-eminence for the Bureau."[1] For the intelligence bureaucrat, the only real lesson of Watergate is "don't get caught," and reform translates into plugging up embarrassing leaks.

A raft of new revelations about fresh abuses came out in the weeks immediately following the publication of the Church Committee's "Final Report," showing how little effect mere exposure without structural change has on the agencies' bureaucratic momentum for interfering with politics. There is still no reason for intelligence officials to believe that the laws apply equally to them as to other citizens.

THE FBI

As the Senate Select Committee's staff report noted, "The Committee has not been able to determine with any greater precision the extent to which COINTELPRO may be continuing."[2] But all the available signs do indicate that COINTELPRO by other names is still going on. In the month of June 1976, for example—just after the official investigation of intelligence abuses had come to an end—a series of items about ongoing FBI activity appeared.

• FBI Director Clarence Kelley was forced to admit in court that, without "one shred of proof," the FBI had issued a nationwide alert against American Indian movement "terrorists" on July 4, 1976. The alert was apparently aimed at provoking violence by fearful law enforcement officials, and had the earmarks of a COINTELPRO-style smear campaign against AIM and the son of Senator James Abourezk, a leading critic of the intelligence community.[3]

• A leaked document showed that the FBI sent the CIA an intelligence report on a peaceful American Indian rally held in early June. The demonstrators had carried placards with anti-CIA slogans on them, and the FBI thought the CIA would be "interested" in who was expressing such lawful, domestic political opinion. In the now familiar scenario, the FBI greeted this charge with a denial, followed by an admission that a "mistake" had been made.[4]

• A damage suit brought by the Socialist Workers party brought to light documents which indicate that the FBI carried out at least eight burglaries of SWP offices during the first half of 1975, after the FBI had offered assurances that such tactics had ended in 1966.[5]

None of this should be surprising—the FBI still has a budget of $80 million per year to devote to intelligence,

COPYRIGHT 1975 BY HERBLOCK IN *THE WASHINGTON POST*

and inevitably that money is used for this kind of activity. All the things that insulated the FBI from reform under Hoover's tenure are still in place, and guidelines issued by the attorney general appear to sanction many past abuses. The bureau can still draw the cloak of secrecy over its activities; it still has extensive files and the implicit threat of blackmail or smear tactics; and there is still no FBI charter to curb its activities, to eliminate that $80 million in the budget, to establish safeguards against abuses, or to enforce the law against its excesses.

THE CIA

If one can judge from what has *not* surfaced, the CIA is not now conducting a massive surveillance program directed at lawful political activity. However, many domestic programs continue. The CIA recruits American and foreign students on domestic campuses. It uses professors and journalists as agents. It spies on foreigners in the United States and Americans abroad. It continues to conduct covert operations. The agency's effort to use Angola for a restaging of the Vietnam disaster was a close call. Leaving the CIA's covert-operations structure intact means that crucial decisions on America's role in the world are still made in secret. The lesson of Angola is that the bureaucracy has not changed, that the clandestine policy-making apparatus that has produced our long line of foreign-policy disasters is still in place and grinding on. The CIA still shores up dictatorships that torture people, it still interferes in democratic elections such as Italy's, and it still is not possible to determine the real scope of its activities. The CIA budget is still secret.

THE NSA

The massive National Security Agency is still reading all American overseas cables; only the techniques have changed. Because of technological advances, the NSA now can read all cables without needing the collusion of the cable companies; and it can eavesdrop on all overseas phone conversations and tie into computer lines.

MILITARY INTELLIGENCE

Military intelligence agencies overseas, as documented in the *Berlin Democratic Club* lawsuit, are still spying on American civilians and interfering in lawful political activities. The present scope of domestic military intelligence activity is unclear. However, the directives governing military practices remain as vague and indefinite as the orders that fostered the abuses of the past.

THE GRAND JURIES

Federal prosecutors continue to twist the constitutional function of the grand jury, using it not as a buffer between the innocent and government harassment but as an inquisition to extract information about political activities. Grand juries are still being used as an intelligence arm of government and people are still being jailed—without due process protection—when they resist; the only change is that the current subjects for such investigations are now the American Indian movement and the Puerto Rican independence movement.

NO ENFORCEMENT

The Justice Department has yet to approach the task of enforcing the laws against the intelligence community with the same zeal that it still uses in dealing with dissidents. In July 1976, Justice Department lawyers recommended against prosecuting CIA officials involved in the mail-opening operation; they decided that presidential knowledge of the program—which neither the Rockefeller Commission nor the congressional investigations were able to find—was enough to authorize CIA officials to violate federal criminal statutes without fear of prosecution.[6] And they decided this despite the fact that there are no provisions in the Constitution, no statutes, and no court decisions that grant the president the authority to make illegal activity legal.

REFORMS—REAL OR COSMETIC?

Politically, the cry for reform cannot be ignored by either the executive branch or the Congress. When it became clear that the intelligence community was keeping files on members of Congress, giving LSD to unsuspecting middle-Americans, and that the White House was using CIA talent to rig a presidential election, the abuses of the intelligence agencies became everyone's problem, and not merely that of the vocal political minority. In a police state, no one is safe. But there is a serious danger that the reform measures which are taken will be cosmetic rather than real—that they will amount to little more than putting a layer of dusting powder over the symptoms of disease in the body politic and pretending that the illness has been cured. And this is precisely what the "reforms" of the Ford administration would do.

President Ford found himself in an election year, holding on to an explosive issue, and he had to do something—not only to deal with his own campaign problems but to deflect the possibility of congressional reforms that would shift the balance of power away from the executive.

The White House has put together a strategy that gives the appearance but not the substance of reform. Its first tack was to repeat that mere revelation is reform. Its second was to promulgate pseudo-reforms. The administration has used the conveniently circular arrangement of using executive branch authority to keep watch against executive branch abuses of authority; it sounds like reform, but it quietly authorizes almost all the activities that the investigations had intended to repudiate. And third, the administration has tried the experiment of using Congress to legitimate its activities—it has submitted a bill to "reform" the use of wiretaps, which would give the intelligence agencies congressional authority to wiretap Americans who have not broken the law, and it seeks secrecy legislation which would provide criminal penalties for future leaks of agency wrongdoing.

REVELATIONS AS REFORM

Administration spokespersons have played upon the seemingly reasonable assumption that to reveal abuses is to reform the situation. The old assurance that "it can't happen here" has been rephrased as "it can't happen again." They will admit that the intelligence bureaucracies had perhaps been carried away in their well-intentioned enthusiasm to guard the nation's security, but now that they are on notice that they should obey the law, the problem, they say, is solved. And the fact that we now know so much more about them than we did before conveys a false sense of having got to the root of the situation.

But the intelligence bureaucracies are still in place, and the programs are still going on. To say that putting the agencies on notice will stop the activities that they have been carrying on for decades is simply not to give the phenomenon of bureaucratic momentum its due. There is no sign from the FBI, for example, that they understand why COINTELPRO was wrong, or even *that* it was wrong, but only that it got them in trouble when it came out. This true response, on the other side of a press release, is to increase secrecy so there will be no more revelations.

EXECUTIVE REFORM OF THE EXECUTIVE

History has created a natural expectation that when some disaster hits the nation the public can look to the president to deal with it. And in the ordinary run of crises this is precisely the role that the Constitution intended for the chief executive. But when the threat to the nation has been the burgeoning of secret power within a clandestine arm of the executive branch, turning to the president's men for help is an inherent contradiction. What is needed in such a situation is a return to a government of laws, and not of men.

The "reforms" of Ford's executive order and Attorney General Edward Levi's new guidelines for the FBI prove the point. Both show the clear marks of having been written by the very people that they are supposed to control. They give the intelligence bureaucrats everything that they've wanted, and at the same time they cover up the fact that there is no reform. The executive order ends up with the presidency giving the president's men in the intelligence community more power, decreased congressional oversight, and still more secrecy. The FBI guidelines, for their part, allow all the investigations that have been discredited.

The provisions of the executive order and the guidelines offer us the president and the attorney general as the primary bulwarks against the future abuse of secret power. When asked what would happen if the president did not take this role seriously, Ford assured the American people that they would not elect an unreliable president, and he offered this assurance a scant four years after the landslide victory of Richard Nixon in 1972; Ford also missed the irony in the fact that he himself is an unelected president, selected by a disgraced predecessor. And while Attorney General Levi may well be the honest and reliable man he seems, there is nothing in the guidelines to protect the nation if the next attorney general is of John Mitchell's mold. With the executive branch alone standing between political freedom and a police state, we do not have a government of laws, but of men; and there is no inherent reason why the nation should expect to be luckier in its officials from now on.

"Reforms" issued by the executive branch can be repealed in total on whim. Officials also assume that they can be repealed on a case-by-case basis; if the president or the attorney general instructs an official to bend the rules of the executive order or the guidelines, there is every reason to expect compliance. Their oral instructions will be seen as superceding the earlier written regulations.

There is another inherent contradiction in offering an executive order as an effective device for reforming the abuses of executive power. Unlike legislation, which requires public debate and a vote if it is to be dropped or altered, an executive order stands or falls at the whim of the current president. The Ford reform package contains an example of this: a 1967 executive order outlawed CIA involvement in universities and voluntary organizations, and the 1976 executive order quietly reauthorizes it.

EXECUTIVE ORDER 11905[7]

Whatever the inherent contradictions, the Ford executive order is now the effective law governing the intelligence agencies. Slickly packaged for television consumption, it uses the rhetoric of the civil libertarian: we need to "preserve and respect our established concepts of privacy and civil liberties" and ensure that intelligence "activities are conducted in a Constitutional and lawful manner and never aimed at our own citizens." To do this, the executive order offers "tough new restrictions," which have a fine ring in a press release but which are quietly canceled out in the fine print. Some of these are listed here.

• Physical surveillance of Americans is prohibited, *unless* approved by the agency's head and directed at someone who is or who was an employee of the agency, a contractor of the agency, an employee of a contractor, or anyone who is in contact with such people. The intelligence agencies now have presidential authority to tail United States citizens.

• The executive order gives new life to CIA's rationale for infiltrating domestic groups; it allows foreign intelligence agencies to collect information on "persons or activities that pose a clear threat to intelligence facilities or personnel." This was the same justification given by the CIA for infiltrating Women Strike for Peace and other nonviolent antiwar groups.

• The executive order allows surveillance of persons "reasonably believed to be acting on behalf of a foreign power," which is another of the oft-repeated reasons the intelligence agencies gave for watching antiwar groups, in spite of the fact that the surveillances never found links to foreign influence.

• An intelligence agency can still claim that it is considering offering someone a job—whether or not the subject would have any interest in working for the agency—as a rationale for investigation.

• The executive order authorizes the National Security Agency to monitor all overseas communications of Americans; anyone who makes any contact with foreigners, including totally legitimate personal or business contacts, becomes fair game under the executive order.

• What the executive order omits is also significant. It places a ban on "political assassination," but fails to mention anything about kidnapping, extortion, bribery, blackmail, paramilitary adventure, coups d'état, torture, etc. By omitting them, it sanctions these tactics.

• And as if to make certain that there are no more embarrassing leaks of the type that started the flow of disclosures about the intelligence bureaucracy's operations, the executive order provides for stricter secrecy. Now, all members of the executive branch and its contractors must sign an agreement not to disclose information about "intelligence sources and methods," the favorite secrecy catch-all. Backing this up, the order claims authority to censor, by giving the agencies the right to impose prior restraints on publication through court orders.

The Ford "reform" package revives the rationales of the old threats to civil liberties, and it does so without even trying to install safeguards against their abuse. The executive order could have tried, for example, to install safeguards that would limit the records on surveillances to information that relates to criminal activities, or it could have included criteria specifying when a surveillance should be ended if no evidence of illegal activity has turned up. Instead, virtually unlimited surveillance is authorized and the only safeguard is the approval of the attorney general. It makes no mention of adhering to the Fourth Amendment's requirement for warrants. Nor does it respond to the fact that past abuses were carried out at all levels of government, from the president and the attorney general on down.

There is also nothing in the order's provisions that tells officials what they have to lose if they once again stretch their authority to bizarre and destructive lengths. There are no provisions for a special prosecutor, for instance, or even for a more aggressive Justice Department program for investigating and prosecuting abuses of power.

The only possible conclusion is that there were no efforts at installing safeguards because it was *not* the executive order's purpose to remedy the abuses of the intelligence agencies. But the Ford administration's package had to present at least the appearance of reform, and it had to present some token solution to the possibility of future abuses of clandestine government power. It does this by keeping everything within the executive branch—by establishing phony oversight mechanisms that are guaranteed to be ineffective. The intelligence community is supposed to self-police itself; the fox is sent to guard the henhouse.

The administration's reforms propose that executive branch employees with knowledge of "questionable activities" in the foreign intelligence agencies should go to the "appropriate authorities." But the president attaches a catch-22: Congress is an appropriate authority only if a regularly constituted committee already knows enough to ask for specific information. Otherwise, the only authority to whom a lower-echelon official with a troubled conscience can turn is the president's Intelligence Oversight Board set up by the executive order. There are literally no provisions for taking information of wrongdoing outside the executive branch's system of self-interests. An official with knowledge of abuses is told to go through channels within the hierarchy that spawned those abuses, a process guaranteed to be ineffective.

While the order specifies that Oversight Board members may not have *present* ties to the agencies they oversee, there is nothing preventing them from being former members of the intelligence community. Ford's appointment of three veterans of the intelligence community is a clear signal that the Intelligence Oversight Board is there for appearances only.

Moreover, lower-echelon officials are not given direct access to the Oversight Board. Reports of questionable activities are, instead, to be filtered through the Office of the Inspectors General, who themselves have a well-established history of assisting cover-ups; they have in the past produced papers on "potential flap activities" that their agencies should take care to conceal.

Even assuming that the board did decide that something was improper, it is only authorized to report it to the president and/or the attorney general. The Ford executive oversight system is designed so that there are no "appropriate authorities" outside the executive branch hierarchy; neither the uneasy official, the inspector general, nor the Oversight Board members are authorized to report wrongdoings to Congress or to a special prosecutor, whether or not the president or the attorney general acts on it.

In spite of the administration's assurances about the integrity of the new post-Watergate bureaucrat, the executive reforms show no sign that official cynicism has lapsed, or, more charitably, that its myopia has improved. Even with the incredibly broad authority for abuse that the executive order gives the intelligence agencies, it provides no measures for enforcing those few restrictions that remain. There are no new structures that could provide some sense that officials will be held accountable. Indeed, the day after the order was issued, the Justice Department announced that it had decided not to prosecute Richard Helms for a burglary that the Rockefeller Commission had cited as clearly illegal.

But perhaps most chilling of all is the knowledge that, although the executive order rides roughshod over the Bill of Rights, its provisions are in fact the law that governs intelligence investigations unless one of three things happens: some future president designs a new executive order more to his liking; the issues reach the courts, giving them a chance to start striking down the most egregious provisions; or Congress takes the initiative and passes legislation that will override it.

THE FBI GUIDELINES[8]

The executive order makes some mention of the functions of the FBI, but it states explicitly that none of the "restrictions" applies to the bureau. The rules that are to control the FBI are found instead in the guidelines covering Domestic Security Investigations, which Attorney General Levi issued. The executive order does authorize the bureau to "detect and prevent . . . subversion . . . on behalf of foreign powers." Such spying and preventive action is nothing more than COINTELPRO revived; it is the meting out of punishments without the safeguards of due process in court to determine whether a crime has been committed or who is guilty. The administration is seemingly unaware that "subversion" is not a crime; it is only what someone in the FBI doesn't approve of.

In the face of this broad grant of power, the FBI guidelines politely ask the bureau to try to be reasonable about who they investigate—but then the bureau has always felt its operations were reasonable. As the comptroller general concluded, ". . . the language in the draft guidelines would not cause any substantial change in the number and type of domestic intelligence investigations initiated."[9] And when one considers that in 1974 there were some 30,000 ongoing intelligence investigations, the scope of the nonsolution is staggering.

All that the guidelines require is an allegation—which could be no more than an anonymous letter—that a person or group will *at some time* use violence for political ends. Inevitably, the FBI will rely on its past practices to determine subjects for its 30,000 intelligence investigations. The guidelines contain nothing to alter the bureaucratic momentum that has long been established; the FBI continues to investigate even those groups which the bureau admits are nonrevolutionary but which might, at some time in the future, be infiltrated or co-opted.

The guidelines' restrictions rely on language so broad that it guarantees expansive interpretation by FBI agents in the field. Domestic security investigations are allowed in order "to ascertain information" concerning the use of "force or violence and the violation of federal law, for the purpose of . . . impairing, for the purpose of influencing U.S. government policies or decisions . . . the functioning of the government of the United States . . . ." Since all political debate is intended ultimately to influence government policies, the most well-intentioned of agents could not possibly determine where to draw the line with such a grant of authority. And as if this were not broad enough, the guidelines toss in the bureau's catch-all category, "impairing . . . interstate commerce." Since crossing state lines has an effect on interstate commerce, this would reauthorize investigations of people traveling to join political meetings, conferences, or demonstrations.

The attorney general's guidelines rely on a distinction between "preliminary" and "full" investigations, which differ in the kinds of investigative techniques that are allowed. Yet past practice gives no reason to believe that this will in fact limit investigative techniques: agents in the field have traditionally thought of such distinctions as a lot of headquarters nonsense, to be honored in the breach. There is nothing in the attorney general's reform program that works against the bureau's established operations. They permit the FBI to remain a clandestine arm of the executive branch, which must justify its actions only to itself, not to the public, or even to a court.

And the guidelines do not apply at all if the bureau believes an American to be an agent of a foreign power.

Due process of law requires hearing *both* sides of an issue, but there is no way that the attorney general's guidelines can be seen as doing that. The attorney general is supposed to be the safeguard for America's political freedom; and while it would be encouraging if such were the case, there is nothing in the traditions of the office that lead one to believe that. As a reform, the guidelines consist of executive oversight of the executive, instead of a balancing of powers in the way that the Constitution mandates.

USING CONGRESS TO LEGITIMATE ABUSES

The third tack that the executive branch has taken amounts to asking Congress to legitimate their abuses. The Ford administration has introduced two bills to Congress—both styled as "reforms"—which provide clear examples of the kind of ambushes waiting on the road to legislating real reforms.

The first bill was presented as part of a package with the executive order. Since the order takes care of any possibility of the intelligence agencies operating illegal programs again—or so the reasoning went—the president was asking for legislation to reform an "abuse" perpetrated against the intelligence agencies: violating the secrecy of "intelligence sources and methods." He conveniently glossed over, however, the fact that this proposed bill of his meant closing off the very leaks that had lifted the cover off intelligence abuses and started the investigations. Regardless of whether or not the information would damage the national security, an official leaking an intelligence scandal could be fined $5,000 and/or imprisoned for five years. Under the terms of the bill, even members of Congress would not be authorized to receive such information; only if an authorized committee requested the information could an official safely release it to them. But this is itself a play upon a well-known executive catch-22—that committees dealing with clandestine agencies generally have no idea what kind of information to be asking for.

The bill also contains a number of dubious provisions making it extremely easy not only to win a conviction but also to take members of the press who publish such leaks before a grand jury to force them to reveal their sources on threat of jail for contempt.

Not much has been heard from Congress about the Ford secrecy bill, fortunately. The administration has had somewhat better luck getting attention for a wiretap bill (S.3197) that it submitted after its proposed secrecy bill. This bill proposes to regulate and control national security wiretaps by requiring warrants for them—the executive still claims that such warrants are not required under the law. The proposed warrant protections, however, are no more than rubber stamps; the bill would limit the court's role to accepting and certifying the findings of the attorney general on whether or not such taps were needed in the interest of national security. At the same time, the bill, if passed, would provide the first congressional authorization for national security wiretaps, which previously have been conducted only with the tenuous catch-all claim of "inherent presidential power." In addition, it would constitute the first congressional authorization in the nation's history of "intelligence" investigations, i.e., investigations of Americans who are not suspected of violating any law. In the name of reform, Congress has been asked to pass S.3197 and to sanction intelligence wiretaps and investigations.

DESIGNING
EFFECTIVE REFORMS

12

The time and the need have clearly come for designing effective reforms; the executive branch's cosmetic reforms—the executive order, the FBI guidelines, and the proposed secrecy and wiretap reform bills—are only diversionary tactics, which lead away from real changes. They perpetuate two problems: first they operate on basic assumptions about what is necessary for maintaining the national security that have already been proved wrong and, second, accountability still relies on human beings in the executive branch rather than on the law.

Patching a few regulations on to the same old activities and restating threadbare exhortations cannot be called reform—these cannot protect civil liberties or lead to less disastrous foreign policy decisions. It is now necessary to challenge the assumptions that have been used to justify the intelligence agencies.

Part of the problem stems from the fact that the intelligence agencies were created on an almost ad hoc basis; they were never really put together with a coherent overview of how they would fit into the nation's constitutional framework, into its basic political design of checks and balances of power. Since their intelligence functions were secret, much of their institutional design has also been kept secret. And in spite of the obvious potentials for abuses of power that come with any clandestine organization, there has never been any counterbalancing system of safeguards designed into their structures.

The abuses of the intelligence agencies are one of the symptoms of the amassing of power in the postwar presidency; the only way to safeguard against future crimes is to alter that balance of power. The documented abuses have been part of the system itself, not merely the excesses of overzealous officials. Therefore the system must also be called to account, and not merely individuals.

Legislated reforms, carefully designed to provide again for basic political values, are needed. Congress must again take on its share of constitutional responsibility for determining the course of the nation in foreign affairs and for keeping the domestic situation open to political debate.

Any system of real, rather than cosmetic, reform of the intelligence agencies requires a three-pronged attack on the problem. First, the basic assumptions about the need for unquestioned presidential power over a clandestine branch of government must be revised. Second, the items in the Bill of Rights which safeguard political debate must be clarified and shored up by legislation. And third, there must be a system of legislated charters that define what the functions of the intelligence agencies are and what penalties are attached to breaking the law; mechanisms for enforcing these laws from outside the executive branch must be established.

FIRST REFORM: END CLANDESTINE GOVERNMENT

The intelligence agencies are in effect a clandestine government operating within the executive branch of the federal government. They act under a cover of secrecy far more impenetrable than that of the overt agencies of the national security apparatus. Even their budgets, in violation of the Constitution, are considered national security secrets. Clandestine government means that Americans give up something for nothing—they give up their right to participation in the political process and to informed consent in exchange for grave assaults on basic rights and a long record of serious policy failures abroad.

To disguise this reality, the secret realm of government has covered itself with a glossy layer of self-issued propaganda, and, under the cover of secrecy, it is able to weave what myths it will about its operations. The recent exposures have revealed a reality that does not come close to justifying the wounds that clandestine government inevitably inflicts on the body polit

The Need for Secrecy: Myth and Reality

The clandestine agencies have taken the "national security secret" and stretched it to the point of absurdity. The Defense Department also has authority to use the classification stamp and, while no one seriously disagrees that it is grossly overused, its secrecy is of an entirely different order. The DoD is not a clandestine organization: the details of its budget are annually subject to lively public debate, its personnel publicly identify themselves, and its bases are there for the world to see. The presumption for this kind of secrecy is that the stamp is supposed to be used only to cover *facts*, which if released would injure the national security.

With the secret realm of government, the organizations themselves and not just specific facts concerning some of their operations are secret. Their budgets are secret; their personnel use covers to conceal their affiliation; their installations are closely guarded secrets—and all this whether or not any specific fact could damage the national security.

Even in ordinary circumstances the classification stamp is routinely overused, but clandestine government by its very nature practices a supersecrecy that insulates it from all accountability and from constitutional processes of government.

The clandestine bureaus maintain that this supersecrecy is essential to the security of the nation. The presidency has zealously guarded what amounts to the office's secret policy; successive presidents have made extravagant claims that the Constitution—somewhere between the lines—grants them the power to carry on secret warfare and to interfere in the affairs of other countries without congressional knowledge or consent and without public support. They have claimed that the intelligence agencies can make secret and unrestricted use of any of the arsenal of morally repugnant covert-action techniques against countries with which America may have, as in the case of Chile, Senate-approved treaties respecting their sovereignty. They have claimed that, whenever they choose, they are entitled secretly to suspend the laws protecting Americans themselves, and to turn these same tactics against the political process within the United States. And to do these things, they claim that all they need say is that the national security requires it and that these activities can and should remain buried forever within the files of the intelligence bureaucracies, which need never come into the open and justify their operations.

The president does have great powers in time of crisis. The commander in chief during time of declared war was certainly meant to have considerable discretion; but only Congress can declare war and it is hardly likely that the framers intended to give the president the power to wage secret war. The president also has the power to declare martial law in times of great domestic crisis; but again, it seems unlikely that the framers ever intended this to mean the right *secretly* to suspend the laws of the land against the critics of his policies in the ordinary course of debate.

Nor is the claim of national security convincing. Generally, the secrecy has been used more to disguise government policy from American citizens than to protect information from the prying eyes of the KGB. The victims of America's covert actions generally know or suspect who stands behind the upheaval. United States government officials admit that experts in the Soviet Union know more about American policies abroad than American citizens do.

Supersecrecy, of course, has other, more pragmatic advantages for the clandestine agencies, which have nothing to do with national security. For example, the secrecy of the clandestine government has enabled executive officials to make exaggerated claims about the need for and utility of covert operations—and no one outside has had the facts to refute them. "Our failures are trumpeted; our successes go unheralded" is the slogan of the CIA. But we now know this is hokum. The operations that CIA officials consider "successes"—like the overthrow of Allende in Chile or the secret war in Laos—most Americans find repugnant. If the agency had any secret successes more convincing, they certainly would have been revealed in the recent investigations. And the agency's "trumpeted failures" have damaged America's international reputation far more than any hidden successes could justify.

Supersecrecy enables the executive officials to control information critical to public debate. As a result, they may manipulate the media by selectively declassifying information that supports their pet projects, by planting and suppressing stories in the "free press," by discrediting critics, by allowing and encouraging disinformation tactics within the United States, and by generally seeing to it that the public and the Congress know only what they want them to.

The logical extension of this mind-set is made clear by the FBI's disruption programs. These operations are predicated on the belief that American democracy cannot work, that if ideas which the bureau decides are "subversive" are allowed to circulate freely, the Communists will "win." The operating assumption is that the public and its congressional representatives cannot be trusted, have no judgment, and therefore must hear only what the intelligence bureaucracy wants them to. The idea was to establish a prepackaged consensus at any cost, even if it was to be a pseudo-consensus based on myth.

For intelligence officials, the need to control information and maintain all-encompassing secrecy over the secret realm of government reaches the level of a maniacal obsession; their reasoning turns upon absurd premises that they cannot recognize. The curious twists and turns of their inbred logic end by, in effect, treating the legitimate interests of the public and the Congress—which they are supposed to be protecting—as if they were identical to those of avowed enemies.

For example, the CIA has claimed that it cannot make public its gross budget figure—as the Constitution requires—because of what the Pike Committee report called some "rather obscure understandings the Russians might derive" from it.[1] Even if one takes this at face value, it is amazing that these self-proclaimed defenders of truth and democracy fail to recognize that their logic is based on a premise that the interests of the American people are either indistinguishable from or subservient to the interests of Russian agents. Even if—and this is doubtful—the Russians might derive some small benefit, could this possibly outweigh the public's constitutional interest in knowing where its money is spent? Yet clandestine government recoils at the thought of balancing its supersecrecy against democratic values, even where national security interests are not genuinely involved.

The supersecrecy of clandestine organizations also comes home in a more insidious, more complex way—it controls the flow of information not only to the public but to the decisionmakers of government. The way in which clandestine intelligence feeds information into the national security apparatus inevitably distorts the way in which critical issues are treated.

The cultish secrecy that they practice ends in crippling their own ability to analyze and use intelligence. Ironies abound: the NSA reports indicating that war was about to break out in the Middle East in 1973 were considered too "sensitive" to be disseminated to a key military analyst—and there was thus no way for him to predict the war.[2]

The mythology of clandestine government is so pervasive that even experts and high officials are not in a position to distinguish fact from fiction. The dissemination of information within the executive branch is controlled in order to discourage dissent among the decisionmakers in the same way that information is controlled in order to discourage dissent among private individuals. The result is that people who might object to the feasibility of schemes, such as the Bay of Pigs fiasco, are simply excluded from the decisionmaking process. Those who do not subscribe to the cold-war cult simply do not rise in the ranks; they lack toughness, we are told.

When clandestine agencies control information, potential critics are cut out of the policy debate at every possible turn—the design of the secrecy system is not só much to protect sensitive information from the Russians as to close off debate, wherever that debate may crop up, whether in the press, the halls of Congress, or the corridors of the CIA. One initial reform must therefore be to reduce secrecy drastically. A common-sense rule of thumb provides an adequate first step: policy decisions and the information necessary to discuss them must be public; the details of technological invention or tactical operations need not be declassified. Thus the budgets and guidelines for the intelligence agencies must be publicly debated. The types of activities undertaken by these agencies must be publicly discussed, and their operations periodically reviewed.

It is paradigmatic that you cannot check on the effectiveness or reliability of a clandestine organization. It is only with the recent intelligence investigations that the intelligence agencies' claims of effectiveness have been measured against real information rather than against propaganda. And the results do not inspire confidence that they can do what they have been set up for.

The CIA was created so that there would never be another Pearl Harbor, and yet it has frequently failed to predict the outbreak of major armed conflicts, from the Tet offensive to the 1973 Middle East War. President Johnson learned of the 1968 Soviet invasion of Czechoslovakia from the Soviet ambassador. The multibillion-dollar intelligence community didn't warn him because it had misplaced the Soviet army in Poland for two weeks. These were not small operations; they were each someone's Pearl Harbor. (The FBI, by the same token, always cites street crime and organized crime when making its plea for ever more authority; yet the statistics show ever increasing street crime, and the Mafia has been alive and well and conspiring with the CIA.)

When the executive justifies its covert operations, it makes claims that they are an absolutely vital part of the nation's foreign policy, that the security of the United States requires such an arsenal—yet the suppressed House Select Intelligence Committee report was unable to find indications "that covert action has been used in furtherance of any particular principle, form of government, or identifiable national interest."[3] CIA defenders offer us the specter of Soviet power, the KGB, and the Chinese hordes. What they fail to mention is more significant: they have never been able successfully to use espionage or covert action techniques against the USSR or China, which are the only two nations that could conceivably threaten the United States. CIA propaganda makes great claims for its cloak-and-dagger operations, but the embarrassing reality is that virtually all our reliable information on these two countries comes from open sources and from technological means such as spy satellites, computers, and electronics. These are all techniques that can be openly acknowledged and do not require a clandestine organization, even if the details of their operations should be kept secret. The "successes" of covert action and espionage, of which the CIA is so proud, have taken place in countries that are no threat to the security of the United States.

As for espionage, once you factor in human error, divided loyalties, and double, triple, and quadruple agents, it becomes clear that the human spy is singularly unreliable and technologically obsolete. Using spies also means that you must invest in a system of special favors, bribes, covers, blackmail, and protection—all of which corrupt American society. And since the most sought-after and valued spies are those who are highly placed in their governments, it becomes clear that using them is not an innocuous, passive intrusion such as a spy satellite; they inevitably become a covert-action technique. This is simply unacceptable in a country with which we are not at war and with which we have treaties of friendship. Spies and covert action are counterproductive as tools in international relations. The costs are too high; the returns too meager. Covert action and spies should be banned and the CIA's Clandestine Services Branch disbanded.

SECOND REFORM: LEGISLATED SAFEGUARDS FOR THE POLITICAL PROCESS

The intelligence agencies, caught in the act of violating state or federal statutes and the Constitution, have responded with a set refrain: we thought there was a national security exemption. And this "national security exemption," it turns out, has been applied to any aspect of the political process about which the intelligence bureaucrats harbored doubts. Remarkable though it may seem, the Senate Select Committee found it necessary to begin its recommendations with this: "There is no inherent constitutional authority for the President or any intelligence agency to violate the law."[4]

The Supreme Court has repeatedly held that the Constitution is not a suicide pact and that it is not necessary to carry its provisions to the lengths of logical absurdity in the face of compelling state interests. But the executive branch has acted as if any claim of overriding national security requirements, no matter how cynical, fatuous, or strained, automatically gave it authority to ride roughshod over constitutional guarantees. The intelligence community has carried its biases to logical absurdities of its own, such as watching the Socialist Workers party in the interest of national security because, among other legal activities, it was trying to undermine the country by "running candidates for public office."

If the intelligence agencies are to be controlled, legislated safeguards must be enacted to ensure that the government cannot stretch legal interpretations to permit it to interfere with the political process. Congress does not have to wait for the courts to declare something unconstitutional; it can pass legislation that makes intelligence agency abuses clearly illegal and it can create structures that will ensure these laws are enforced.

Preventive Action   The intelligence agencies have made extensive use of programs designed to disrupt, discredit, and "neutralize" the political activity of people and organizations they did not approve of. Such programs are euphemistically called "preventive action." They are supposed to prevent violence, often by using violent covert-action techniques. Preventive action has been the rationale for the entire range of COINTELPRO activities against people and organizations that officials felt might someday, in the indefinite future, develop into a criminal conspiracy. In effect, this has allowed bureaucrats to act as judge and jury, and to mete out punishments for crimes that have not been committed, according to their prejudices, with no regard to the due-process safeguards of the Fifth Amendment.

To defend its prerogatives for carrying out "preventive action" the FBI relies on horror stories; it paints vivid pictures of an epidemic of terrorism breaking out if it is not allowed total discretion. It neglects to mention that it already has the legal power to deal with actual threats of violence.

What preventive action really means is the right to carry out covert operations against political activity. Legislation should outlaw it completely; to allow any leeway is an open invitation to continue COINTELPRO.

"Intelligence" Investigations: Unconstitutional   The intelligence agencies have maintained that the Bill of Rights does not apply to their operations. Constitutional

safeguards, they say, apply only to criminal, not "intelligence," investigations, because the latter do not lead to prosecution. This reasoning leads to the logical conclusion that if you are a criminal, you are fully protected by the Constitution; but if you are a politically minded citizen, the government can investigate all your personal and public activities and even engage in "preventive action" if it dislikes your goals.

Intelligence investigations are unconstitutional, and legislation should mandate that the *only* lawful investigations are for crime—never politics. First, the record shows that such investigations are designed to chill the freedom of speech and association that the First Amendment guarantees. Second, they are not based on the Fourth Amendment standard, which requires a judicial warrant issued by an impartial magistrate and based on probable cause to believe that a crime has been or is about to be committed. Third, the record shows that information collected by "intelligence" investigations *does* end in criminal prosecutions. Legislation should put an end to this legal fiction that the executive has created for itself.

Speech Crimes There is, however, one catch to safeguarding political debate by allowing only criminal investigations—the cold-war era's "speech crimes" contained in 18 U.S.C. 2383-2386, which are still on the books. The Smith Act makes it a crime to advocate the overthrow of the government by violence, and the Voorhis Act tries to control the right of free political association. The Supreme Court has narrowed the meaning of the statutes so that the proscribed speech and association must involve activity that actually incites others to overthrow the government. In practice, all that these statutes provide now is the excuse the FBI needs for investigating political activity— mere speech *might*, they say, in spite of the Court's limitations making it almost impossible to secure convictions under the acts, still turn out to be criminal. The Justice Department's new guidelines for controlling FBI investigations continue to authorize use of the Smith Act as the basis for preliminary investigations. As long as these speech crimes remain on the books, political debate will be treated as suspect, and political surveillance will continue.

Investigative Techniques The intelligence agencies have been able to move major covert operations through loopholes that they have cut in the Bill of Rights for investigative techniques. These should be subject to legislation; the techniques used are such an important aspect of the government's power to intrude on all aspects of personal and political life that it is essential they be carefully restricted.

Wiretaps and other telecommunications and electronic taps should be banned outright; they can never fulfill the standards of the Fourth Amendment because they can never avoid the vacuum-cleaner effect—picking up personal information about not only the subject, but about other people who have no connection with the investigation under way. They sweep up everything before it, including any vestige of privacy. "Surreptitious entry" should be seen for what it is—the common crime of burglary—and treated as such.

Mail openings, mail covers, and searches of bank records and phone records should be allowed only with a judicial warrant, issued under Fourth Amendment standards and with minimization procedures to protect those aspects of citizens' lives that do not relate to the criminal investigation at hand.

The use of informers has been a particularly thorny legal problem. On the theory that the Fourth Amendment does not protect people from having bad judgment about their friends, the Court has in the past not placed any restrictions on the use of informers. Yet informers have been one of the most destructive and dubious investigative techniques in use. They are often people of disreputable character, without training or discipline, working only for the money and passing all information—both personal and political—into the files of the intelligence agencies. Since informers are paid on the basis of how much information they bring in, it is in their interest to distort or create facts to fit what sells well back at the bureau or the agency. For example, bureau informant Timothy Redfearn testified that, in response to "pressure" from the FBI to earn his $400 a month informer's fee, he twice burglarized Socialist Workers Party offices in Denver and gave the documents to his "handler," John Almon. Redfearn has, according to court records, been under a psychiatrist's care for several years for "intermittent depression."[5]

In a number of ways, informers are a far more serious problem to political freedom than are wiretaps and bugs, which are at least a passive intrusion; informers are human beings who work their way into someone's trust and actively pry out statements. And informers, posing as real members of an organization, influence events and distort the political process by voting and by taking positions of leadership within organizations. At their worst, informers have acted as agents provocateurs, inciting violence and supplying weapons and know-how, encouraging the very violence they claim to be preventing.

The use of paid informers should be eliminated, but citizens should be able to exchange information about criminal activity for promises of protection if that seems appropriate. In no circumstances should informers be planted in political groups, since informers in such groups must participate in and distort the political process.

The enormous recordkeeping and dissemination systems of the government constitute another loophole in the Bill of Rights—one which the framers of the Constitution could not have foreseen. The Privacy Act of 1974 is only a step toward protecting individuals from some of the implications of the government's singular ability to collect information on people. The Senate Select Committee recommended that the FBI be prohibited from disseminating information to the White House, the public, or the press for political or improper use. The only information that it should be possible to exchange should be evidence of a specific crime, and then only to the agency responsible for enforcement.

The Grand Juries   The Justice Department has taken the grand jury, originally included in the Bill of Rights as a safeguard against harassing prosecution, and transmuted it into a technically legal intelligence arm of the government. Legislation should be passed to reestablish and safeguard the role that the framers intended for it. A number of bills for reforming grand jury abuse have been proposed; the most comprehensive take the following measures:

• Witnesses should have a right to counsel in the grand jury room, a right against compelled self-incrimination, a right to be notified whether they are a potential defendant, and a right to know what the subject of the investigation is.

• Witnesses should be given at least seven days' notice that they must appear, and should be notified of their newly established rights before the grand jury.

• The witness should have a right to ask for a change of venue. "Use immunity" should be abolished, only "transactional immunity" should be permitted, and then only on a voluntary basis.

• The rules of evidence should be the same as in courts: no more use of hearsay, the fruits of illegal searches and warrantless wiretaps, or irrelevant and prejudicial evidence.

• Contempt sentences for refusing to testify should be limited to six months; double jeopardy should be ended by making this six-month limit apply to all testimony on the same subject before later grand juries.

• Indictments should be handed down only if the evidence on which they are based is legally sufficient, competent, and admissible in court, and if the government has presented all the exculpatory evidence in its possession.

• Finally, a statute to reform grand jury proceedings should require that jurors be instructed of their rights, powers, and functions—that they are not a rubber stamp for the prosecutor but an independent body historically intended to safeguard people from government harassment.

THIRD REFORM: LAWS TO GOVERN THE INTELLIGENCE AGENCIES

The third prong for reforming the intelligence agencies is to establish legislated charters that will make explicit what they may and may not do, who will be enforcing these restrictions, and what the penalties will be for violation of the law.

Abuses of power have stemmed from a combination of several factors, but one of the most apparent is that the agencies were beyond the rule of law partly because there was often no clear or enforceable rule of law to obey. The intelligence agencies' charters have been remarkably fuzzy, self-determined, accomplished by executive fiat, or indeed nonexistent. In many cases, agencies repeatedly avoided going to Congress for legislative authority to do something precisely because they knew that vagueness would increase their power in the long run.

The record shows that, since clandestine agencies are not accountable to public opinion, they can and will choose to interpret their authority broadly. For instance, the authority of the director of Central Intelligence to protect "intelligence sources and methods" has expanded until it has covered virtually everything touching upon the CIA. In other situations, such as when the CIA developed Operation CHAOS, the agency clearly and by any standard violated its charter—but the charter included no provisions to enforce that restriction.

The CIA Charter As noted, the covert operations of the CIA have cost more than they are worth and its human espionage activities are technologically obsolete. At the same time, not enough resources have gone into its intended function: the analysis of intelligence data. The

CIA should be restructured, and its resources channeled into developing better methods of analysis and coordinating intelligence from other sources. By charter, the Covert Operations Branch of the CIA should be terminated. All covert operations, including human espionage in peacetime, should be ended. In addition, as the Senate Select Committee recommended, secret CIA publications, academic activities, and media connections should be outlawed. The charter should also state the the CIA cannot arrange for the intelligence services of foreign allies to do for it what it is not authorized to do itself.[6]

The FBI Charter[7]   The investigative jurisdiction of the FBI should be established by legislative charter: the FBI's only legitimate function should be the investigation of *crimes*, and never politics; speech-crime laws should be repealed. Since espionage, sabotage, and violent actions are criminal, this jurisdiction can take care of the nation's genuine security needs without the FBI having to function as a political policeman again. The House Select Committee on Intelligence recommended that the "intelligence" function be eliminated by abolishing the bureau's Internal Security Branch, and that the Counter-Intelligence Division be limited to the investigation of actual espionage. The loopholes which currently exist should also be plugged; legislation should explicitly forbid the FBI's farming out to state and local police forces the activities that it is not itself authorized to carry out.

The charter should also make explicit that "preventive action" will not be tolerated. As discussed above, the FBI already has the authority to protect the public from impending *crimes*. Any greater authorization than this will inevitably resurrect COINTELPRO.

There is an additional area of danger, which the new FBI charter must deal with if the intelligence bureaucracy is not to turn its energy to creating a new system of escape hatches. In some cases a bona-fide criminal investigation may be directed against persons or organizations also involved in legitimate First Amendment activities. The

270

COPYRIGHT 1976 BY *THE PHILADELPHIA INQUIRER*. WASHINGTON POST WRITERS GROUP.

charter should establish a system of safeguards to ensure that such criminal investigations are not conducted as a pretext for a political investigation. Whenever an investigation is to be begun against a person or a group that runs candidates for public office, advocates legislation, or takes stands on public issues, or where some element of the alleged crime involves political beliefs, authorization should come from outside the FBI. When such an investigation is begun, a system should be designed in order to keep the intrusion on protected First Amendment rights to a minimum.

Security Investigations Security-clearance investigations on "prospective" job applicants have been one of the areas the intelligence agencies have used to justify surveillance. And while it is necessary to have reliable people in sensitive jobs, giving the FBI the job of conducting such checks is tantamount to giving it the political power to decide who is going to be in the government, and authority to gather information with blackmail potential.

A separate agency should be set up for security investigations, one whose charter will ensure that such investigations cannot be used as a pretext for spying on people for other reasons. Security investigations should be done only with the applicant's authorization, and files should be kept separate from all other files; safeguards should be established that would limit their use to their intended purpose. The current exceptions to the Privacy Act should be eliminated; citizens should have the right to confront and refute the information collected on them.

The National Security Agency A legislated charter should take the NSA out of the Department of Defense and bring it under civilian control. Strict limitations should be placed on the messages that it is allowed to intercept. Currently, there is no statute or executive directive limiting the NSA's ability to monitor telecommunications of Americans as long as one end of the exchange is not within the United States; not even a judicial warrant is required. The safeguards of the Fourth Amendment must be applied to all communications of citizens, whether they take place at home or abroad. Since electronic eavesdropping is impossible to narrow enough so that it is not a general warrant prohibited by the Constitution, such NSA intercepts must be banned, whether they be conducted via telecommunication, computer lines, or any new technological method.

Military Intelligence Legislation should prohibit military intelligence from playing any role in the surveillance of civilians, including situations where troops have been called in to control civil disturbances; in such situations the intelligence collection authority should be limited to the geography as it relates to crowd control.

The constitutional rights of military personnel should also be protected—the military should not be authorized to collect intelligence on any lawful activities, whether at home or abroad.

The Internal Revenue Service The IRS should be li-

DESIGNING EFFECTIVE REFORMS

mited to the function that it was originally created for—collecting taxes. Its investigations should deal only with tax liability and tax crimes; it should have no access to records on the political views or activities of taxpayers; it should have no authority to compile its own records on such matters.

Other Government Agencies There are about seventy agencies that have some sort of intelligence function. Congress may find it necessary to reevaluate them, since they may be pressed into the intelligence vacuum if the reform charters limit the intelligence functions of the CIA, the FBI, the NSA, military intelligence, and the IRS.

ENFORCING THE LAW

None of these restrictions on the intelligence community will make any difference unless a real system of enforcement is available to back them up. Effective enforcement should be designed into several mutually reinforcing systems, each supporting the others. The courts allow for both criminal and civil penalties, congressional oversight can be strengthened, and the right of the public and the Congress to know what the executive branch is doing must be protected.

The Courts: Criminal Penalties Violating the charters, including carrying out activities that go beyond what is explicitly authorized, should be subject to criminal penalties. Without sanctions in court, the limits on the intelligence community will be nothing more than exhortation, easily ignored. There should be criminal penalties for

• violating the limits imposed by charter on the intelligence agencies, and on using the authority of the intelligence agencies to violate the laws that apply to the rest of the nation;

• intentionally deceiving Congress or the public about intelligence agency activities that violate the law and their charters;

• failing to report such violations to the special prosecutor and the congressional oversight committees.

At the same time, all information relating to violations of the law should be automatically exempt from classification. But having criminal penalties on the books is only the first step—there must be effective procedures for calling violators to account.

Special Prosecutor[8]   The Justice Department has been visibly reluctant to prosecute officials for crimes carried out under cover of the law. The Watergate experience showed that it takes a special prosecutor to get around the problems involved in enforcing the law against executive-branch officials; if officials are not to be told in effect that they are above even the most explicitly drawn laws, Congress must create a special prosecutor before the statute of limitations on past crimes runs out.

In some situations, special prosecutors have compiled their own records of abuse; there is a realistic fear that, once begun, a special prosecutor can get out of control and end as another overzealous official accountable to no one. This can be handled in one of two ways. If Congress sets up a permanent special prosecutor as part of its plan for enforcing the charters, it can also put limits on the length of time that a given individual can serve. Alternatively, Congress can arrange for a temporary special prosecutor whose appointment is triggered when there is reason to believe that officials have broken the law.

The Justice Department has been resisting the idea of establishing a special prosecutor as if it were a slur on the integrity of individual officials within the department. A special prosecutor would be an incursion on to what is ordinarily exclusive Justice Department territory. But when billions of dollars have been spent on secret programs that violated the law and ruined lives, ordinary solutions are not sufficient. The basic principle of a government of law and not of men is that accountability is set out in the legal structures, and does not depend on the integrity of a few individuals.

The investigation of something as serious as official criminal activity must be carried out with the appearance of impartiality, so that the public can be assured that, whatever the outcome of the investigation, the matter is settled. And the Justice Department, for several reasons, is not in a position to give this appearance of impartiality, no matter what the integrity of its present officials. First, the FBI is a part of the Justice Department, and there is at least implied collusion. Second, the Justice Department has in the past acknowledged that the CIA was above the law: there was an agreement between the CIA and the Justice Department that if the CIA general counsel decided that a prosecution would require the release of classified information the charges would be dropped. Third, the Justice Department is currently representing intelligence officials who are being sued for damages in civil court—a conflict of interest. And finally, no matter how sincerely an attorney general may want to prosecute, there will be problems of maintaining loyalty and morale within the department among officials who may, if only by lack of vigilance, have been implicated in the illegality under investigation.

In short, if public confidence in government is to be restored, a special prosecutor is imperative. He or she should have a mandate to probe all government agencies to find violations, have access to all intelligence agency files, and be able to use any information necessary to a successful prosecution.

The Courts: Civil Remedies[9]   Justice is meted out in civil as well as criminal courts. Ensuring that people can readily use the civil courts to enforce the law and to protect themselves is another established line of defense for civil liberty. The civil suit provides a channel for discovering the details of secret government programs; courts can decide that a program is illegal and issue an injunction against it; the threat of being sued for damages is an effective deterrent for an official considering some questionable operation; and lawsuits provide some redress for the victims, many of whose lives have been left in ruins.

But current law is weighted against the citizen's suit against the government and its officials; legislation should be passed that would make it easier to sue in court for both damages and injunctive relief.

As recommended by the Church Committee, people should be notified by the government of the illegal files that are held on them and of their rights in civil litigation.[10] The Privacy and Freedom of Information Acts should be amended to give citizens greater access to the information in their files.

Congress should also pass legislation making the civil suit available to citizens of ordinary means. Where the plaintiffs substantially prevail, they should get attorneys' fees and court costs. It should not be necessary to prove a concrete injury in order to get an award of damages; establishing only that constitutional rights have been violated should be enough to justify an award of damages.

And finally, government officials should be held to the same standard of guilt as other citizens; claiming that illegal actions were done "in good faith and reasonable belief" that they were legal should not be a basis for relieving officials of their liability.

Congressional Oversight Congress provides an essential counterbalance to power within the executive branch, but there is a danger that congressional oversight will be treated as a panacea. In reality, it is only part of the solution.

As the executive branch is fond of reminding us, we already have had committees to oversee the intelligence agencies, but these simply have not done their job effectively. While this does not absolve the responsibility of executive officials, it does provide some lessons about congressional oversight. Without a tremendous amount of public attention focusing on an issue, oversight tends to become lost among the daily activities in Congress. Right now such attention exists, but eventually it will die down and, unless effective remedies have been installed, the best that can be expected is a repeat of the usual oversight situation—inaction.

There are a number of changes that would enable the setting up of an oversight structure that would respond even to a mini-scandal, something that would improve the situation greatly over what has existed in the past. The Senate has already established an Oversight Committee that has the earmarks of being more than a rubber stamp. It has full access to intelligence agency information and it has the power of the purse to back up its authority; if the intelligence bureaucracy does not cooperate, the committee can withhold its appropriations. The House should establish a separate committee; competition between the two would increase the likelihood of aggressive oversight.

The oversight committees must also have ways to avoid being limited to official channels of information. Obviously, if public attention is a prerequisite for effective oversight, then there must be ways of generating that attention. Encouraging whistle-blowing is an essential element.

The reform charters should place an affirmative obligation for officials to blow the whistle, and authorize reporting illegal activities to the Congress, the special prosecutor, and the public; it is not hard to envision evidence of a scandal getting lost, for a variety of reasons, on the desk of some committee. The right to report it to the public serves as insurance that such things will be taken seriously.

But merely requiring officials to report illegal activities will not be enough to guarantee overcoming the bureaucratic tradition of secrecy. Whistle-blowers will need to be protected. All groups with an esprit de corps have "informal" sanctions to discourage their members from revealing their secrets to outsiders. Unless protection is offered, officials will have to gamble between risking formal sanctions or informal sanctions. On the one hand, if they do not reveal an activity they *may* be subject to criminal and civil sanctions, but if they do reveal it, they will certainly ruin their chances for promotion within their agency. The case of Ernest Fitzgerald, who revealed the C-5 cost overrun, is a singular example of this. In that situation the Department of Defense tried a number of tactics to oust Fitzgerald from his job; it has taken specific congressional action to protect him. Congress should set up a system of guarantees that a whistle-blowing official can rely on.

The Government Accounting Office (GAO) is an investigative arm of Congress and another potential channel for funneling information to an oversight committee. When GAO investigators find evidence of illegal actions, they should be empowered to release their report not only to the Oversight Committee but to the public as well so that popular support can be generated for reform. As part of the power of the purse, both the Senate and the House Select Committees recommended that GAO be given full and unrestricted audit authority over the intelligence agencies.

Whether or not an oversight committee should have the right to go public with information in a dispute between the executive and legislative branches is the difference between effective and cosmetic congressional oversight. Without the ability to generate public support, congressional oversight is a watchdog without a bark, which is what the executive branch's oversight recommendations were designed to produce. In the Ford scheme for congressional oversight, for example, anything short of a two-thirds vote of both houses to release information constitutes a "leak"—a proposition that is absurdly weighted against any balance of power between the branches of government. Instead, legislation should confirm that individual members of Congress, like everyone else, can release to the public any information that gives evidence of illegal or improper activity going beyond the statutory authority of the intelligence agencies. The Angola controversy provides a case in point. There, the executive branch tried to conceal the fact that it was carrying on a covert paramilitary adventure. Without public opposition, it would be continuing still.

CONCLUSION

The process of remedying the abuses of the intelligence agencies will not be an easy one, but it is absolutely vital if, after the close call in postwar America, democracy is to be alive and well in 1984. It is now clear that the same lawlessness that has characterized America's foreign policy has come home and threatens the country's political process.

To date, only a few patchwork elements of reform have been put into effect. At every turn the executive branch continues to fight any major changes and, instead, offers "reforms" that end up authorizing for the future the abuses of the past. If there is to be any real insurance against a repetition of past excesses under the cover of increased secrecy, major changes in the people's assumptions and in America's structures must be made and a balance of power within the federal government restored. Clandestine government accountable to no one must end; a government of laws must be put in its place.

NOTES

INTRODUCTION

1. Quoted in Victor Marchetti and John Marks, *The CIA and the Cult of Intelligence* (New York: Dell, 1974), p. 347.

1

THE CIA'S CAMPAIGN AGAINST SALVADOR ALLENDE

1. Tad Szulc, "Exporting Revolution," *The New Republic*, Sept. 21, 1974, p. 23.

2. Seymour Hersh, "Kissinger Called Chile Strategist," *New York Times*, Sept. 11, 1974.

3. Seymour Hersh, "Censored Matter in Book about CIA," *New York Times*, Sept. 11, 1974.

4. Seymour Hersh, "Kissinger Called Strategist," *New York Times*, Sept. 15, 1974.

5. Interview with Saul Landau, Frank Mankiewicz, and Kirby Jones; July 1974 (on file at the Institute for Policy Studies).

6. Staff Report of the Select Committee to study Governmental Operations with respect to Intelligence Activities, United States Senate, "Covert Action in Chile 1963-1973" (Washington, D.C.: U.S. Government Printing Office, 1975), pp. 1, 15. (Hereafter cited as "Chile Report.")

7. Philip Agee, *Inside the Company: CIA Diary* (Harmondsworth, Eng.: Penguin, 1974), p. 382.

8. "Chile Report," pp. 11-13.

9. Interview by John Marks with a retired CIA man.

10. "Chile Report," pp. 7-8, 17-19.

11. "Chile Report," pp. 19-23.

12. "Chile Report," p. 23.

13. "Chile Report," p. 23.

14. "Chile Report," p. 33.

15. "Chile Report," p. 25.

16. "Chile Report," pp. 25-26.

17. An Interim Report of the Select Committee to Study Governmental Operations with Respect to Intelligence Activities, U.S. Senate, "Alleged Assassination Plots Involving Foreign Leaders" (Washington, D.C.: U.S. Government Printing Office, 1975), pp. 227-228. (Hereafter cited as "Assassination Report.")

18. "Assassination Report," p. 226.

19. "Assassination Report," p. 254.

20. "Chile Report," pp. 26-28, 32-35.

21. John Marks and Victor Marchetti, *The CIA and The Cult of Intelligence* (New York: Dell, 1974), p. 368.

22. "Chile Report," p. 29.

23. Fred Landis, "The CIA Makes Headlines," *Liberation Magazine*, March/April, 1975.

24. "Chile Report," pp. 29-30.

25. Marlisle Simons, "The Brazilian Connection," *Washington Post*, Jan. 6, 1974.

26. "Chile Report," pp. 30-31.

27. "Chile Report," pp. 38.

28. Seymour Hersh, "CIA Chief Tells," *New York Times*, Sept. 8, 1974.

29. "Chile Report," p. 8.

30. "Chile Report," p. 38.

31. "Assassination Report," p. 254.

32. Gerald Ford, text of News Conference, Sept. 15, 1974, in *New York Times*, Sept. 16, 1974.

33. Ford News Conference (see note 32).

2
THE CIA COVERT ACTION
AROUND THE WORLD

1. Seymour Hersh, "Censored Matter on Book on the CIA," *New York Times*, Sept. 11, 1974.

2. Gary Wills, "The CIA from Beginning to End," *New York Review of Books*, Jan. 22, 1976.

3. Final Report of the Select Committee to Study Governmental Operations with respect to Intelligence Activities, U.S. Senate, "Foreign and Military Intelligence," p. 128. (Hereafter cited as Final Report, Book I.)

4. Final Report, Book I, p. 128.

5. Final Report, Book I, p. 132.

6. 50 U.S.C. 403(d).

7. Final Report, Book I, p. 105.

8. Final Report, Book I, p. 50.

9. Victor Marchetti and John Marks, *The CIA and the Cult of Intelligence* (New York: Dell, 1974), p. 337. (Hereafter cited as *Cult of Intelligence*.)

10. Victor Marchetti and John Marks, "Undercovering the CIA," *More* magazine, Spring 1974.

11. Nicholas M. Horrock, "Panal Says Jackson Gave Secret Advice to CIA," *New York Times*, Jan. 26, 1976.

12. Seymour Hersh, "Huge CIA Operation Reported in US against Anti-War Forces, and other Dissidents in Nixon Years," *New York Times*, Dec. 22, 1974.

13. Final Report, Book I, p. 132.

14. Final Report, Book I, p. 31.

15. Final Report, Book I, p. 153.

16. Interview with an ex-CIA official who served in Germany.

17. "The CIA Report," *Village Voice*, Feb. 16, 1976.

18. Seymour Hersh, "CIA and Reports Evoke Ford Anger," *New York Times*, Jan. 8, 1976.

19. Final Report, Book I, pp. 108-109.

20. Final Report, Book I, pp. 109-112.

21. *Cult of Intelligence*, p. 95.

22. *Cult of Intelligence*, p. 46.

23. *Cult of Intelligence*, pp. 47-49.

24. *Cult of Intelligence*, p. 362.

25. Thomas Ross and David Wise, *The Invisible Government* (New York: Random House, 1964).

26. Final Report, Book I, p. 57.

27. Final Report, Book I, pp. 146-147.

28. Final Report, Book I, p. 155.

29. Philip Agee, *Inside the Company: CIA Diary* (Harmondsworth, Eng.: Penguin, 1974). (Hereafter cited as *CIA Diary*.)

30. *Village Voice*, "The CIA REPORT."

31. Final Report, Book I, p. 154.

32. David Wise, "Covert Operations around the World," in Robert Borosage and John Marks, *The CIA File* (New York: Grossman/Viking, 1976), p. 21.

33. *Cult of Intelligence*, pp. 51-52.

34. David Wise, "Covert Operations around the World," p. 20.

35. *Cult of Intelligence*, p. 54.

36. *Cult of Intelligence*, p. 54.

37. Fred Branfman, on the Grenada television documentary "The Rise and Fall of the CIA."

38. Branfman (see note 37).

39. John Marks, "How to Spot a Spook," *Washington Monthly*, November 1974.

40. Fred Branfman, "The President's Secret Army: A Case Study—The CIA in Laos, 1962-1972," in Robert Borosage and John Marks, *The CIA File*.

41. Interview with Continental official, May 1976.

42. Edward Landsdale, "Memo on 'Unconventional Warfare Resources,' " in *The Pentagon Papers*; quoted from Marchetti and Marks, *The CIA and the Cult of Intelligence*, pp. 149-150.

43. *1970 World Aviation Directory*.

44. Taylor Branch and George Crile, "The Kennedy Vendetta: Our Secret War," *Harper's* magazine, August 1975. (Hereafter cited as "Kennedy Vendetta.")

45. An Interim Report of the Select Committee to Study Governmental Operations with respect to Intelligence Activities, the U.S. Senate, "Alleged Assassination Plots Involving Foreign Leaders, November 1975." (Hereafter cited as "Assassination Report.")

46. "Assassination Report," p. 46.

47. "Assassination Report," p. 4.

48. "Assassination Report," p. 5.

49. *Cult of Intelligence*, pp. 236-237.

50. John Marks, "The CIA's Corporate Shell Game," *Washington Post*, July 11, 1976.

51. Taylor Branch and John Marks, "Tracking the CIA," *Harper's Weekly*, January 24, 1975.

52. John Marks, "The CIA Won't Quite Go Public," *Rolling Stone* magazine, July 18, 1974.

53. *CIA Diary*, p. 372.

54. Staff Report of the Select Committee to Study Govern-

mental Operations with respect to Intelligence Activities, U.S. Senate, "Covert Action in Chile 1963-1973" (Washington, D.C.: U.S. Government Printing Office, 1975), pp. 11-13. (Hereafter cited as Senate Report on Chile.)

55. Allan Frank, "John Marks Talks about the CIA," *Washington Star*, May 13, 1975.

56. Robert M. Smith, "Ashland Oil Paid by CIA in Secret," *New York Times*, July 9, 1975.

57. Thomas W. Braden, "I'm Glad the CIA Is Immoral," *Saturday Evening Post*, May 20, 1967.

58. Neil Sheehan, "News Guild Aided by Groups Linked to CIA Conduits," *New York Times*, Feb. 19, 1967.

59. Grenada television documentary, "The Rise and Fall of the CIA."

60. Final Report, Book I, p. 193.

61. Final Report, Book I, pp. 191-201.

62. Final Report, Book I, p. 198.

63. Final Report, Book I, p. 201.

64. Stuart H. Loory, "The CIA's Use of the Press: A Mighty Wurlitzer," *Columbia Journalism Review*, September/October 1974.

65. Final Report, Book I, pp. 201-203.

66. John Marks, "The CIA's Church Connection: Missionaries as Informants," National Catholic News Service, July 23, 1975.

67. Final Report, Book I, pp. 189-190.

68. Final Report, Book I, pp. 181-192.

69. *Cult of Intelligence*, p. 234.

70. Final Report, Book I, pp. 185-186.

71. Richard Harwood, "O What a Tangled Web the CIA Wove," *Washington Post*, Feb. 26, 1967.

72. Final Report, Book I, pp. 187-188.

73. "Kennedy Vendetta."

74. Final Report, Book I, p. 158.

75. Final Report, Book I, p. 57.

3
THE FBI'S VENDETTA AGAINST MARTIN LUTHER KING, JR.

1. Robert M. Bleiweiss, ed., *Marching to Freedom: The Life of Martin Luther King, Jr.* (New York: Signet, 1968), pp. 67-68. (Hereafter cited as *Marching*.)

2. *Marching*, p. 65.

3. *Marching*, p. 77.

4. *Marching*, p. 77-78.

5. Final Report of the Select Committee to Study Governmental Relations with Respect to Intelligence Activities, United States Senate, Supplementary Detailed Staff Reports on Intelligence Activities and the Rights of Americans, Book III, "Dr. Martin Luther King, Jr., Case Study" (Washington, D.C.: U.S. Government Printing Office, 1976), p. 87, Memorandum from Director, FBI to Special Agent in Charge, Atlanta, 9/20/57. (Hereafter cited as Book III, with report title.)

6. Book III, "Dr. Martin Luther King, Jr., Case Study," p. 87 (emphasis added).

7. Book III, "Dr. Martin Luther King, Jr., Case Study," p. 88.

8. Book III, "Dr. Martin Luther King, Jr., Case Study," p. 88.

9. See "The Bureau in War and Peace," below, pp. 55-62.

10. Victor Navasky, *Kennedy Justice* (New York: Atheneum, 1971), p. 149. (Hereafter cited as Navasky.)

11. Book III, "The Development of FBI Domestic Intelligence Investigations," p. 451.

12. For example, see Navasky, pp. 110-112.

13. Book III, "Dr. Martin Luther King, Jr., Case Study," p. 88, n. 30.

14. The Senate Select Committee on Intelligence called King's two advisers, who were labeled Communist by the FBI, "Adviser A" and "Adviser B." However, in 1971, Navasky named Stanley Levison and Jack O'Dell as the two advisers. It is clear from Navasky and the Senate Report that "Adviser A" is Levison and "Adviser B" is O'Dell. (See Navasky, chapter 3, "Civil Rights: The Movement and the General," and Book III, "Dr. Martin Luther King, Jr., Case Study.")

15. Book III, "Dr. Martin Luther King, Jr., Case Study," p. 89.

16. Book III, "Dr. Martin Luther King, Jr., Case Study," pp. 87-88, and n. 26, for explanation of Reserve Index.

17. See Navasky, chapter 3, for identification of O'Dell as Adviser B, and Book III, "Dr. Martin Luther King, Jr., Case Study," p. 88, for quote from Memorandum from Frederick Baumgardner to William Sullivan, 10/22/62.

18. Book III, "Dr. Martin Luther King, Jr., Case Study," pp. 95-96.

19. Book III, "Dr. Martin Luther King, Jr., Case Study," p. 96.

20. Book III, "Dr. Martin Luther King, Jr., Case Study," p. 96.

21. Book III, "Dr. Martin Luther King, Jr., Case Study," p. 86.

22. Book III, "Dr. Martin Luther King, Jr., Case Study," p. 90.

23. Book III, "Dr. Martin Luther King, Jr., Case Study," p. 90.

24. Navasky, pp. 121-123.

25. Book III, "Dr. Martin Luther King, Jr., Case Study," p. 91.

26. Navasky, pp. 112-115.

27. Book III, "Dr. Martin Luther King, Jr., Case Study," p. 87, Airtel from SAC, Atlanta to Director, FBI, 11/21/61.

28. Book III, "Dr. Martin Luther King, Jr., Case Study," p. 101, n. 94.

29. Navasky, p. 148.

30. Navasky, p. 148.

31. Book III, "Dr. Martin Luther King, Jr., Case Study," p. 95.

32. Book III, "Dr. Martin Luther King, Jr., Case Study," p. 89.

33. Navasky, p. 143.

34. Book III, "Dr. Martin Luther King, Jr., Case Study," p. 86, n. 23, for quote from FBI *Manual* (emphasis added).

35. *Marching*, p. 88.

36. Martin Luther King, Jr., *Why We Can't Wait* (New York: Signet, 1963), pp. 80-81.

37. *Marching*, p. 95.

38. *Marching*, p. 100.

39. Book III, "Dr. Martin Luther King, Jr., Case Study," p. 86, n. 23, for quote from FBI *Manual*.

40. Book III, "Dr. Martin Luther King, Jr., Case Study," pp. 92, 95-98.

41. Book III, "Dr. Martin Luther King, Jr., Case Study," p. 97, n. 74, for quote from Andrew Young's testimony before Senate Select Committee on Intelligence.

42. Book III, "Dr. Martin Luther King, Jr., Case Study," p. 97.

43. Book III, "Dr. Martin Luther King, Jr., Case Study," p. 97.

44. Book III, "Dr. Martin Luther King, Jr., Case Study," p. 99, n. 86, for description of 6/30/63 article in *Birmingham News*.

45. Book III, "Dr. Martin Luther King, Jr., Case Study," p. 103.

46. Navasky, p. 146.

47. Book III, "Dr. Martin Luther King, Jr., Case Study," p. 115.

48. See generally, Book III, "Dr. Martin Luther King, Jr., Case Study," pp. 104-111.

49. Book III, "Dr. Martin Luther King, Jr., Case Study," p. 106.

50. Book III, "Dr. Martin Luther King, Jr., Case Study," p. 107.

51. Book III, "Dr. Martin Luther King, Jr., Case Study," p. 107.

52. Book III, "Dr. Martin Luther King, Jr., Case Study," pp. 107, 110.

53. Book III, "Dr. Martin Luther King, Jr., Case Study," pp. 107-108 (emphasis added).

54. Book III, "Dr. Martin Luther King, Jr., Case Study," p. 108.

55. Book III, "Dr. Martin Luther King, Jr., Case Study," pp. 110-111.

56. Book III, "Dr. Martin Luther King, Jr., Case Study," p. 115.

57. Book III, "Dr. Martin Luther King, Jr., Case Study," p. 133.

58. Book III, "Dr. Martin Luther King, Jr., Case Study," p. 133.

59. See generally, Book III, "Dr. Martin Luther King, Jr., Case Study," pp. 120-130.

60. Book III, "Dr. Martin Luther King, Jr., Case Study," p. 121.

61. Book III, "Dr. Martin Luther King, Jr., Case Study," p. 135.

62. Book III, "Dr. Martin Luther King, Jr., Case Study," p. 141.

63. Book III, "Dr. Martin Luther King, Jr., Case Study," p. 143.

64. Book III, "Dr. Martin Luther King, Jr., Case Study," pp. 142-143.

65. For Royko, see Navasky, pp. 137-138; see Book III, "Dr. Martin Luther King, Jr., Case Study," p. 133, n. 220, for quote from Rowan's article of 6/20/69 in *Washington Evening Star*, "FBI Won't Talk about Additional Wiretappings."

66. Book III, "Dr. Martin Luther King, Jr., Case Study," pp. 111-120, 146-154.

67. Book III, "Dr. Martin Luther King, Jr., Case Study," p. 154.

68. David Halberstam, *The Best and the Brightest* (New York: Random House, 1972), p. 436.

69. Book III, "Warrantless FBI Electronic Surveillance," pp. 346-347.

70. Book III, "Warrantless FBI Electronic Surveillance," p. 347.

71. Book III, "Dr. Martin Luther King, Jr., Case Study," p. 155.

72. Book III, "Dr. Martin Luther King, Jr., Case Study," p. 155.

73. Book III, "Dr. Martin Luther King, Jr., Case Study," p. 155.

74. Book III, "Dr. Martin Luther King, Jr., Case Study," p. 156; see also Navasky, p. 153.

75. Book III, "Dr. Martin Luther King, Jr., Case Study," pp. 157-158.

76. Book III, "Dr. Martin Luther King, Jr., Case Study," p. 162.

77. Book III, "Dr. Martin Luther King, Jr., Case Study," pp. 163-170.

78. Book III, "Dr. Martin Luther King, Jr., Case Study," p. 160.

79. Book III, "Dr. Martin Luther King, Jr., Case Study," p. 137.

80. Book III, "Dr. Martin Luther King, Jr., Case Study," pp. 173-174.

81. Book III, "Dr. Martin Luther King, Jr., Case Study," p. 174.

82. Book III, "Dr. Martin Luther King, Jr., Case Study," p. 183.

83. Book III, "Dr. Martin Luther King, Jr., Case Study," p. 146.

84. Book III, "Dr. Martin Luther King, Jr., Case Study," p. 145, and "The Internal Revenue Service: An Intelligence Resource and Collector," p. 855.

85. Book III, "Dr. Martin Luther King, Jr., Case Study," p. 178 (Ford Foundation) and p. 145 (National Science Foundation).

86. Book III, "Dr. Martin Luther King, Jr., Case Study," p. 144.

87. See Hearings before the Select Committee to Study Governmental Operations with Respect to Intelligence Activities, United States Senate, 94th Congress, 1st Session, Volume 6, Federal Bureau of Investigation, p. 389, for memo on King and black messiah; and p. 24, for explanation of it. See also, Book III, "Dr. Martin Luther King, Jr., Case Study," p. 181.

88. Book III, "Dr. Martin Luther King, Jr., Case Study," p. 119.

89. Book III, "Dr. Martin Luther King, Jr., Case Study," p. 184.

4

THE BUREAU IN WAR AND PEACE

1. For a study of the FBI today, see Sanford J. Ungar, *FBI* (Boston: Little, Brown, 1975). (Hereafter cited as Ungar.) For percentage of overall resources: Ungar, p. 146; comparison with organized crime: Final Report of the Select Committee to Study Governmental Relations with Respect to Intelligence Activities, United States Senate, 94th Congress, 2nd Session, Supplementary Detailed Staff Reports on Intelligence Activities and the Rights of Americans, Book III (Washington, D.C.: U.S. Government Printing Office, 1976), "The Use of Informants in FBI Intelligence Investigations," p. 228. (Hereafter cited as Book III, name of report.)

2. Ungar, pp. 37-63; see also generally, Don Whitehead, *The FBI Story: A Report to the People* (New York: Random House, 1951) (this is a bureau-approved book); and Max Lowenthal, *The Federal Bureau of Investigation* (New York: William Sloane Associates, 1950). (Hereafter cited as Lowenthal.)

3. Fred J. Cook, *The FBI Nobody Knows* (New York: Macmillan, 1964). (Hereafter cited as *The FBI Nobody Knows*.) Other accounts by ex-agents include, William W. Turner, *Hoover's FBI: The Men and the Myth* (New York: Dell, 1971), and Joseph L. Schott, *No Left Turns: The FBI in Peace and War* (New York: Praeger, 1975).

4. Citizens' Commission to Investigate the FBI, "The Complete Collection of Political Documents Ripped-off from the FBI Office in Media, Pa., March 8, 1971," *WIN*, vol. VIII, nos. 4 and 5, March 1972. (Hereafter cited as Media Papers.)

5. Statement of Information, Hearings before the Committee on the Judiciary, House of Representatives, 93rd Congress, 2d Session, Book VII, "White House Surveillance Activities and Campaign Activities, May-June 1974." See also documents on file in *Morton H. Halperin, et al.* v. *Henry A. Kissinger, et al.*, Civil Action No. 1187-73 (DCDC); and summary in Jerry J. Berman and Morton H. Halperin, eds., *The Abuses of the Intelligence Agencies* (Washington, D.C.: Center for National Security Studies, 1975), pp. 36-40. (Hereafter cited as Abuses book.)

6. *Socialist Workers Party* v. *Attorney General* 73 Civ. 3160 (SDNY).

7. Commission on CIA Activities within the United States, *Report to the President* (Washington, D.C.: U.S. Government Printing Office, 1975), pp. 101-115, 232. (Hereafter cited as Rockefeller Report.)

8. See generally, Final Report of the Select Committee to Study Governmental Operations with Respect to Intelligence Activi-

ties, United States Senate, 94th Congress, 2nd Session, Intelligence Activities and the Rights of Americans, Book II (Washington, D.C.: U.S. Government Printing Office, 1976). (Hereafter cited as Book II.) See also generally Book III.

9. Book II, p. 70.

10. The FBI's basic statutory investigatory authority is 18 U.S.C. 533.

11. Book III, "The Development of FBI Domestic Intelligence Investigations," pp. 388-391.

12. Book III, "The Development of FBI Domestic Intelligence Investigations," pp. 378-380, 382.

13. Book III, "The Development of FBI Domestic Intelligence Investigations," p. 381.

14. Book III, "The Development of FBI Domestic Intelligence Investigations," pp. 380-382.

15. Book III, "The Development of FBI Domestic Intelligence Investigations," pp. 382-388.

16. *The FBI Nobody Knows*, p. 138, and Book III, "The Development of FBI Domestic Intelligence Investigations," pp. 388-390.

17. See generally Lowenthal.

18. Book III, "The Development of FBI Domestic Intelligence Investigations," p. 394.

19. Book III, "Warrantless FBI Electronic Surveillance," p. 279.

20. Book III, "The Development of FBI Domestic Intelligence Investigations," p. 393.

21. Book III, "The Development of FBI Domestic Intelligence Investigations," pp. 393-394.

22. Book III, "The Development of FBI Domestic Intelligence Investigations," p. 404.

23. Book III, "The Development of FBI Domestic Intelligence Investigations," pp. 403-407. See also, Report to the House Committee on the Judiciary by the Comptroller General of the United States, *FBI Domestic Intelligence Operations—Their Purpose and Scope: Issues that Need to be Resolved* (Washington, D.C.: General Accounting Office, 1976), Appendix IV.

24. Book III, "The Development of FBI Domestic Intelligence Investigations," p. 392.

25. Book III, "The Development of FBI Domestic Intelligence Investigations," p. 408.

26. Book III, "The Development of FBI Domestic Intelligence Investigations," p. 410.

27. Book III, "The Development of FBI Domestic Intelligence Investigations," p. 396.

28. Book III, "The Development of FBI Domestic Intelligence Investigations," p. 399.

29. Book III, "The Development of FBI Domestic Intelligence Investigations," pp. 412-417.

30. Book III, "The Development of FBI Domestic Intelligence Investigations," pp. 414-415.

31. Book III, "The Development of FBI Domestic Intelligence Investigations," p. 417.

32. Book III, "Warrantless FBI Electronic Surveillance," p. 279.

33. Book III, "Warrantless FBI Electronic Surveillance," p. 317.

34. Book III, "Domestic CIA and FBI Mail Opening," p. 640.

35. Book III, "The Development of FBI Domestic Intelligence Investigations," p. 413.

36. Book III, "The Development of FBI Domestic Intelligence Investigations," pp. 413-414.

37. Book III, "The Development of FBI Domestic Intelligence Investigations," p. 413.

38. Book III, "The Development of FBI Domestic Intelligence Investigations," pp. 420-421.

39. Hearings before the Select Committee to Study Governmental Operations with Respect to Intelligence Activities, United States Senate, 94th Congress, 1st Session, vol. 6, "Federal Bureau of Investigation" (Washington, D.C.: U.S. Government Printing Office, 1976). Exhibit 36, "Political Abuse and the FBI: Staff Report," pp. 471-472. (Hereafter cited as Hearings, with volume number.) See also, Hearings before the Subcommittee on Civil and Constitutional Rights of the Committee on the Judiciary, House of Representatives, 94th Congress, 1st Session, "FBI Oversight" (Washington, D.C.: U.S. Government Printing Office, 1975), pp. 8-11.

40. Hearings, vol. 6, pp. 471-472.

41. Book III, "The Development of FBI Domestic Intelligence Investigations," p. 408.

42. Book III, "The Development of FBI Domestic Intelligence Investigations," pp. 457-458.

43. John M. Blum, et al., *The National Experience* (New York: Harcourt, Brace & World, 1963), pp. 752-754. (Hereafter cited as *National Experience*.) See also *The FBI Nobody Knows*, pp. 270-302, 367-376.

44. *National Experience*, p. 772; see also Arthur S. Link, *American Epoch* (New York: Alfred A. Knopf, 1962), pp. 646-648.

45. Book III, "The Development of FBI Domestic Intelligence Investigations," p. 436.

46. Hearings, vol. 6, pp. 58-59; see also, *The FBI Nobody Knows*, p. 33.

47. Richard O. Wright, ed., *Whose FBI?* (New York: Open Court, 1974), p. 199. (Hereafter cited as *Whose FBI?*)

48. Book III, "The Development of FBI Domestic Intelligence Investigations," p. 463.

49. Book III, "The Development of FBI Domestic Intelligence Investigations," p. 431.

50. Book III, "The Development of FBI Domestic Intelligence Investigations," p. 463.

51. John H. Schaar, *Loyalty in America* (Berkeley: University of California Press, 1957), p. 141. (Hereafter cited as *Loyalty*.)

52. Book III, "The Development of FBI Domestic Intelligence Investigations," p. 437.

53. Book III, "The Development of FBI Domestic Intelligence Investigations," pp. 427-428.

54. Book III, "The Development of FBI Domestic Intelligence Investigations," pp. 433-435.

55. Book III, "The Development of FBI Domestic Intelligence Investigations," p. 434.

56. Book III, "The Development of FBI Domestic Intelligence Investigations," p. 463.

57. Book III, "COINTELPRO: The FBI's Covert Action Programs against American Citizens," p. 5; see also "The Development of FBI Domestic Intelligence Investigations," pp. 449-452, 479-487.

58. Hearings, vol. 6, p. 59.

59. Book III, "The Development of FBI Domestic Intelligence Investigations," p. 451.

60. Book III, "The Development of FBI Domestic Intelligence Investigations," p. 449.

61. Book III, "The Development of FBI Domestic Intelligence Investigations," p. 434, n. 221, for Clark Clifford's testimony before the Senate Select Committee on Intelligence, which explains these figures.

62. See John M. Goshko, "Shadowy World of Police Informers," *Washington Post*, Sept. 26, 1975; Goshko and others have reported that the bureau has two informers for every agent. This number is based on that assumption.

63. See generally Book III, "The Use of Informants in FBI Intelligence Investigations."

64. Book III, "The Development of FBI Domestic Intelligence Investigations," p. 451.

65. Book III, "The Use of Informants in FBI Intelligence Investigations," p. 229.

66. Book III, "The Use of Informants in FBI Intelligence Investigations," pp. 255-259.

67. Book II, p. 53.

68. Book III, "Warrantless FBI Electronic Surveillance," p. 282.

69. Book III, "Warrantless FBI Electronic Surveillance," p. 301.

70. Book III, "Warrantless FBI Electronic Surveillance," pp. 295-296, 301.

71. Book III, "Domestic CIA and FBI Mail Opening," p. 640.

72. See generally Book III, "Warrantless Surreptitious Entries: FBI 'Black Bag' Break-ins and Microphone Installations."

73. Book III, "Warrantless Surreptitious Entries: FBI 'Black Bag' Break-ins and Microphone Installations," p. 360.

74. Book III, "The Development of FBI Domestic Intelligence Investigations," pp. 419, 429, 438-439.

75. See generally Walter Goodman, *The Committee* (New York: Farrar, Straus & Giroux, 1968).

76. *National Experience*, pp. 753-754, 772-774; *The FBI Nobody Knows*, p. 289; I. F. Stone, *The Haunted Fifties* (London: Merlin Press, 1963), pp. 23-30.

77. See generally *Loyalty: National Experience*, pp. 752-753; Book III, "The Development of FBI Domestic Intelligence Investigations," pp. 431-435.

78. Book III, "The Development of FBI Domestic Intelligence Investigations, p. 427; *National Experience*, p. 753; *Whose FBI?* pp. 194-196.

79. *Dennis* v. *United States* 341 U.S. 494, 510-511 (1951).

80. Book III, "The Development of FBI Domestic Intelligence Investigations," pp. 442-447.

81. *Yates* v. *United States* 354 U.S. 298, 325 (1957).

82. Book III, "The Development of FBI Domestic Intelligence Investigations, p. 435.

83. Book III, "COINTELPRO: The FBI's Covert Action Programs against American Citizens," pp. 3, 10-11; see also *Whose FBI?*

84. See generally Justice Department Report, "FBI COIN-TELPRO Activities," prepared by Assistant Attorney General Henry Petersen, Nov. 18, 1974; Book III, "COINTELPRO: The FBI's Covert Action Programs against American Citizens," p. 15.

85. Book III, "COINTELPRO: The FBI's Covert Action Programs against American Citizens," p. 3, and report generally.

86. Book III, "COINTELPRO: The FBI's Covert Action Programs against American Citizens," pp. 33-34.

87. Book III, "COINTELPRO: The FBI's Covert Action Programs against American Citizens," pp. 5, 17.

88. Book III, "COINTELPRO: The FBI's Covert Action Programs against American Citizens," p. 8; note 24 on that page cites bureau admissions that COINTELPRO activities "may" have violated various United States laws.

89. Book III, "COINTELPRO: The FBI's Covert Action Programs against American Citizens," pp. 64-73.

90. Frank Donner, "Let Him Wear a Wolf's Head: What the FBI Did to William Albertson," *Civil Liberties Review*, vol. 3 no. 1 (April/May 1976): 12-22.

91. Book III, "The Development of FBI Domestic Intelligence Investigations," pp. 479-489.

92. Book III, "COINTELPRO: The FBI's Covert Action Programs against American Citizens," pp. 17-18.

93. Hearings, vol. 6, p. 389, for 3/4/68 Airtel from Director FBI to SAC Albany.

94. Book III, "COINTELPRO: The FBI's Covert Action Programs against American Citizens," pp. 23-27; and "The Development of FBI Domestic Intelligence Investigations," p. 507.

95. Book III, "The Development of FBI Domestic Intelligence Investigations," p. 471.

96. Book III, "The Development of FBI Domestic Intelligence Investigations," pp. 492-493, for Attorney General Clark's memorandum to FBI Director, 9/14/67.

97. Book III, "Warrantless FBI Electronic Surveillance," pp. 346-349.

98. Book III, "The Development of FBI Domestic Intelligence Investigations," pp. 483-489.

99. See "The Other Agencies at Home," below, for detailed discussion of the intelligence activities of other agencies.

100. Book III, "The Development of FBI Domestic Intelligence Investigations," pp. 537-539.

101. Book III, "Warrantless FBI Electronic Surveillance," pp. 349-351.

102. See generally Book III, "National Security, Civil Liberties, and The Collection of Intelligence: A Report on the Huston Plan," pp. 921-982.

103. Book II, p. 6.

104. See generally Book III, "The Development of FBI Domestic Intelligence Investigations," pp. 454-518, for explanations of bureau actions against these groups.

105. Hearings, vol. 2 ("Huston Plan"), p. 117, testimony of Charles Brennan; see also Final Report of the Select Committee to Study Governmental Operations with Respect to Intelligence Activities, United States Senate, 94th Congress, 1st Session, Foreign and Military Intelligence, Book I (Washington, D.C.: U.S. Government Printing Office, 1976), p. 171.

106. See generally Book III, "The Internal Revenue Service: An Intelligence Resource and Collector," pp. 835-920.

107. FBI Documents released under the Freedom of Information Act on August 14, 1975 relating to COINTELPRO activities directed at White Hate Groups and the Communist Party USA, Memorandum of September 2, 1965 from Director FBI to the Attorney General. (Hereafter cited as COINTELPRO documents.)

108. Book II, p. 75.

109. Book III, "The Use of Informants in FBI Domestic Intelligence Investigations," p. 236.

110. See generally Book III, "Warrantless FBI Electronic Surveillance," p. 271-351.

111. Nicholas Horrock, "Car Burnings and Assaults on Radicals Linked to FBI Agents in Last Five Years," *New York Times*, July 11, 1976. (Hereafter cited as "Car Burnings.") Warrants in all domestic security wiretaps and bugs were required after *United States* v. *United States District Court* 407 U.S. 297 (1972).

112. See generally Book III, "National Security Agency Surveillance Affecting Americans."

113. See generally Book III, "Domestic CIA and FBI Mail Opening Programs," pp. 561-677; see also Rockefeller Report, pp. 101-115.

114. Book III, "Warrantless Surreptitious Entries: FBI 'Black Bag' Break-ins and Microphone Installations," pp. 360-361.

115. "Car Burnings."

116. Hearings, vol. 6 ("Federal Bureau of Investigation"); "Political Abuse and the FBI: Staff Report," pp. 470-485; see also Book III, "Warrantless FBI Electronic Surveillance," pp. 349-351.

117. Hearings, vol. 6 ("FBI"), p. 19.

118. Book III, "The Development of FBI Domestic Intelligence Investigations," p. 503.

119. Book III, "The Development of FBI Domestic Intelligence Investigations," pp. 519-521; see also "The Other Agencies at Home," below.

120. Book III, "COINTELPRO: The FBI's Covert Action Programs against American Citizens," pp. 15-23.

121. See generally COINTELPRO documents.

122. Book III, "The Use of Informants in FBI Domestic Intelligence Investigations," pp. 239-244.

123. Book III, "COINTELPRO: The FBI's Covert Action Programs against American Citizens," p. 41.

124. Book III, "COINTELPRO: The FBI's Covert Action Programs against American Citizens," pp. 40-43, and generally, "The FBI's Covert Action Program to Destroy the Black Panther Party," pp. 185-223.

125. According to the FBI, COINTELPRO was terminated in 1971. However, recent revelations indicate that COINTELPRO has continued after 1971, at least unofficially, or, if approved by headquarters, on an "individual" basis. The letters terminating the programs establish that individual actions could be approved by the bureau. In any event, COINTELPRO activity did not end in 1971. See particularly, "Car Burnings."

126. Book III, "COINTELPRO: The FBI's Covert Action Programs against American Citizens," p. 51.

127. Milton Viorst, "FBI Mayhem," *New York Review of Books*, vol. XXIII, no. 4 (March 18, 1976): 21-28.

128. Lawrence Stern, "FBI Tipster: Led Draft Board Raid," *Washington Post*, Nov. 19, 1975.

129. Media Papers, p. 28, for 9/16/70 FBI memo.

130. "Car Burnings."

131. Nelson Blackstock, *COINTELPRO: The FBI's Secret War on Political Freedom* (New York: Vintage Books, 1975), and Abuses book.

132. Book III, "COINTELPRO: The FBI's Covert Action Programs against American Citizens," pp. 23-27.

133. Book III, "COINTELPRO: The FBI's Covert Action Programs against American Citizens," p. 25.

134. Book III, "COINTELPRO: The FBI's Covert Action Programs against American Citizens," p. 7.

135. Book III, "COINTELPRO: The FBI's Covert Action Programs against American Citizens," p. 26.

136. Book III, "COINTELPRO: The FBI's Covert Action Programs against American Citizens," pp. 28-33.

137. See "The Internal Revenue Service," below, for information on the IRS.

138. Abuses book, pp. 80-83.

139. See "The CIA," below, for information on the CIA.

140. See "Military Intelligence," below, for information on military intelligence.

141. See generally *Washington Post* and *New York Times* articles in the spring and summer of 1976 for details of the revelations in connection with the Socialist Workers party suit.

142. Ungar, p. 198.

5
THE CIA

1. Victor Marchetti, and John Marks, *The CIA and the Cult of Intelligence*, (New York: Alfred A. Knopf, 1974), p. 227.

2. "House Committee on Expenditures in the Executive Departments," Hearings on H.R. 2319 National Security Act of 1947, 80th Congress, April 2-July 1, 1947, p. 555.

3. *Congressional Record*, 95: 6949.

4. "National Security Council Intelligence Directive No. 7," Domestic Exploitation, Approved 2/12/48 (available at CNSS).

5. "Memorandum for the Record," September 22, 1948, accompanying letter from Frank G. Wisner, assistant director for policy coordination, CIA, to Mr. D. Milton Ladd, assistant to the director, FBI, September 22, 1948 (available at CNSS).

6. George Volsky, "Cuban Exiles Recall Domestic Spying and Picketing for CIA," *New York Times*, January 4, 1975.

7. Ibid.

8. "Organization and Functions," Domestic Operations Division and Station memorandum, February 11, 1963 (available at CNSS). (Re-designated the Foreign Resource Division on January 28, 1972.)

9. Final Report of the Select Committee to Study Governmental Relations with Respect to Intelligence Activities, United States Senate, Supplementary Detailed Staff Reports on Intelligence Activities and the Rights of Americans, Book III (Washington, D.C.: U.S. Government Printing Office, 1976), "CIA Intelligence Collection about Americans: CHAOS Program and the Office of Security," pp. 701-702. (Hereafter cited as Book III, with report title.)

10. Book III, "CIA Intelligence Collection about Americans," p. 702.

11. Marchetti and Marks, *The CIA and the Cult of Intelligence*, p. 237.

12. Final Report of the Select Committee to Study Governmental Operations with Respect to Intelligence Activities, United States Senate, Intelligence Activities and the Rights of Americans, Book II (Washington, D.C.: U.S. Government Printing Office, 1976), "The Growth of Domestic Intelligence, 1936 to 1976," p. 97. (Hereafter cited as Book II, with report title.)

13. Seymour M. Hersh, "CIA Kept Eartha Kitt File," New York Times News Service, *Washington Star News*, January 3, 1975.

14. Book III, "Domestic CIA and FBI Mail Opening," p. 571.

15. Book III, "Domestic CIA and FBI Mail Opening," p. 605.

16. Book III, "Domestic CIA and FBI Mail Opening," p. 609.

17. Book III, "Domestic CIA and FBI Mail Opening," p. 577.

18. Book III, "Domestic CIA and FBI Mail Opening," p. 574.

19. Book III, "Domestic CIA and FBI Mail Opening," p. 631.

20. Book III, "Domestic CIA and FBI Mail Opening," pp. 628-630.

21. Book III, "Domestic CIA and FBI Mail Opening," p. 574.

22. Ibid.

23. Book III, "Domestic CIA and FBI Mail Opening," p. 575.

24. Book III, "Domestic CIA and FBI Mail Opening," p. 576

25. Book III, "Domestic CIA and FBI Mail Opening," p. 590.

26. Book III, "Domestic CIA and FBI Mail Opening," p. 571.

27. Report to the President by the Commission on CIA Activities within the United States, June 1975 (Washington, D.C.: U.S. Government Printing Office), 163. (Hereafter cited as the Rockefeller Report.)

28. Rockefeller Report, p. 163.

29. Rockefeller Report, p. 164.

30. William Greider and George Lardner, "New Conflict in Account by Helms Seen," *Washington Post*, Jan. 29, 1975.

31. Rockefeller Report, pp. 164-165.

32. Rockefeller Report, p. 161.

33. Book III, "CIA Intelligence Collection about Americans: CHAOS Program and the Office of Security," p. 723.

34. Rockefeller Report, p. 154.

35. Book III, "CIA Intelligence Collection about Americans: CHAOS Program and the Office of Security," p. 725.

36. See generally CIA file on Women Strike for Peace, received under the Freedom of Information Act, on file at CNSS.

37. Rockefeller Report, pp. 294-295.

38. Rockefeller Report, p. 296.

39. Rockefeller Report, p. 249.

40. Rockefeller Report, p. 238.

41. Book III, "CIA Intelligence Collection about Americans: CHAOS Program and the Office of Security," p. 720.

42. Book II, "The Growth of Domestic Intelligence, 1936 to 1976," p. 94.

43. Book III, "CIA Intelligence Collection about Americans: CHAOS Program and the Office of Security," p. 690.

44. Book III, "CIA Intelligence Collection about Americans: CHAOS Program and the Office of Security," p. 691.

45. Warren Brown, "U.S. Citizens Spied on by CIA Abroad," *Washington Post*, July 17, 1976.

46. Book III, "CIA Intelligence Collection about Americans: CHAOS Program and the Office of Security," p. 692.

47. Book III, "CIA Intelligence Collection about Americans: CHAOS Program and the Office of Security," p. 692.

48. Book III, "CIA Intelligence Collection about Americans: CHAOS Program and the Office of Security," p. 699.

49. Book III, "CIA Intelligence Collection about Americans: CHAOS Program and the Office of Security," p. 720.

50. Rockefeller Report, p. 136.

51. Book III, "CIA Intelligence Collection about Americans: CHAOS Program and the Office of Security," p. 712.

52. Book III, "CIA Intelligence Collection about Americans: CHAOS Program and the Office of Security," p. 704.

53. Book III, "CIA Intelligence Collection about Americans: CHAOS Program and the Office of Security," p. 694.

54. Rockefeller Report, p. 140.

55. Book III, "CIA Intelligence Collection about Americans: CHAOS Program and the Office of Security," p. 700.

56. Book III, "CIA Intelligence Collection about Americans: CHAOS Program and the Office of Security," p. 718.

57. Intelligence Activities, Senate Resolution 21, Hearings before the Select Committee to Study Governmental Operations with Respect to Intelligence Activities, U.S. Senate, 94th Congress, vol. 4, "Mail Opening," Oct. 21, 22, 24, 1975, p. 220.

58. Book III, "CIA Intelligence Collection about Americans: CHAOS Program and the Office of Security," p. 697.

59. Book III, "CIA Intelligence Collection about Americans: CHAOS Program and the Office of Security," p. 705-706.

60. Address to the American Society of Newspaper Editors, April 14, 1971, as reprinted in *U.S. News and World Report*, April 26, 1971.

61. "CIA Activities in the United States," memorandum to the deputy director for intelligence from W. E. Colby, dated April 21, 1972 (available at CNSS).

62. Rockefeller Report, p. 130.

63. Rockefeller Report, p. 144.

64. In general, see President Ford's executive order #11905, issued on Feb. 18, 1976.

6

MILITARY INTELLIGENCE

1. "Military Surveillance of Civilian Politics," A Report of the Subcommittee on Constitutional Rights, Committee on the Judiciary, United States Senate, 93rd Congress, 1st Session, Committee Print 1973, p. 29. (Hereafter cited as "Military Surveillance": Committee Report.)

2. "Military Surveillance": Committee Report, p. 4.

3. "Military Surveillance," Hearings before the Subcommittee on Constitutional Rights of the Committee on the Judiciary on S.2318, United States Senate, 93rd Congress, 2nd Session, 1974, p. 16. (Hereafter cited as Hearings on S.2318.)

4. For information on the Military Intelligence Division in World War I, see Joan M. Jensen, *The Price of Vigilance* (Chicago: Rand McNally, 1968).

5. An excellent discussion on the history of military intelligence operations in general can be found in a prepared statement by Joan M. Jensen, entitled "Military Surveillance of Civilians, 1917-1967" published in Hearings on S.2318, pp. 169-177. (Hereafter cited as Jensen's Statement.)

6. Roger Daniels, *The Bonus Marchers: An Episode of the Great Depression* (Westport, Conn.: Greenwood Publishing Corp., 1971). This book gives a fairly detailed account of the role of then Chief of Staff Douglas MacArthur and the use of military intelligence.

7. Jensen's Statement, p. 173.

8. Hearings on S. 2318, p. 174.

9. *Korematsu* v. *United States*, 323 US 214. See also Barbara Tuchman, *Stilwell and the American Experience in China*. (New York: Macmillan, 1971).

10. For a very brief discussion on the Deliminations Agreement, see "Federal Data Banks, Computers and the Bill of Rights," Hearings before the Subcommittee on Constitutional Rights of the Committee on the Judiciary, United States Senate, 92nd Congress, 1st Session, Part I, 1971, p. 149. (Hereafter cited as Federal Data Bank Hearings, Part I.)

11. Jensen's Statement, p. 175.

12. Jensen's Statement, p. 175.

13. Federal Data Bank Hearings, Part I, p. 381.

14. Hearings on S. 2318, p. 176.

15. Paul J. Scheeps, *The Role of the Army in the Oxford, Mississippi Incident, 1962-1963*, Office of the Chief of Military History, Monograph No. 73 M (Washington, D.C.: Department of the Army, 1965), p. 284.

16. Data Bank Hearings, Part I, p. 381.

17. "Military Surveillance": Committee Report, p. 16.

18. "Military Surveillance": Committee Report, p. 18.

19. "Military Surveillance": Committee Report, p. 17.

20. Ibid.

21. Hearings on S. 2318, p. 179.

22. Final Report of Cyrus R. Vance, Special Assistant to the Secretary of Defense, Concerning the Detroit Riots, July 23 through August 2, 1967: Department of Defense Press Release No. 856-67, 9/12/67, p. 51.

23. "Military Surveillance": Committee Report, pp. 28-29.

24. Annex B (intelligence) to the Department of the Army Civil Disturbance Plan (U) dated February 1, 1968, cited in "Federal Data Banks, Computers, and the Bill of Rights," Hearings before the Subcommittee on Constitutional Rights of the Committee on the Judiciary, United States Senate, 92nd Congress, 1st Session, Part II, 1971, pp. 1119-1122. (Hereafter cited as Federal Data Bank Hearings, Part II.)

25. Request from General William Yarborough to the director of the National Security Agency, included in Hearings exhibits in "Intelligence Activities, Senate Resolution 21," Hearings before the Select Committee to Study Governmental Operations with Respect to Intelligence Activities, United States Senate, 94th Congress, 1st Session, vol. 5, *The National Security Agency and Fourth Amendment Rights*.

26. "Army Surveillance of Civilians: A Documentary Analysis," by the Staff of the Subcommittee on Constitutional Rights, Senate Committee on the Judiciary, 92nd Congress, 2d Session (1972), p. 89. (Hereafter cited as "Army Surveillance of Civilians Analysis.")

27. Final Report of the Senate Committee to Study Governmental Relations with Respect to Intelligence Activities, United States Senate, Supplementary Detailed Staff Reports on Intelligence Activities and the Rights of Americans, Book III, "Improper Surveillance of Private Citizens by the Military" (Washington, D.C.: U.S. Government Printing Office, 1976), p. 789. (Hereafter cited as Book III, name of report.)

28. Statement of Robert F. Froehlke, then assistant secretary of defense (administration), before the Senate Subcommittee on Constitutional Rights in Federal Data Bank Hearings, Part I, p. 388.

29. Statement of Robert F. Froehlke, then assistant secretary of defense (administration), before the Senate Subcommittee on Constitutional Rights in Federal Data Bank Hearings, Part I, p. 422.

30. "Military Surveillance": Committee Report, p. 13.

31. "Army Surveillance of Civilians Analysis," p. 96.

32. Agent Letter No. 25 dated 2/18/71, reports by Military Intelligence Agents cited in Federal Data Bank Hearings, Part II, p. 1498.

33. Department of the Army Civil Disturbance Information Collection Plan (ACDP) (U), dated May 2, 1968, cited in Federal Data Bank Hearings, Part II, pp. 1123-1139.

34. "Army Surveillance of Civilians Analysis," p. 7.

35. Statement of Christopher H. Pyle, attorney and former captain in army intelligence, before the Senate Subcommittee on Constitutional Rights, in Federal Data Bank Hearings, Part I, pp. 197-198. See also statement of Ralph M. Stein, formerly assigned to the Domestic Intelligence section of the Counter-Intelligence Analysis Branch, before the Senate Subcommittee on Constitutional Rights in Federal Data Bank Hearings, Part I, pp. 272-273.

36. Statement of Joseph J. Levin Jr., former military agent, before the Senate Subcommittee on Constitutional Rights, in Federal Data Bank Hearings, Part I, p. 290.

37. Statement of Christopher H. Pyle before the Senate Subcommittee on Constitutional Rights, in Federal Data Bank Hearings, Part I, pp. 185, 200-201.

38. "Army Surveillance of Civilians Analysis," pp. 30-31.

39. "Army Surveillance of Civilians Analysis," p. 22.

40. "Army Surveillance of Civilians Analysis," p. 42.

41. "Military Surveillance": Committee Report, p. 6.

42. "Army Surveillance of Civilians Analysis," p. 9.

43. "Military Surveillance": Committee Report, p. 67.

44. "Military Surveillance": Committee Report, p. 33.

45. See OPLAN GARDEN PLOT documents on file at the Center for National Security Studies. OPLAN GARDEN PLOT, which went into effect on Feb. 1, 1968, finds roots in several previous intelligence plans. The GARDEN PLOT plans operational procedures stem from the wider specifications of DOD intelligence directives to squash civil disorders.

46. Attorney General's First Annual Report, *Federal Law Enforcement and Criminal Justice Assistance Activities* (Washington D.C.: U.S. Government Printing Office, 1972), p. 325.

47. 6th U.S. Army Final Report, Command Post Exercise Cable Splicer III, Section III, Field Operations, pp. 11-12. This document, also available at CNSS, is part of a larger file on CABLE SPLICER obtained by Ron Ridenhour. His article, "Arizona's Anti-Riot Plans Revealed," written with Al Senia in *New Times*, vol. VII, no. 26, March 24-30, 1976, discusses an Arizona operational "war-game" exercise of CABLE SPLICER III.

48. The attendance roster for this meeting is on file at CNSS.

49. Christopher H. Pyle, "CONUS Intelligence: The Army Watches Civilian Politics," *Washington Monthly* (January 1970), pp. 4-16. Also see the statement of Christopher H. Pyle before the Senate Subcommittee on Constitutional Rights, in Federal Data Bank Hearings, Part I, pp. 147-169.

50. The use of federal troops is governed by the Posse Comitatus Act (18 U.S.C. §1385) and may occur only within the provisions of U.S.C. §331-334. For a more detailed discussion see "Military Surveillance of Civilian Political Activities: Report and Recommendations for Congressional Action," by the Committee on Civil Rights, the Association of the Bar of the City of New York, reprinted in Hearings on S. 2318, pp. 145-148.

51. "Military Surveillance": Committee Report, pp. 19-20.

52. Statement of Morris Janowitz, professor of sociology, before the Senate Subcommittee on Constitutional Rights, in Federal Data Bank Hearings, Part I, p. 347.

53. Lynch directive, Federal Data Bank Hearings, Part II, pp. 1099-1102.

54. Hearings on S. 2318, p. 4.

55. 40 Federal Register 35204, Aug. 18, 1975.

56. "Military Surveillance": Committee Report, p. 95.

57. Book III, "Improper Surveillance of Private Citizens by the Military," pp. 816-818.

58. Hearings on S. 2318, pp. 223-225, 229, 235-236, 238, 239, 247, 250-251.

59. Hearings on S. 2318, p. 205.

60. Hearings on S. 2318, p. 226.

61. Department of Defense Directive 5200.27, Dec. 8, 1975. (Hereafter cited as December 1975 DOD Directive 5200.27.)

62. December 1975 DOD Directive 5200.27, p. 4.

63. "Use of the Armed Forces to Conduct Surveillance of Civilians," Senate Subcommittee on the Judiciary Report to Accompany S.84, March 1976, p. 11.

7

THE NATIONAL SECURITY AGENCY

1. Richard Lyons, "Church Warns of U.S. Tyranny," *Washington Post*, Aug. 18, 1975, p. A3.

2. Final Report of the Select Committee to Study Governmental Operations with Respect to Intelligence Activities, United States Senate, Supplementary Detailed Staff Reports on Intelligence Activities and the Rights of Americans, Book III (Washington, D.C.: U.S. Government Printing Office, 1976), p. 738. (Hereafter cited as Book III, name of report.)

3. Philip Agee, *Inside the Company* (New York: Stonehill Publishing Co., 1975), p. 43.

4. Huston Memorandum, May 15, 1973, in "Statement of Information," Hearings before the Committee on the Judiciary, House of Representatives, 93rd Congress, 2d Session, Book VII, p. 438.

5. See Book III, "National Security Agency Surveillance Affecting Americans," pp. 736-738.

6. Book III, "National Security Agency Surveillance Affecting Americans," p. 765.

7. Book III, "National Security Agency Surveillance Affecting Americans," p. 740.

8. "Foreign Wireless and Radio Monitoring," National Security Council Intelligence Directive No. 6, Dec. 12, 1947.

9. Book III, "National Security Agency Surveillance Affecting Americans," p. 770.

10. Book III, "National Security Agency Surveillance Affecting Americans," p. 750.

11. Book III, "National Security Agency Surveillance Affecting Americans," p. 746.

12. Book III, "National Security Agency Surveillance Affecting Americans," p. 746.

13. Book III, "National Security Agency Surveillance Affecting mericans," p. 739.

14. Book III, "National Security Agency Surveillance Affecting Americans," p. 749.

15. Book III, "National Security Agency Surveillance Affecting Americans," pp. 753-756.

16. *Katz* v. *U.S.*, 389 U.S. 347 (1967), together with the decision in *Berger* v. *New York*, 388 U.S. 41 (1967), held that electronic surveillance is a search and seizure under the Fourth Amendment.

17. Book III, "National Security Agency Surveillance Affecting Americans," p. 741.

18. Book III, "National Security Agency Surveillance Affecting Americans," p. 755.

19. Quoted in Book III, "National Security Agency Surveillance Affecting Americans," p. 756.

20. Book III, "National Security Agency Surveillance Affecting Americans," p. 755.

21. 407 U.S. 297.

22. Book III, "National Security Agency Surveillance Affecting Americans," p. 760.

23. Book III, "National Security Agency Surveillance Affecting Americans," p. 739.

24. Book III, "National Security Agency Surveillance Affecting Americans," p. 759.

25. Book III, "National Security Agency Surveillance Affecting Americans," p. 759.

26. Book III, "National Security Agency Surveillance Affecting Americans," p. 739.

27. Book III, "National Security Agency Surveillance Affecting Americans," p. 777.

28. Book III, "National Security Agency Surveillance Affecting Americans," p. 766.

29. Book III, "National Security Agency Surveillance Affecting Americans," p. 760.

30. Book III, "National Security Agency Surveillance Affecting Americans," p. 742.

31. See Book III, "NSA Personnel Security and Related Matters," pp. 777-783.

32. Commission on CIA Activities within the United States, *Report to the President*, June 1975, p. 142.

33. *Halkin* v. *Helms*, Civ. Action No. 75-1773 (D.D.C.), a civil suit brought by the ACLU for damages resulting from the Operation CHAOS contribution to the MINARET watch list.

34. The Fourth Amendment to the Constitution reads as fol-

lows: "The right of the people to be secure in their persons, houses, papers and effects, against unreasonable searches and seizures, shall not be violated, and no warrants shall issue, but upon probable cause, supported by Oathe or affirmation, and particularly describing the place to be searched, and the persons or things to be seized."

35. Statement of Lt. General Lew Allen, Jr., director, National Security Agency, before the House Select Committee on Intelligence, Aug. 6, 1975, pp. 7-8.

36. Executive Order #11905, promulgated Feb. 18, 1976.

37. Book III, "National Security Agency Surveillance Affecting Americans," p. 764.

8

THE INTERNAL REVENUE SERVICE

1. "Statement of Information," Hearings before the Committee on the Judiciary, House of Representatives, 93rd Congress, 2nd Session, pursuant to H. Res. 803, Book VII, "Internal Revenue Service, May-June, 1974." (Hereafter cited as Impeachment Book VIII.)

2. Impeachment Book VIII, p. 54.

3. Impeachment Book VIII, pp. 138-144.

4. Final Report of the Select Committee to Study Governmental Operations with Respect to Intelligence Activities, Book III, "Supplementary Detailed Staff Reports on Intelligence Activities and the Right of Americans, U.S. Senate, April 14, 1976." (Hereafter cited as Final Report, Book III.)

5. *Reuben G. Lenske* v. *United States*, 383 F 2d (CA 9, 1967), p. 27.

6. *Reuben G. Lenske* v. *United States*, 383 F 2d (CA 9, 1967), p. 27.

7. *Communist Party U.S.A.* v. *Commissioner of Internal Revenue*, 332 F 2d 325 (App. D.C. 1967), p. 329. The case was concluded in 1967 when the Court of Appeals again reversed a Tax Court ruling and held that CPUSA had shown its central contention that, like other political parties, it was not subject to federal income taxes (*Communist Party U.S.A.* v. *Commissioner of Internal Revenue*, 373 F 2d 682, 1967).

8. Final Report, Book III, p. 891.

9. Final Report, Book III, p. 893.

10. Final Report, Book III, p. 891. At the time, Rogovin was also serving as the CIA's contact at the IRS working to head off tax audits of CIA proprietary companies and private foundations passing funds for the agency. For a detailed account of Rogo-

vin's role, see Taylor Branch, "Playing Both Sides against the Middle," *Esquire*, Sept. 1976, pp. 17-18.

11. Memorandum, director, Audit Division, to assistant commissioner (Compliance), March 9, 1963, cited in Final Report, Book III, p. 892.

12. Final Report, Book III, p. 892.

13. Investigation of the Special Service Staff of the Internal Revenue Service, Staff of the Joint Committee on Internal Revenue Taxation, 94th Congress, 1st Session (Committee Print 1975), p. 106. (Hereafter cited as Special Service Report 1975.)

14. Special Service Report 1975, p. 108.

15. Final Report, Book III, p. 896.

16. Final Report, Book III, p. 896.

17. Special Service Report 1975, p. 14.

18. Memorandum from F. J. Baumgardner to W. C. Sullivan, 5/10/65, cited in Final Report, Book III, p. 847.

19. Final Report, Book III, p. 847.

20. Final Report, Book III, p. 850.

21. Memorandum from C. D. Brennan to W. C. Sullivan, 2/3/69, "New Left Movement, IS—Miscellaneous." Final Report, Book III, p. 851.

22. Final Report, Book III, p. 855.

23. Memorandum from Midwest City Field Office to FBI headquarters, 8/1/68, cited in Final Report, Book III, p. 854.

24. Memorandum from FBI headquarters to Midwest City Field Office, 8/6/68, cited in Final Report, Book III, p. 854.

25. Memorandum from Baumgardner to W. C. Sullivan, 5/6/64, cited in Final Report, Book III, p. 855.

26. Final Report, Book III, p. 857.

27. CIA memorandum captioned "Subject: Victor Marchetti," cited in Final Report, Book III, p. 858.

28. CIA memorandum dated 2/2/67, captioned "IRS Briefing on Ramparts," cited in Final Report, Book III, p. 859.

29. Memorandum from Tom Huston to H. R. Haldeman, Sept. 21, 1970, cited in the Hearings before the Select Committee on Presidential Campaign Activities of the United States Senate, Phase I: Watergate Investigation—Book 3, 93d Congress, 1st Session (1973), p. 1338. (Hereafter cited as Watergate Book 3.)

30. Special Services Report 1975, p. 17.

31. Memorandum [to file] from Commissioner Thrower, 6/16/69, cited in Final Report, Book III, p. 877.

32. Special Service Report 1975, p. 24.

33. Memorandum from D. O. Virdin for file, July 2, 1969, cited

in Political Intelligence in the Internal Revenue Service: The Special Service Staff, Staff of the Subcommittee on Constitutional Rights of the Senate Committee on the Judiciary, 93rd Congress, 2nd Session (Committee Print 1974), pp. 120-121. (Hereafter cited as Special Service Report 1974.)

34. Memorandum from D. W. Bacon to assistant commissioners, cited in Special Services Report 1974, p. 123 (July 18, 1969).

35. D. O. Virdin memorandum for file, "Activist Organizations Committee," July 31, 1969; D. O. Virdin, "Memorandum to Mr. [Harold E.] Snyder. Activist Organizations Committee," May 2, 1968, cited in Final Report, Book III, p. 879.

36. Final Report, Book III, p. 881.

37. Final Report, Book III, p. 881-882.

38. Special Service Report 1974, p. 329.

39. Memorandum from Tom Huston to H. R. Haldeman, Sept. 21, 1970, Impeachment Book VIII, p. 44.

40. Final Report, Book III, p. 885.

41. Nov. 1-2, 1972, IRS report; Subject: the Special Service Staff, Its Origin, Mission and Potential, cited in the Hearings before the Select Committee to Study Governmental Operations with Respect to Intelligence Activities of the U.S. Senate, 93rd Congress, 1st session, vol. 3, titled "Intelligence Activities Senate Resolution 21," Oct. 2, 1975, p. 39. (Hereafter cited as "Senate Resolution 21.")

42. Unsigned memorandum composed by D. O. Virdin 7/24/69. Cited in Final Report, Book III, p. 880.

43. Special Service Report 1975, pp. 50, 57.

44. Special Service Report 1975, p. 48.

45. Special Service Report 1975, p. 50.

46. For a more detailed description of the *Compendium*, see "Military Surveillance of Civilian Politics," Report of the Subcommittee on Constitutional Rights of the Committee on the Judiciary, U.S. Senate, 93rd Congress, 1st Session (1973), pp. 52-57.

47. Special Service Report 1975, p. 39.

48. Special Service Report 1975, p. 51.

49. Final Report, Book III, p. 890.

50. "Church Says IRS Tax Data Used to 'Harass' U.S. Citizens," *Washington Post*, Oct. 3, 1975, p. A3. (Hereafter cited as IRS Data Article.)

51. Special Service Report 1974, p. 40.

52. Special Service Report 1975, p. 45.

53. IRS Data Article.

54. Documents released by the Internal Revenue Service to the Tax Reform Research Group, 133 C Street, S.E., Washington, D.C., and on file at the Center for National Security Studies, 122 Maryland Avenue, N.E., Washington, D.C. (Hereafter cited as IRS Documents.)

55. Special Service Report 1975, p. 42.

56. Special Service Report 1975, p. 41.

57. *Treasury, Postal Service, and General Government Appropriations Fiscal Year 1976*. Hearings Before the Senate Committee on Appropriations, Part 1, 94th Congress, 1st Session, 1975, p. 461. (Hereafter cited as FY 76 Appropriations Hearings.)

58. Final Report, Book III, p. 899.

59. Report of Task Force on Intelligence Gathering and Retrieval System, June 25, 1969, Internal Revenue Service Intelligence Division, cited in Final Report, Book III, p. 901.

60. Final Report, Book III, p. 897.

61. Final Report Book III, p. 907.

62. Frank Donner, "The Internal Revenue Service: the Search for a Sanction," chapter from an unpublished manuscript, p. 56. Donner's source for this information was a selective print-out of 172 names leaked to the public in late spring 1975, presumably by an IRS employee. (Hereafter cited as Donner.)

63. Donner, p. 56.

64. Final Report, Book III, p. 915.

65. Final Report, Book III, p. 915.

66. Johnnie Walters affidavit, June 10, 1974, cited in Impeachment Book VIII, p. 218.

67. Charles Colson memorandum, June 12, 1972, cited in Impeachment Book VIII, p. 216.

68. Impeachment Book VIII, p. 25.

69. Impeachment Book VIII, p. 196. A November 1971 "talking paper" discussed specifically the problem of making IRS politically responsive to the White House. It read, in part: ". . . The Republican appointees appear afraid and unwilling to do anything with IRS that could be politically helpful. For example:

- We have been unable to obtain information in the possession of IRS regarding our political enemies
- We have been unable to stimulate audits of persons who should be audited
- We have been unsuccessful in placing RN supporters in the IRS bureaucracy.

70. Memorandum from Tom Huston to H. R. Haldeman, dated Sept. 21, 1970, cited in Special Service Report 1975, p. 70.

71. Impeachment Book VIII, p. 32, and *Center for Corporate Responsibility* v. *Schultz*, 368 F Supp. 863, pp. 871-872.

72. "IRS Accused of Recent Spying," *New York Times*, April 13, 1975, p. 17, and Final Report, Book III, p. 874.

73. Memorandum, IRS Special Agent Neuhauser, Chicago, to Assistant Regional Commissioner—Intelligence, Midwest Region, undated, p. 2, cited in Final Report, Book III, p. 875.

74. Final Report, Book III, p. 875.

75. Final Report, Book III, p. 875.

9
THE GRAND JURIES

1. *U.S.* v. *Dionesio*, 410 U.S. 1 (1973).

2. Hearsay: *Costello* v. *U.S.*, 350 U.S. 359 (1955). Illegal searches: *U.S.* v. *Calandra*, 94S.Ct.613 (1974). Warrantless wiretap: *U.S.* v. *Gelhard*, 408 U.S. 41 (1972).

3. *U.S.* v. *Mandujano*, 44 U.S.L.W. 4629, (May 19, 1976). (May 19, 1976).

4. See generally *Memorandum on the Grand Jury*, prepared by the Office of Policy and Planning, U.S. Department of Justice, for the House Judiciary Committee, Subcommittee on Immigration, Citizenship and International Law, June 6, 1976, pp. 59-63.

5. "A Kind of Immunity That Leads to Jail: The New Grand Jury," by Paul Cowan, *New York Times* magazine, April 29, 1973. (Hereafter cited as Cowan article.)

6. *Blair* v. *U.S.*, 250 U.S. 273,282 (1919).

7. *Branzburg* v. *Hayes*, 408 U.S. 665,668 (1972).

8. "Annals of Law: Taking the Fifth," by Richard Harris, *New Yorker*, April 19, 1976.

9. See generally *Kastigar* v. *U.S.*, 406 U.S. 44 (1972).

10. Cowan article.

11. Cowan article.

12. Cowan article.

13. Normal conviction rate: "The Organized Crime Control Act or Its Critics: Which Threatens Civil Liberties?" McClellan, 46 *Notre Dame Lawyer*, 55, 60 (1970), cited in *The Grand Jury* by Leroy Clark (New York: Quadrangle, 1975), p. 50. ISD conviction rate: "Who Is Guy Goodwin and Why Are They Saying Those Terrible Things about Him?" by Lacey Fosburgh, *Juris Doctor*, January 1973.

14. The testimony of Senator Edward M. Kennedy, Hearings on the Fort Worth Five and Grand Jury Abuse before the House Judiciary Subcommittee No. 1, March 13, 1973.

15. Clark, *The Grand Jury*, pp. 47-48.

16. Grand Jury "Horror" Stories, compiled by Barry Winograd, March 15, 1973: Seattle, p. 6; Tucson, p. 4; Detroit, p. 6. Available from Coalition to End Grand Jury Abuse, 105 2nd St., N.E., Washington, D.C. 20002.

17. "Arrest in Capitol Bombing Called 'Fishing Expedition,' " by Timothy S. Robinson, *Washington Post*, Oct. 17, 1975.

18. Frank J. Donner and Richard I. Lavine, "Kangaroo Grand Juries," *The Nation*, Nov. 19, 1973.

19. *U.S.* v. *Briggs*, 514 F 2nd 794, 805-806 (5th Circuit 1975).

20. 8 Moore's Federal Practice 6.02[1][b].

21. Cowan article.

22. In re Grand Jury Investigation, Des Moines, Iowa, in the matter of Martha Copleman, U.S. District Court, Southern District of Iowa, M-1-59.

23. "The FBI Connection," *Grand Jury Report*, published by Coalition to End Grand Jury Abuse (Winter 1976), p. 5.

24. "Grand Juries: A History of Repression," *Quash*, published by Grand Jury Project, 853 Broadway, New York City 10003, January 1976, pp. 13, 15.

25. Barry Winograd and Martin Tassler, "The Political Question," *Trial*, January/February 1973, p. 16.

10
THE LAWLESS STATE

1. Final Report of the Select Committee to Study Governmental Operations with Respect to Intelligence Activities, U.S. Senate, Book I, p. 7. (Hereafter cited as Final Report, book no.)

2. Final Report, Book II, p. 2.

3. Quoted in Victor Marchetti and John Marks, *The CIA and the Cult of Intelligence* (New York: Alfred A. Knopf, 1974), p. 343.

4. Final Report, Book I, p. 149.

5. The program is described in an exchange of correspondence between the Justice Department and the CIA in 1948, on file at the Center for National Security Studies, Washington, D.C.

6. *Richardson* v. *United States*, 42 LW 5086 (1974).

7. *United States* v. *Marchetti*, 466 F 2d 1309 (4th Cir. 1972).

8. *United States* v. *Hoffa*, 385 U.S. 293 (1966); and e.g., *United States* v. *Brown*, 484 F 2d 413 (5th Cir. 1973), *cert. den.* 415 US 960 (1974).

9. *United States* v. *Nixon.*

10. Final Report, Book IV, p. 157.

11. *United States* v. *Lee*, 106 U.S. 196, 220 (1882).

12. *Washington Post*, Oct. 23, 1975.

13. Hearings before the Select Committee to Study Governmental Operations with respect to Intelligence Activities, vol. 4, "Mail Opening." pp. 259-260. (Hereafter cited as Mail-Opening Hearings.)

14. Final Report, Book II, p. 141.

15. Final Report, Book II, pp. 140, 142.

16. Commission on CIA Activities within the United States, *Report to the President* (Washington, D.C.: Government Printing Office, 1975), p. 134.

17. Final Report, Book II, p. 144.

18. Final Report, Book II, p. 266.

19. Final Report, Book II, p. 283.

20. Interim Report of the Select Committee to Study Governmental Operations with Respect to Intelligence Activities, United States Senate, "Alleged Assassination Plots Involving Foreign Leaders," p. 9. (Hereafter cited as "Assassination Report.")

21. Mail-Opening Hearings, p. 45.

22. "Assassination Report," p. 10.

23. "Assassination Report," p. 11.

24. Ibid.

25. "Assassination Report," p. 107.

26. "Assassination Report," pp. 38-39.

27. Hannah Arendt, *Crises of the Republic* (New York: Harcourt, Brace, 1969), p. 137.

28. "Assassination Report," p. 319.

29. CIA cable from Dominican Republic, on file at the Center for National Security Studies, Washington, D.C.

30. Quoted in Jonathan Schell, *The Time of Illusion* (New York: Alfred A. Knopf, 1976), p. 159.

31. Quoted in Marchetti and Marks, *The CIA and the Cult of Intelligence*, p. 243.

32. Final Report, Book II, p. 4.

33. Final Report, Book II, p. 208.

34. *Village Voice*, "The CIA Report," Feb. 16, 1976.

11
HAVE THE CRIMES STOPPED?

1. *New York Times*, June 17, 1976, p. 18.

2. Final Report of the Select Committee to Study Governmental Relations with Respect to Intelligence Activities, United States Senate, 94th Congress, 2nd Session, Supplementary Detailed Staff Reports on Intelligence Activities and the Rights of Americans, Book III (United States Government Printing Office: 1976), p. 13 (hereinafter Senate Report).

3. Paul Delany, "FBI Chief Testifies on Indian Alert," *New York Times*, July 8, 1976, p. 13.

4. Hefferey Oppenheimer, "CIA Says FBI in Error in Forwarding Report," *Washington Star*, June 25, 1976, p. 4.

5. Robert L. Jackson and Ronald J. Ostrow, "Recent FBI Burglaries are Alleged," *Washington Post*, June 23, 1976, p. 11.

6. "CIA Mail Opening Program not Criminal, Probers Say," *Washington Star*, July 27, 1976, p. 3.

7. For a fuller discussion of Executive Order 11905, see two newsletters: *First Principles: National Security and Civil Liberties*, March 1, 1976, and *Intelligence Report*, "President Ford's Intelligence Proposals: A Charter for Abuse," March 1976. Both may be ordered from the Center for National Security Studies, 122 Maryland Ave N.E., Washington, D.C. 20002.

8. For a fuller discussion see Jerry J. Berman, "How to Curb the FBI," *The Nation*, April 26, 1976.

9. Comptroller General of the United States, *Report to the House Committee on the Judiciary, FBI Domestic Intelligence Operations: Their Purpose and Scope: Issues That Need to Be Resolved* (Washington, D.C.: United States General Accounting Office, 1976) p. 150.

12
DESIGNING EFFECTIVE REFORMS

1. "The Select Committee's Investigation Record," *The Village Voice*, February 16, 1976, p. 76 (hereinafter Pike Report).

2. Pike Report, p. 77.

3. Pike Report, p. 83.

4. Senate Report, Note I, Book II, p. 297.

5. John M. Crewdson, "Burglary Report Delayed by FBI," *New York Times*, July 30, 1976.

6. Senate Report, Book 1, p. 459.

7. For a fuller discussion of the issues involved in drafting an

FBI Charter, see Jerry J. Berman, "The Case for a Legislated Charter," and Morton H. Halperin, "Protecting First Amendment Rights in FBI Criminal Investigations," *First Principles*, June 1976.

8. See generally, Committee on Civil Rights of the Association of the Bar of the City of New York, *Intelligence Agency Abuses: The Need for a Temporary Special Prosecutor*, available from the Bar Association at 42 West 44th St., New York, New York 10006.

9. See generally, John H. F. Shattuck, "Tilting at the Surveillance Apparatus," *The Civil Liberties Review*, Summer 1974, pp. 59ff.

10. Senate Report, Book II, p. 336.

BIBLIOGRAPHY OF
MAJOR SOURCES

GENERAL

Hearings and Final Reports of the Committee on the Judiciary, House of Representatives, 93rd Congress, 2d Session, pursuant to H. Res. 803. (Impeachment Hearings.)

Hearings of the Select Committee on Intelligence, House of Representatives, 94th Congress, 1st Session. (Portions of the report of this committee were printed in the Feb. 16 and 23, 1976 issues of the *Village Voice*. The remainder has not been made public.)

Hearings and Final Reports of the Select Committee on Presidential Campaign Activities, United States Senate, 93rd Congress, 2d Session. (Watergate Hearings.)

Hearings and Final Reports of the Select Committee to Study Governmental Operations with Respect to Intelligence Activities, U.S. Senate, 94th Congress, 1st and 2d Sessions.

Report to the President by the Commission on CIA Activities within the United States (Washington, D.C.: U.S. Government Printing Office, June 1975). (Rockefeller Commission Report.)

THE CENTRAL INTELLIGENCE AGENCY

Agee, Philip. *Inside the Company: CIA Diary*. Harmondsworth, Eng.: Penguin Books, 1975.

Borosage, Robert, and Marks, John D., eds. *The CIA File*. New York: Grossman Publishers, 1976.

Copeland, Miles. *Without Cloak or Dagger*. New York: Simon and Schuster, 1974.

Marchetti, Victor, and Marks, John D. *The CIA and the Cult of Intelligence*. New York: Alfred A. Knopf, 1974.

Ross, Thomas B., and Wise, David. *The Invisible Government*. New York: Vintage Books, 1974.

THE FEDERAL BUREAU OF INVESTIGATION

Navasky, Victor. *Kennedy Justice*. New York: Atheneum, 1971. See particularly chapter 3 for a discussion of the FBI program against the Reverend Martin Luther King, Jr.

Report to the House Committee on the Judiciary by the Comptroller General of the United States, *FBI Domestic Intelligence Operations—Their Purpose and Scope: Issues that Need to Be Resolved*. Washington, D.C.: General Accounting Office, 1976.

Ungar, Sanford J. *FBI*. Boston: Little Brown, 1975.

Watters, Pat, and Gillers, Stephen, eds. *Investigating the FBI*. New York: Ballantine Books, 1974.

THE INTERNAL REVENUE SERVICE

Investigation of the Special Service Staff of the Internal Revenue Service, Staff of the Joint Committee on Internal Revenue Taxation, 94th Congress, 1st Session (Committee Print: 1975).

Political Intelligence in the Internal Revenue Service: The Special Service Staff, Staff of the Subcommittee on Constitutional Rights of the Senate Committee on the Judiciary, 93rd Congress, 2d Session (Committee Print: 1974).

MILITARY INTELLIGENCE

"Army Surveillance of Civilians: A Documentary Analysis," By the Staff of the Subcommittee on Constitutional Rights, Senate Committee on the Judiciary, 92nd Congress, 2d Session (Committee Print: 1972).

"Federal Data Banks, Computers and the Bill of Rights," Hearings before the Subcommittee on Constitutional Rights of the Committee on the Judiciary, U.S. Senate, 92nd Congress, 1st Session (1971) (Part I).

"Military Surveillance," Hearings before the Subcommittee on Constitutional Rights of the Committee on the Judiciary, U.S. Senate, 93rd Congress, 2d Session, on S.2318 (1974).

"Military Surveillance of Civilian Politics," a Report by the Subcommittee on Constitutional Rights, Committee on the Judiciary, U.S. Senate, 93rd Congress, 1st Session (Committee Print: 1973).

Pyle, Christopher, "CONUS Intelligence: The Army Watches Civilian Politics," *Washington Monthly*, vol. 1, no. 12 (January, 1970): 4-16.

THE GRAND JURIES

Clark, Leroy. *The Grand Jury*, New York: Quadrangle, 1975.

Coalition to End Grand Jury Abuse, 105 2nd Street, N.E., Washington, D.C. 20002 (newsletter: *Grand Jury Report*, and various reprints available).

Donner, Frank, and Lavine, Richard. "Kangaroo Grand Juries." *The Nation*, Nov. 19, 1973.

Grand Jury Project, 853 Broadway, New York City 10003 (newsletter: *Quash*, and various other publications available).

Harris, Richard. "Annals of Law: Taking the Fifth." *New Yorker*, April 5, 12, 19, 1976.

Representation of Witnesses before Federal Grand Juries. 2nd ed. London: Clark Boardman Co., 1976.

CONTROLLING THE INTELLIGENCE AGENCIES

Commission on the Organization of the Government for Foreign Policy. Washington, D.C.: Government Printing Office, June 1975.

"Developments in the Law—the National Security Interest and Civil Liberties." *Harvard Law Review* 85 (April 1972): 1130.

Dorsen, Norman, and Gillers, Stephen. *None of Your Business: Government Secrecy in America*. New York: The Viking Press, 1974.

Executive Privilege, Secrecy in Government, Freedom of Information. Hearings before the Subcommittee on Intergovernmental Relations of the Committee on Government Operations and the Subcommittee on Separation of Powers and Administrative Practice and Procedure of the Committee on the Judiciary, U.S. Senate, 93rd Congress, 1st Session.

Government Secrecy. Hearings before the Subcommittee on Intergovernmental Relations of the Committee on Government Operations, U.S. Senate, 93rd Congress, 2d Session.

Surveillance. Hearings before the Subcommittee on Courts, Civil Liberties, and the Administration of Justice of the Committee on the Judiciary, House of Representatives, 94th Congress, 1st Session.

INDEX

Abernathy, Ralph David, 62, 121, 124
Abrams, Creighton, 161
Acree, Vernon, 189, 208
AFL, 48, 159
AFL-CIO, 20, 26
Alexander, Donald, 203
Allen, Lew, Jr., 179, 184
African-American Institute, 54
Agee, Philip, 19, 40-41
Agency for International Development (AID), 19, 43, 46
Air America, 43-44
Albania, 39
Albee, Edward, 142
Albertson, William, 115-16
Allende, Salvador, 2, 15-29, 36
Almon, John, 267
America First, 99
American Civil Liberties Union (ACLU), 107, 165, 205
American Destiny Party, 99
American Friends of the Middle East, 54
American Friends Service Committee, 106-107, 121, 142, 156
American Indian Movement, 121, 213, 219, 240-41, 243
American Nationalist Party, 99
American Nazi Party, 121
American Newspaper Guild, 48
American Protective League, 157, 158
Americans for Democratic Action, 165, 203
Anaconda Copper Co., 19
Anderson, Jack, 145
Angleton, James, 142, 225
Angola, 36
Antioch College, 121
Arbenz, Jacobo, 39-40
Arendt, Hannah, 232
Army Counter-Intelligence Analysis Branch, 155, 163
 Compendium, 166, 202
Army Signals Security Agency, 173

Ashland Oil Co., 47-48
Atlanta Constitution, 83
"Attorney General's List," 105, 110, 112
Augusta Chronicle, 67

Bacon, Leslie, 215
Baker, Howard, 233
Baldwin, Hanson, 123
Baptist Foundation of America, 205
Bay of Pigs, 34, 44
Bentley, Elizabeth, 103
Betar, Sam, 213
Birmingham News, 75
Bissell, Richard, 25, 39, 232
Black Panther Party, 121, 125-26, 146, 213
Bolivia, 50, 56
Bradley, Thomas, 205
Brandt, Willy, 37, 81
Brazil, 26, 41
Bridges, Harry, 96
British Guiana, 48
Brown, Irving, 48
Brown, Sam, 121
Brownell, Herbert, 225-26
Bundy, McGeorge, 65
Bureau of Narcotics and Dangerous Drugs (BNDD), 172, 176, 177-78
Burke, Marshall, 64, 70, 74, 79, 83
Burma, 42
Burns, Arthur, 198
Bush, Vannevar, 136

CABLE SPLICER, 3, 156, 167
California Migrant Ministry, 203
Cambodia, 42
Campbell, William, 211
Carmichael, Stokeley, 121
Carter, Marshall S., 232
Castro, Fidel, 16, 18-19
Caulfield, John, 189
Center for Corporate Responsibility, 207
Central Intelligence Agency (CIA), 2, 79, 166

assassination plots, 44-46
beginnings, 4-5, 6-7, 31-34, 102
collaboration with other agencies
  FBI, 123, 124, 130, 151, 240-241
  IRS, 197
  Justice Dept., 223-24
  NSA, 152, 172, 176, 177-78
departments
  Clandestine Services, 11, 36, 38
  Counter-Intelligence Division, 136, 148
  Domestic Contact Service (DCS), 138-39, 151
  Domestic Operations Division, 138, 145
  Office of Security, 3, 143-46
  Special Operations Group, 148-49
  Technical Service Division, 44
domestic operations, 3, 120, 135-54. *See also* CHAOS; MERRIMAC; RESISTANCE
  current state of, 11, 154, 242
  justification given for extralegal, 1, 8, 143-48, 225-26, 230-31, 260
  secret infrastructure, 46
drug testing and behavior modification, 51-53
foreign covert activity, 30-47
  in Albania, 39
  in Bolivia, 50, 56
  in Brazil, 26, 41
  in British Guiana, 48
  in Burma, 42
  in Cambodia, 42
  in Chile, 15-29, 36, 47, 50
  in China, 39, 41
  in Colombia, 50
  in Congo, 45
  in Cuba, 44
  in Dominican Republic, 45, 233
  in Eastern Europe, 39

in Ecuador, 40-41
in Germany, 37
in Guatemala, 39-40, 41
in Indonesia, 41-42, 43
in Iran, 39-40, 41
in Iraq, 41
in Italy, 37-38
in Laos, 42-43
in Panama, 47
in Poland, 39
in Soviet Union, 39, 261-62
in Ukraine, 39
in Uruguay, 39
in Vietnam, 41, 42, 45-47, 50, 51
in Western Europe, 37-39
ineffectiveness, 259, 261-62
legislative charter needed, 269-270
Mafia association, 44, 45, 213
mail-opening program, 8, 140-143, 225-26
proprietaries, 43-44, 46-47
use made of non-governmental entities
churches and missionaries, 49-50
corporations, 47-48
émigré groups, 54
foundations and voluntary organizations, 53-54
labor unions, 48
press and publishing industry, 48
universities, 50-51
Central Intelligence Agency Act of 1949, 136
Chambers, Whittaker, 103
CHAOS, 3, 134, 136, 139, 142, 148-54, 183
Chaplin, Mortimer, 192-93
Chavez, Cesar, 124
Chicago Daily, 83
Chile, 2, 15-29, 30-31, 36, 47, 50
China, 39, 41, 142
Christian Front, 99
Christian Mobilizers, 99
Christian Nationalist Crusade, 121

Church, Frank, 2, 143, 171, 181. *See also* Senate Select Intelligence Committee
Church League of America, 203
CIA *see* Central Intelligence Agency
Civil Air Transport (CAT), 42, 43-44
Civil Disturbance Plan, 163
Clark, Ramsey, 89, 118-19, 205
Clergy and Laity Concerned, 121
COINTELPRO, 3, 10, 126
and civil rights movement, 79, 88, 131
establishment, 8, 112-16, 226
secrecy and non-oversight, 131, 229, 240
Colby, William, 27, 34-35, 46, 47, 49
Colombia, 50
COMINFIL, 106-107, 117, 121
and civil rights movement, 64, 68-71, 73, 79
COMINT (Communications Intelligence), 173, 179
Commerce, U.S. Dept. of, 104
Communications Act of 1934, 173-74
Communications Intelligence, *see* COMINT
Communist Control Act of 1954, 105
Communist Labor Party, 94
Communist Party (U.S.), 103, 111-12
FBI investigation of, 94, 99, 104-106
FBI-alleged connection of Martin Luther King, Jr. to, 65, 67-85, 113
IRS investigation of, 190, 203, 205
COMSEC, departments, 172-73
CONARC, 156
Congo, 45
Congress, U.S.
legislation needed to govern intelligence agencies, 269-73

Congress, U.S. (cont.)
  non-oversight of intelligence
      agencies, 222-23, 244-45,
      253-54, 256
    of CIA, 35, 36
    of FBI, 97-98, 100-101, 115,
      131-32
  oversight function, 276-78
Congress for Cultural Freedom,
    54
Congress of Industrial Organiza-
    tions (CIO), 159
Congress of Racial Equality
    (CORE), 62, 64, 65, 84,
    117, 146
Connor, Bull, 71, 72
Continental Armies (CONUS),
    156, 160-61
Cooper, Wayne, 46
Cotter, William, 143
CORE, see Congress of Racial
    Equality
Coughlin, Father, 96, 99
Counter Terror (CT) program, 46
Cuba, 16, 18-19, 34, 44
Cuban exiles, 44, 54, 138

Davis, Nathaniel, 24-25
Davis, Sammy, Jr., 124
Day, J. Edward, 225, 230
Dean, John, 234
Defense, U.S. Dept. of (DOD), 79,
    104, 162, 176, 257, 278
  domestic intelligence operations,
    155, 164, 169
  see also Military intelligence
Defense Investigative Review
    Council (DIRC), 169
DeLoach, Cartha, 67, 84, 86
Dennis case, 111
Diem, Ngo Dinh, 42, 45
Diem, Nhu Dinh, 45
Directorate for Civil Disturbance
    Planning and Operations,
    155, 156, 164
Dominican Republic, 45, 233
Donovan, William, 32
Downey, John, 41

Dulles, Allen, 32, 53, 230

Eisenhower, Dwight D., 7, 44
El Mercurio, 21, 25
Ellender, Allen, 222
Ellsberg, Daniel, 213, 234
Encounter, 54
Espionage Act, 94
Ervin, Sam, 169
Evans, Courtney, 75

Fair Play for Cuba Committee,
    192
Farmer, James, 62, 65
FBI, see Federal Bureau of Inves-
    tigation
Fecteau, Richard, 41
Federal Bureau of Investigation
    (FBI), 1, 3, 217, 262
  beginnings, 90-91, 93-98
  collaboration with CIA, 123-24,
    130, 137, 139, 142, 151,
    240-41
    with IRS, 108, 113, 122, 130,
    188, 190, 192, 194-97, 199
    with Military Intelligence,
    160, 161, 166, 167
    with NSA, 123-24, 172, 176,
    180
  disruption programs, 130-32,
    259
  and domestic communism, 102-
    116
  guidelines for, current Justice
    Dept., 251-53, 265-66
  intelligence activities: current,
    120, 130-32, 240-42
  intelligence activities: origin, ex-
    tent, and legality of, 4-5, 7-
    8, 91-101, 121, 123, 265
  and 1960s dissent, 116-18, 124-
    130
  and Martin Luther King, Jr.,
    61-89
  legislative charter needed, 270
  "snitch jackets," 114, 116
  and wiretapping, 123, 225-26

see also COINTELPRO; CO-
MINFIL; Hoover, J.
Edgar
Federation of American Scientists,
142
Feldman, Myer, 193
Fielding, Lewis, 234
54/12 Committee, *see* Operations
Advisory Group
First National City Bank, 47
Fitzgerald, Desmond, 49
Fonda, Jane, 121
Ford, Gerald R., 2, 28, 29
executive order on domestic in-
telligence, 154, 246-51
legislative program to reform
intelligence agencies, 244-
245, 253-54
Forman, James, 62
Forrestal, James, 174
40 Committee, 18, 21-23, 25, 26.
See also Operations Advi-
sory Group
Frankfurter, Felix, 111
Free Speech Movement (Berke-
ley), 117
Freedom of Information Act, 227,
276
Froehlke, Robert, 164-65

G-2, 157-58, 159
GARDEN PLOT, 3, 156, 167
Gelter, Michael, 145
Germany, 37. *See also* Nazi Ger-
many
Giancana, Sam, 44, 213
Gibbons, Harold, 206
Glomar Explorer, 35
Goldwater, Barry, Jr., 124
Goodell, Charles, 203
Goodwin, Guy, 211-12, 213-16
Government Accounting Office
(GAO), 278
Grace Shipping Lines, 41
Greece, 30-31
Green, Leon C., 198-99
"Green Berets," 42
Grusse, Ellen, 218

Guatemala, 30-31, 39-40, 41
Guy, Ralph, 217

Haig, Alexander, 24
Haldeman, H. R., 234
Harrington, Michael, 28-29, 36
Hart, Philip, 222
Hawkins, Augustus, 205
Hayden, Tom, 121
Hecksher, Henry, 24
Helms, Richard, 22-23, 145, 148,
152, 232
lack of concern over illegalities,
226
lying to conceal CIA activities,
9, 53, 135, 153
Hennessy, John M., 19, 24
Hersh, Seymour, 35-36, 124
Hiss, Alger, 91, 103
Hoover, Herbert, 34, 158
Hoover, J. Edgar, 94, 152, 167,
224
and adverse FBI publicity, 10,
227-28
and civil rights movement, 66-
67, 69, 77
and COINTELPRO, 8, 112,
115
on Communist threat, 103-104,
109
and Lyndon Johnson, 83-84,
118, 119
and Martin Luther King, Jr.,
63, 67-71, 74-76, 82, 85-86
responsibility for growth and
character of FBI, 91, 95,
97, 98, 102, 229
use of blackmail, 81, 92, 235
Hoover Commission, 4, 34
House Appropriations Committee,
82, 97, 101, 115
House Intelligence Committee, 2,
235, 260
House Un-American Activities
Committee (HUAC), 102-
104, 107, 109-110, 146
Houston, Lawrence, 178, 230
HT-LINGUAL, 3

Hufstedler, Shirley, 219
Hughes, Howard, 35
Humanist Society, 7
Hunt, E. Howard, 236
Huston, Thomas Charles, 149, 198, 200, 206, 229, 234
Huston Plan, 10, 120, 130, 229

Independent Voters of Illinois, 99
Indonesia, 41-42, 43
Inside the Company: CIA Diary (P. Agee), 40-41
Institute for Policy Studies, 121
Intelligence Evaluation Committee, 166
Intelligence Gathering and Retrieval System (IGRS), 204
Intelligence Oversight Board, 249-250
Internal Revenue Service (IRS)
 collaboration with FBI, 108, 112, 113, 188, 190, 192, 194-97, 199
 collaboration with other intelligence agencies, 195, 197
 computerized intelligence gathering, 204-206
 illegal disclosure of files, 194-97
 investigative capacity and authority, 3, 187-89
 legislation necessary, 272-73
 organized crime and, 189-90, 204
 political use of, 1, 8, 88, 130, 134, 190, 191-93
 Special Services Staff (SSS), 189, 190, 198-204
Internal Security Act of 1950, 105
International Commission of Jurists, 54
International Police Services, 46
International Telephone and Telegraph Co. (ITT), 47, 173
 in Chile, 19-20, 21, 22
Iran, 30-31, 39-40, 41
Iraq, 41
IRS, *see* Internal Revenue Service

ISD, *see* Justice, U.S. Dept. of: Internal Security Division
Italy, 37-38
ITT, *see* International Telephone and Telegraph Co.

Jackson, Henry, 35
Janowitz, Morris, 168
Jenkins, Walter, 82, 83
Jewish Defense League, 123
John Birch Society, 121
Johnson, Lyndon B., 7-10, 54, 80, 88, 112, 194
 and CIA, 16, 135-36, 148, 261
 and FBI, 64, 83-84, 118-19, 124, 141
Johnson, Louis, 174
Jordan, Robert E., III, 157
Justice, U.S. Dept. of, 80, 104, 120
 campaign against subversion, 109, 111, 112
 collaboration with intelligence agencies, 152, 164, 188, 193, 223-24
 and FBI campaign against Martin Luther King, Jr., 65-66, 69, 71, 73-74, 75
 grand juries used for intelligence gathering and harrassment, 134, 209-19, 243, 268-69
 Interdivisional Information Unit (IDIU), 120, 124
 Internal Security Division (ISD), 211-12, 213-17
 need for special prosecutor for intelligence abuses, 274-75
 non-oversight of FBI by, 69, 71, 73-74, 76-77, 90-93, 100, 111
 non-prosecution of intelligence community, 10, 88, 243-44, 250, 274-75
 and wiretapping, 80, 225

Karemessines, Thomas, 24, 28
Karenga, Ron, 125

Katz case, 177
Katzenbach, Nicholas, 64, 83, 89,
    162, 229, 231
Keith case, 179-80
Kelley, Clarence, 132, 180, 228,
    236, 239-40
Kennan, George, 37
Kennedy, Edward, 143, 214
Kennedy, John F., 7, 72-73, 81,
    162
  and CIA, 16, 44
  and FBI, 69
  and IRS, 192-93
  and Martin Luther King, Jr.,
    65, 74, 75, 79-80
Kennedy, Robert F., 67, 192
  and CIA, 44
  and FBI, 75, 115, 119
  and Martin Luther King, Jr.,
    64, 69-71, 76-77, 79, 82,
    231
King, Coretta, 65, 80, 124
King, Martin Luther, Jr., 131,
    140, 196-97
  and FBI, 61-89, 117, 121, 123
Kissinger, Henry, 17-18, 23-24, 30,
    41, 152
Kitt, Eartha, 140
Kiwanis Club, 99
Kleindienst, Richard, 179, 217
Korry, Edward, 21, 24
Ku Klux Klan (KKK), 72, 118,
    121-26, 131, 165, 194, 203
Kurds, 41

Labor Youth League, 70
Laird, Melvin, 179
Lansdale, Edward, 42
Laos, 34, 36, 42-43
Law Enforcement Policy Commit-
    tee, 166
League of Fair Play, 99
Lenske, Reuben G., 190-91
LEPRECHAUN, 3, 10, 205
Levi, Edward, 217, 246, 251-53
Levison, Stanley, 67, 68, 69-71,
    73-77

Lewis, John, 62
Lexington Rehabilitation Center
    (Kentucky), 52
Lindsay, John, 203
Loyalty and Security Program
    (1947), 104
Lumumba, Patrice, 45
Lynch, Robert, 168-69

MacArthur, Douglas, 159
McCarthy, Joseph, 103, 110, 112
McCone, John, 20, 141, 236
McGill, Ralph, 83
McGovern, George, 206
McKissick, Floyd, 117
Mafia, 44, 45
Malcolm X, 123, 151
Marchetti, Victor, 197, 224
Mardian, Robert, 211, 217
Maroney, Ken, 217
Marquette University, 82
Marshall Plan, 37
Massachusetts Institute of Tech-
    nology, 50-51
"Media Papers," 92, 130
Medical Committee for Human
    Rights, 205
Meany, George, 48
MERRIMAC, 3, 146-47
Michigan State University, 51
Military Intelligence, 3, 79
  collaboration with FBI, 124,
    160-61, 166-67
  domestic operations, 134, 1?
    169, 243
  legislation needed to gover[n]
    272
MINARET, 3, 134, 173, 1?
    179-80
Minutemen (San Diego), [?]
Mississippi Freedom Dem[ocratic]
    Party, 119
Mitchell, John, 179, 217
MKULTRA, 52
MONGOOSE, 44
Morse, Wayne, 119
Mossadegh, Mohamm[ed]

Movimiento Chicano, 213
Moyers, Bill, 64, 82, 83
Mulroney, Michael, 232
Muskie, Edmund, 124

Narcotics, U.S. Bureau of, 52
Nation of Islam, 121
National Association for the Advancement of Colored People (NAACP), 62, 63, 64, 107, 108, 156
National Council of Churches, 82
National Education Association, 54
National Lawyers Guild, 107, 190-191
National Reconnaissance Office, 133
National Science Foundation, 88
National Security Act of 1947, 32-33, 36, 136
National Security Agency (NSA), 163
  collaboration with other agencies, 120, 123, 152, 172, 176, 177-78
  Communications Intelligence, see COMINT; SHAMROCK
  domestic surveillance: legal and illegal, 1, 3, 8, 11-12, 134, 185-86, 242-43
  information gathering capacity and mission, 171-73, 183-

  congressional over-
         86
  legislative charter, 272
  Council (NSC),
         137
  Council Intelligence directives
         172,

         121
         51,

Nazi Germany, 4, 96, 103
New Mobilization to End the War in Vietnam, 121
New York Daily News, 127
New York Times, The, 34, 35-36, 49
Newspaper Guild, 96
Nixon, Richard M., 1, 8, 10, 81, 124, 143
  and CIA, 16, 22-23, 24, 26, 150
  and FBI, 120
  and IRS, 198-99, 206-208
  justification for extralegal intelligence activities, 224-25, 234
  use of grand juries against dissent, 211-13, 216-17
North Korea, 142
NSA, see National Security Agency
NSC, see National Security Council

Ober, Richard, 148-49, 151-52
O'Brien, Lawrence, 206
O'Dell, Jack, 67-68, 70, 73-77
Office of Strategic Services (OSS), 4, 31-32, 37
Olson, Alice, 52
Olson, Frank, 51, 52-53
Operations Advisory Group, 56
Organized Crime Control Act of 1970, 212
Osborn, Howard, 141

Paiva, Glycon de, 26
Palmer, A. Mitchell, 94-95
Pan American Airlines, 47
Panama, 47
Parks, Rosa, 61, 62
Patria y Libertad, 26
Paul VI (pope), 81-82
Pauling, Linus, 203
The Penkovskiy Papers, 49
Petersen, Henry, 180
PHOENIX, 46
Pike, Otis, 2, 235
Poland, 39

Poor People's March (1968), 88, 165
Posse Comitatus Act of 1878, 168
Powers, Katharine, 217
Privacy Act of 1974, 267, 272, 276
Progressive Labor Party, 129
Psychological Assessment Associates, 46
Puerto Rican Independence Movement, 213, 218-19, 243
Puerto Rican Nationalist Party, 218
Puerto Rican Socialist Party, 218
Pyle, Christopher, 168

Raborn, Admiral, 141, 236
Radford, Charles E., 123
Radio Free Europe, 54
Radio Liberty, 54
Ramparts, 148, 197
Randolph, A. Philip, 63
Raymond, Jill, 218
RCA Global, 173
Redfearn, Timothy, 267
Registration Act, 105
RESISTANCE, 3, 145
"Restless Youth" (CIA), 151, 152, 227
Reuther, Walter, 48
Richardson, Elliot, 180
Richey, Charles R., 207
Rockefeller, Nelson, 82
Rockefeller Commission, 243-44
  on CIA abuses, 2, 92, 145, 153
  on FBI abuses, 92
  on NSA abuses, 181, 184
Rodgers, William, 115
Rogovin, Mitchell, 192, 193
Rooney, John, 82
Roosevelt, Franklin D., 4, 31, 91, 95-97, 99
  created OSS, 31
Rosselli, John, 44
Rotary Club, 99
Rowan, Carl, 83
Royko, Mike, 83
Rustin, Bayard, 70

Saltonstall, Leverett, 223
SANE, 107, 121
Santiago, Edgar Maury, 219
Saxe, Susan, 217
Schippers, David, 213
Schlesinger, James, 179, 181, 227
Schneider, René, 23, 45
SDS, *see* Students for a Democratic Society
Secret Service, 124, 130, 166, 172
Seigenthaler, John, 192
Senate Foreign Relations Committee, 148
Senate Internal Security Committee, 103, 109-110
Senate Judiciary Committee, 165
Senate Select Intelligence Committee, 2, 10, 181
  recommendations for correcting intelligence abuses, 263, 267, 276
  report on intelligence activities, *passim*
Senate Subcommittee on Constitutional Rights, 165, 168
SETTER, 3
SHAMROCK, 3, 10, 173-75, 181
Smith, Gerald L.K., 121
Smith Act of 1940, 97, 109, 111-112, 115-16, 265
Socialist Workers Party
  FBI investigations and disruptions of, 106, 117, 122-23, 124, 127, 129, 267
  suit against FBI, 92, 131, 241
Somers, John, 210
Southern Air Transport, 44
Southern Capital and Management Corporation, 46
Southern Christian Leadership Conference (SCLC), *see* King, Martin Luther, Jr.
Southern Regional Council (SRC), 66-67, 68
Soviet Union, 37, 38, 102-103
  CIA and, 39, 140-42, 261, 262
Special Service Staff (SSS), 3
Spellman, Francis Cardinal, 82

State, U.S. Dept. of, 22, 23, 49,
    79, 104, 166
Steinbeck, John, 142
Stone, Harlan Fiske, 95
STUDEM, 3, 121
Student Nonviolent Coordinating
    Committee (SNCC), 62,
    64, 84, 123, 203
Students for a Democratic Society
    (SDS), 197
  and CIA, 151
  and FBI, 121, 123, 128-29
  and IRS, 200
Sukarno, President, 42
Sullivan, William, 69, 87-88, 226
Supreme Court, U.S., 112, 123,
    224, 263, 265

303 Committee, *see* Operations
    Advisory Group
Throckmorton, John, 162
Thrower, Randolph, 198
Time, 81-82
Tordella, Louis, 174
Torres, Lureida, 218-19
Tower, John, 181
Trafficantes family, 44
Treasury, U.S. Dept. of, 22
Trujillo, Rafael, 45, 233
Truman, Harry S., 172
  and CIA, 32, 36
  and FBI, 102, 108
  and Loyalty Program, 104, 105-
    106
Turgeon, Terry, 218
Turkey, 37

Ukraine, 39
Union of Soviet Socialist Repub-
    lics, *see* Soviet Union
United Auto Workers, 48
United Farmworkers Union, 114
United Mine Workers, 96

United Slaves, 125
United States Intelligence Board,
    179, 226
Urban League, 7, 165, 203
Uruguay, 56

Vance, Cyrus, 162-63
Vekemans, Roger, 50
VIDEM, 3, 121
Vietnam, 30-31, 41-42, 50-51, 128,
    142
Vietnam Veterans against the
    War, 122, 213, 216
Village Voice, 2
Voorhis Act of 1941, 98, 109, 265
Voter Education Project, 62

Wachtel, Harry, 89
Walters, Johnnie, 189
War Resisters League, 146
Warren, Raymond, 24-25
Washington Ethical Society, 146
Washington Monthly, 168
Washington Post, 49, 145
Weather Underground, 121, 123
West Coast Longshoremen's
    Union, 96
Western Union, 173
Wheeler, Earle G., 161
Whitten, Les, 145
Wilkins, Roy, 62, 86
Wilson, Dagmar, 146
WI/ROGUE, 45
Women Strike for Peace, 7, 121,
    146-47
Wright, Paul, 200

Yarborough, William, 163
Young, Andrew, 74

Zaïre, *see* Congo
"Z-Coverage," 99, 109

Katz case, 177
Katzenbach, Nicholas, 64, 83, 89,
    162, 229, 231
Keith case, 179-80
Kelley, Clarence, 132, 180, 228,
    236, 239-40
Kennan, George, 37
Kennedy, Edward, 143, 214
Kennedy, John F., 7, 72-73, 81,
    162
  and CIA, 16, 44
  and FBI, 69
  and IRS, 192-93
  and Martin Luther King, Jr.,
    65, 74, 75, 79-80
Kennedy, Robert F., 67, 192
  and CIA, 44
  and FBI, 75, 115, 119
  and Martin Luther King, Jr.,
    64, 69-71, 76-77, 79, 82,
    231
King, Coretta, 65, 80, 124
King, Martin Luther, Jr., 131,
    140, 196-97
  and FBI, 61-89, 117, 121, 123
Kissinger, Henry, 17-18, 23-24, 30,
    41, 152
Kitt, Eartha, 140
Kiwanis Club, 99
Kleindienst, Richard, 179, 217
Korry, Edward, 21, 24
Ku Klux Klan (KKK), 72, 118,
    121-26, 131, 165, 194, 203
Kurds, 41

Labor Youth League, 70
Laird, Melvin, 179
Lansdale, Edward, 42
Laos, 34, 36, 42-43
Law Enforcement Policy Commit-
    tee, 166
League of Fair Play, 99
Lenske, Reuben G., 190-91
LEPRECHAUN, 3, 10, 205
Levi, Edward, 217, 246, 251-53
Levison, Stanley, 67, 68, 69-71,
    73-77

Lewis, John, 62
Lexington Rehabilitation Center
    (Kentucky), 52
Lindsay, John, 203
Loyalty and Security Program
    (1947), 104
Lumumba, Patrice, 45
Lynch, Robert, 168-69

MacArthur, Douglas, 159
McCarthy, Joseph, 103, 110, 112
McCone, John, 20, 141, 236
McGill, Ralph, 83
McGovern, George, 206
McKissick, Floyd, 117
Mafia, 44, 45
Malcolm X, 123, 151
Marchetti, Victor, 197, 224
Mardian, Robert, 211, 217
Maroney, Ken, 217
Marquette University, 82
Marshall Plan, 37
Massachusetts Institute of Tech-
    nology, 50-51
"Media Papers," 92, 130
Medical Committee for Human
    Rights, 205
Meany, George, 48
MERRIMAC, 3, 146-47
Michigan State University, 51
Military Intelligence, 3, 79
  collaboration with FBI, 124,
    160-61, 166-67
  domestic operations, 134, 155-
    169, 243
  legislation needed to govern,
    272
MINARET, 3, 134, 173, 176-77,
    179-80
Minutemen (San Diego), 126, 203
Mississippi Freedom Democratic
    Party, 119
Mitchell, John, 179, 217
MKULTRA, 52
MONGOOSE, 44
Morse, Wayne, 119
Mossadegh, Mohammed, 39-40

Movimiento Chicano, 213
Moyers, Bill, 64, 82, 83
Mulroney, Michael, 232
Muskie, Edmund, 124

Narcotics, U.S. Bureau of, 52
Nation of Islam, 121
National Association for the Advancement of Colored People (NAACP), 62, 63, 64, 107, 108, 156
National Council of Churches, 82
National Education Association, 54
National Lawyers Guild, 107, 190-191
National Reconnaissance Office, 133
National Science Foundation, 88
National Security Act of 1947, 32-33, 36, 136
National Security Agency (NSA), 163
    collaboration with other agencies, 120, 123, 152, 172, 176, 177-78
    Communications Intelligence, see COMINT; SHAMROCK
    domestic surveillance: legal and illegal, 1, 3, 8, 11-12, 134, 173-86, 242-43
    information gathering capacity and mission, 171-73, 183-186, 248
    need for Congressional oversight, 183-86
    need for legislative charter, 272
National Security Council (NSC), 32, 33-34, 56, 137
National Security Council Intelligence Directives (NSCIDs), 36, 102, 172, 174
National States Rights Party, 121
National Student Association, 51, 54, 148, 203
Navasky, Victor, 76

Nazi Germany, 4, 96, 103
New Mobilization to End the War in Vietnam, 121
New York Daily News, 127
New York Times, The, 34, 35-36, 49
Newspaper Guild, 96
Nixon, Richard M., 1, 8, 10, 81, 124, 143
    and CIA, 16, 22-23, 24, 26, 150
    and FBI, 120
    and IRS, 198-99, 206-208
    justification for extralegal intelligence activities, 224-25, 234
    use of grand juries against dissent, 211-13, 216-17
North Korea, 142
NSA, see National Security Agency
NSC, see National Security Council

Ober, Richard, 148-49, 151-52
O'Brien, Lawrence, 206
O'Dell, Jack, 67-68, 70, 73-77
Office of Strategic Services (OSS), 4, 31-32, 37
Olson, Alice, 52
Olson, Frank, 51, 52-53
Operations Advisory Group, 56
Organized Crime Control Act of 1970, 212
Osborn, Howard, 141

Paiva, Glycon de, 26
Palmer, A. Mitchell, 94-95
Pan American Airlines, 47
Panama, 47
Parks, Rosa, 61, 62
Patria y Libertad, 26
Paul VI (pope), 81-82
Pauling, Linus, 203
The Penkovskiy Papers, 49
Petersen, Henry, 180
PHOENIX, 46
Pike, Otis, 2, 235
Poland, 39